Impartial Justice

Impartial Justice

The Real Supreme Court Cases that Define the Constitutional Right to a Neutral and Detached Decisionmaker

Eric T. Kasper

LEXINGTON BOOKS
Lanham • Boulder • New York • Toronto • Plymouth, UK

Published by Lexington Books
A wholly owned subsidiary of The Rowman & Littlefield Publishing Group, Inc.
4501 Forbes Boulevard, Suite 200, Lanham, Maryland 20706
www.rowman.com

10 Thornbury Road, Plymouth PL6 7PP, United Kingdom

British Library Cataloguing in Publication Information Available

Library of Congress Cataloging-in-Publication Data
Kasper, Eric T.
Impartial justice : the real Supreme Court cases that define the constitutional right to a neutral and detached decisionmaker / Eric T. Kasper.
pages cm
Includes bibliographical references and index.
ISBN 978-0-7391-7721-1 (cloth : alk. paper) -- ISBN 978-0-7391-7722-8 (electronic)
1. Fair trial--United States--Cases. 2. United States. Supreme Court. I. Title.
KF4765.K37 2013
347.73'50264--dc23
2013005239

™ The paper used in this publication meets the minimum requirements of American National Standard for Information Sciences—Permanence of Paper for Printed Library Materials, ANSI/NISO Z39.48-1992.

Printed in the United States of America

Dedicated to my son, Jackson, in the hope that he may grow up in a more just world

Contents

Acknowledgements ix

Preface xi

Introduction: A Short History of What It Means to Be a Neutral, Impartial, and Unbiased Decisionmaker in Anglo-American Law 1

Part One: An Impartial Jury Trial in Criminal Cases 19

1. Prejudicial Pretrial Publicity: *Sheppard v.Maxwell* (1966) 21
2. Avoiding Mob Justice: *Frank v. Mangum* (1915) and *Moore v. Dempsey* (1923) 29
3. Racial Discrimination in Jury Selection: *Batson v. Kentucky* (1986) and *Miller-El v. Dretke* (2005) 41
4. Sex Discrimination in Jury Selection: *Hoyt v. Florida* (1961) and *Taylor v. Louisiana* (1975) 55
5. Death-Qualified Juries: *Witherspoon v. Illinois* (1968) and *Lockhart v. McCree* (1986) 67

Part Two: Due Process and the Right to an Impartial Judge 79

6. Mayor-Judges with a Financial Stake in the Outcome: *Tumey v. Ohio* (1927) and *Ward v. Village of Monroeville* (1972) 81
7. A Judge Hearing a Contempt Proceeding after Being Vilified by the Defendant: *Mayberry v. Pennsylvania* (1971) 89
8. Non-Lawyer Judges: *North v. Russell* (1976)` 101

9. The Judge Who Was Bribed in Other Cases: *Bracy v. Gramley* (1997) 111

10. A Judge Deciding a Case Involving a Major Campaign Supporter: *Caperton v. A.T. Massey Coal Co.* (2009) 121

Part Three: Due Process and the Right to an Impartial Decisionmaker in Quasi-Judicial, Non-Court Settings 135

11. Parole Revocation: *Morrissey v. Brewer* (1972) 137

12. Medical License Review: *Withrow v. Larkin* (1975) 147

13. Mental Health Commitments for Juveniles: *Parham v. J.R.* (1979) 159

14. Prison Discipline: *Edwards v. Balisok* (1997) 175

15. Enemy Combatant Cases: *Hamdi v. Rumsfeld* (2004) 181

Conclusions 193

Catalog of Cases 201

Bibliography 205

Index 213

Acknowledgments

This is the third book I have written, and as was the case with the first two, I feel incredibly privileged to have had such great support from family, friends, and colleagues. It is with this in mind that I happily thank all of those who helped me along the way.

I began writing this manuscript after spending much of early to mid-2010 researching about procedural due process. I knew that I wanted to write something about that topic, but I wasn't quite sure what it was. Finally, I stumbled upon something which was not discussed much in the literature: a connection between the Sixth Amendment right to an impartial jury and the Fourteenth Amendment due process right to a neutral judge. The connection to the due process right to a neutral decisionmaker in other contexts soon followed. Early on in this process, I wrote two papers that eventually became the basis for portions of the book. At the 68th Midwest Political Science Association (MPSA) Annual National Conference in April 2010, I presented a paper titled "Within the Framework of the Law: Supreme Court Decision-Making in Enemy Combatant Cases," which eventually became the basis for chapter fifteen of this book. I thank Jennifer Barnes Bowie and Christina Leah Boyd for their helpful feedback on that paper. In addition, at the 70th MPSA Annual National Conference in April 2012, I presented a paper titled, "Judicial Impartiality and Campaign Finance: A Critical Analysis of the U.S. Supreme Court's Due Process Jurisprudence in *Caperton v. A.T. Massey Coal*," which was the starting point for chapter ten. I thank Howard Katz, Ross Astoria, and William James Nancarrow for their helpful comments on that paper. Invaluable insight was later provided by Nichole Kathol into what is now chapter four. Although one should not "judge a book by its cover," I also thank Troy and Melissa Kozma for their work in helping to choose a design for the outside of this book.

It goes without saying that I am very thankful to everyone, including the fantastic staff at Lexington Books of the Rowman & Littlefield Publishing

Group, who did editing, reviewing, and typesetting for me. In particular, I deeply appreciate the efforts of the editors who worked on this book, including Melissa Wilks, A. Lenore Lautigar, Justin Race, and Robert Westfall. Alison Northridge and Alissa Parra of Lexington Books also labored to ensure that the book would be of the highest quality. Benjamin Schoening's efforts were crucial in typesetting the manuscript, and the feedback of an anonymous reviewer strengthened the text immensely. Finally, Alice Kasper helped me do one final check of the manuscript to make sure that it was camera-ready, and Dawn Dodge assisted in printing it.

Most importantly, I would like to thank the love and support given to me by my family, including my in-laws, Dick, Carol, Amy, Andy, Marshall, and Cole. My parents, Clint and Sharon, have always encouraged me in my work, and this book was no different. I also am quite appreciative of the patience of my daughter, Madison, and my son, Jackson, who were able to put up with me slaving over a computer screen during countless weekends and evenings. And of course, none of this would have book possible without the love of my life, my wife, Julie.

Finally, if I have forgotten to thank anyone, I sincerely apologize. The oversight was purely accidental.

Preface

In February 2011, former Luzerne County, Pennsylvania Judge Mark A. Ciavarella was on trial for thirty-nine criminal charges.[1] Anytime that a judge faces criminal charges it makes for a juicy story in the media, as it allows reporters to produce an ironic narrative. This case was more than juicy, however. It involved allegations that were nearly unbelievable and were, in many respects, appalling. Ciavarella and a fellow former judge, Michael T. Conahan, had been indicted for actions prosecutors claimed they took *as* judges. Indeed, according to various newspaper stories, Ciavarella and Conahan were involved in what was dubbed the "kids for cash" scandal, where Conahan shut down the county's juvenile detention center by cutting off public funds for it; prosecutors claimed that both judges then sent a great number of children to two new detention centers, privately owned by the judges' friends, who had given Ciavarella and Conahan $2.6 million in a *quid pro quo*.[2] Federal prosecutors also claimed that Conahan agreed to send the private facility $1.3 million per year in public funds as part of a conspiracy that lasted from 2003 to 2008.[3]

The stories from Ciavarella's juvenile courtroom that emerged during his criminal trial became too much to bear. News reports indicate that when he was judge, Ciavarella presided over countless trials that lasted as little as one or two minutes. Many children were then quickly sent to serve time in these new detention centers, often without being able to speak in their own defense and without being represented by counsel. Children were sentenced to serve time in many cases where probation officers did not recommend it and where the crime was a relatively minor nonviolent offense. Examples of these cases include the following:

- A twelve-year-old boy took his mother's car for a joyride and was involved in a minor accident. Neither he nor anyone else was injured. The boy was a first offender, he had no attorney, and he was confused how to plead at his court appearance. At the end of his day in court, his punishment was two years in a juvenile detention center.

- A thirteen-year-old boy was sent to a detention center for several days for failing to appear at a hearing as a witness. The boy's family claimed that they had never been notified about the hearing and the boy had already told school officials that he had not seen anything. This boy had never been in trouble with the law before.
- A fourteen-year-old boy appeared in court for being involved in a minor fight after school. In his first court appearance, the boy was not allowed to speak. After approximately four minutes, he was sentenced to a juvenile detention center.
- A fifteen-year-old girl appeared in court without an attorney after building a MySpace page that mocked her assistant principal. The girl, who was a good student on her first offense, was sentenced to three months in a juvenile detention center.
- A seventeen-year-old boy who was jailed by Ciavarella for a minor infraction was never the same after he was released, becoming bitter, angry, and plagued by depression. He later committed suicide by shooting himself in the chest.[4]

It has been estimated that from 2003-2008 Ciavarella presided over approximately 6,500 juvenile cases involving up to 4,000 different children. More than half of these juveniles were without the aid of an attorney to defend them. According to reports, more than half of the children who appeared before Ciavarella were sentenced to some type of juvenile detention. During the time that authorities claim this kickback scheme was occurring, Ciavarella sentenced juveniles to secure detention outside the home at a rate approximately twice the state average.[5]

If these stories are true, how could something like this happen? As a Wisconsin municipal judge, I shudder at this type of abuse of power. My state, like every other state, has ethics rules that prohibit judges from presiding over cases where there is a conflict of interest. For example, of particular relevance to Wisconsin judges is a state statute which states that "No local public official may use his or her public position or office to obtain financial gain or anything of substantial value for the private benefit of himself or herself or his or her immediate family, or for an organization with which he or she is associated."[6] Wisconsin judges are also held accountable by a code of judicial conduct, which states in relevant part that a judge shall recuse himself or herself when the "judge knows that he or she...has an economic interest in the subject matter in controversy;" the Wisconsin statutes likewise prohibit a judge from hearing a case when "a judge has a significant financial or personal interest in the outcome of the matter."[7] The American Bar Association (ABA) has model rules of professional conduct for judges that are often used as a starting point when states and the federal government write their respective rules. The ABA's model rule on this point requires judicial disqualification if the "judge knows that he or she, individually or as a fiduciary, or the judge's spouse, domestic partner, parent, or child, or any other member of the judge's family residing in the judge's household, has an economic interest in the subject matter in controversy."[8] The federal system and every state, including Ciavarella's Pennsylvania, have similar ethics rules for judges.

Of course, the financially-based conflicts of interest that arouse in the courtrooms of Michael Conahan and Mark Ciavarella are but one way for a judge to be biased. Indeed, there is a myriad of rules and laws to ensure impartiality of judges in other situations. For instance, I would have to disqualify myself from hearing a case where I am related to any party or attorney or their spouses within a third degree of kinship (a third degree of kinship includes great-grandparents, grandparents, parents, aunts, uncles, brothers, sisters, children, grandchildren, great grandchildren, nieces, and nephews), and the *ABA Model Code of Judicial Conduct* prohibits judicial action under these circumstances too.[9] The disqualification here should be obvious, as no person can be expected to be impartial when his or her close family is involved in the case. After all, if my daughter or son were a party in a case, how could the other party have any confidence that I would render a fair and impartial decision?

I would also have to disqualify myself in any case where I am a party to the case or a material witness, or if I previously acted as legal counsel to any party in the case.[10] It should be quite clear here too why it would be assumed that a judge in this situation might be biased, as one would either be ruling over one's own case or where one has some substantial stake in the outcome. Finally, there is a general catch-all conflict of interest statute for judges in Wisconsin, which prohibits judges from hearing a case when "a judge determines that, for any reason, he or she cannot, or it appears he or she cannot, act in an impartial manner."[11] This provision, which is also represented in the ABA's model rules, ensures that if a party is a close friend of mine, or if a party is someone I detest due to a prior incident, or for virtually any other reason that would impede my ability to remain neutral, then I would need to step down and let another judge hear that case. Statutes and rules such as these are a reflection of the principle that parties in a trial or hearing have the right to a detached decisionmaker who has no personal stake in the outcome of the case. And even if a judge in these types of cases thinks he or she could be unbiased, it is better to recuse oneself, because so much as the appearance of partiality is enough to call into question the fairness of a decision.

These rules protecting the rights of parties have been opined in many cases by the highest court in the land. Indeed, the U.S. Supreme Court has interpreted the U.S. Constitution to protect one's right to a neutral decisionmaker. This rests primarily in the right to procedural due process, which is located in both the Fifth and Fourteenth Amendments. Furthermore, the right in criminal cases to an impartial jury is protected by the Sixth and Fourteenth Amendments. Throughout this book, you will read about cases involving these rights, which ultimately are the core of fairness and justice. Sometimes the facts of these cases are just as shocking as what you have already read in this preface; sometimes they are even more stunning. From here forward, you will learn how the U.S. Supreme Court has ruled in these cases. These rulings, along with the facts of these cases, will bring to life and thoroughly explain this concept of having a neutral, impartial, and unbiased person or group deciding the outcome of a case.

This right to a neutral decisionmaker dates back centuries in Anglo-American law to Magna Carta, through the development of English law, to the establishment of the U.S. Constitution and Bill of Rights. The progression of this right will be examined in the introduction. The definitions of "neutral," "unbiased," and "impartial," as they are currently understood, will also be surveyed in the introduction. This will give us the proper backdrop to look in more depth at how the rights to an impartial jury in criminal cases and to procedural due process in many different types of cases ensure an unbiased decisionmaker.

Part One will specifically focus on the constitutional right for the accused to have an impartial jury. Part Two examines the due process right to a neutral judge in criminal and civil cases. Finally, Part Three looks at the right to a neutral decisionmaker and procedural due process in contexts outside of civil and criminal trials. This includes prisoner and parolee hearings, mental health commitments, license reviews, and enemy combatant tribunals.

As for the judges noted at the beginning of the preface, Michael Conahan pleaded guilty to fraud charges and was sentenced to seventeen years and six months in prison and forced to pay close to $900,000 in fines and restitution.[12] Mark Ciavarella was found guilty on twelve of the charges against him, including racketeering and conspiracy to launder money.[13] As journalist Anthony Pitts stated upon Ciavarella's guilty verdicts (but before Ciavarella was sentenced), "[h]e had time to hear and rebut the evidence against him. He had a lawyer. And when he is sentenced, he will face a judge who, we may assume, has no financial interest in his punishment. That's called justice."[14] For his acts, Ciavarella was sentenced to twenty-eight years in prison.[15] It is easy to argue that a sentence of that length or more is justified for such a blatant disregard of the rights of so many young defendants. Making sure that what Conahan and Ciavarella did will not happen to future people appearing before a judge, jury, or other decisionmaker is the focus of the constitutional right to a neutral trier of fact.

Notes

1. "Pennsylvania: Mixed Verdict for Disgraced Judge," *The New York Times*, February 18, 2011, http://www.nytimes.com/2011/02/19/us/19brfs-Judge.html?_r=1&ref=markaciavarella (accessed July 14, 2011).

2. Dave Janoski, "Ciavarella, Conahan Withdraw Guilty Pleas," *The Citizens' Voice*, August 24, 2009, http://citizensvoice.com/news/ciavarella-conahan-withdraw-guilty-pleas-1.208291#axzz1S6aJWL7n (accessed July 14, 2011); Leonard Pitts, Jr., "Kids Denied Due Process," *The Miami Herald*, February 27, 2011, http://www.miamiherald.com/2011/02/27/2086108/kids-denied-due-process.html#storylink=misearch (accessed July 14, 2011).

3. Thomas Frank, "Lock 'Em Up: Jailing Kids Is a Proud American Tradition," *The Wall Street Journal*, April 1, 2009, http://online.wsj.com/article/SB123854010220075533.html (accessed July 14, 2011). It should also be noted that Ciavarella has maintained that none of his decisions were influenced by money.

4. Pitts, "Kids Denied Due Process,"; Ian Urbina, "Despite Red Flags About Judges, a Kickback Scheme Flourished," *The New York Times*, March 27, 2009, http://www.nytimes.com/2009/03/28/us/28judges.html?_r=1 (accessed July 14, 2011); Juvenile Law Center, "Luzerne County 'Kids-For-Cash' Juvenile Court Scandal," http://www.jlc.org/luzerne/ (accessed July 14, 2011); "Distraught Mother Confronts Ciavarella Outside Courthouse, *The Times Leader*, February 18, 2011, http://www.timesleader.com/news/Deliberations-resume-in-CIavarella-trial.html (accessed July 14, 2011).

5. "Luzerne County 'Kids-For-Cash' Juvenile Court Scandal;" Urbina, "Despite Red Flags About Judges, a Kickback Scheme Flourished."

6. Wis. Stat. § 19.59(1)(a).

7. Wis. SCR 60.04(4)(d); Wis. Stat. § 757.19(2)(f).

8. American Bar Association, *ABA Model Code of Judicial Conduct*, Rule 2.11(A)(3), http://www.americanbar.org/content/dam/aba/administrative/professional_responsibility/2010_mcjc_final_for_website.authcheckdam.pdf, adopted February 2007 and amended August 2010 (accessed June 7, 2012).

9. Wis. Stat. § 757.19(2)(a); Wis. Stat. § 990.001(16); American Bar Association, Rule 2.11(A)(2).

10. Wis. Stat. § 757.19(2)(b); Wis. Stat. § 757.19(2)(c).

11. Wis. Stat. § 757.19(2)(g).

12. Michael Rubinkan, "Pa. Judge Gets 28 Years in 'Kids for Cash' Case," *Forbes*, August 11, 2011, http://www.forbes.com/feeds/ap/2011/08/11/general-us-courthouse-kickbacks_8618656.html (accessed August 11, 2011); "Former Luzerne Judge Conahan Sentenced to 17.5 years," *The Scranton Times-Tribune*, September 23, 2011, http://thetimes-tribune.com/news/former-luzerne-judge-conahan-sentenced-to-17-5-years-1.1207994 (accessed July 10, 2012).

13. "Pennsylvania: Mixed Verdict for Disgraced Judge."

14. Pitts, "Kids Denied Due Process."

15. Rubinkan, "Pa. Judge Gets 28 Years in 'Kids for Cash' Case."

Introduction:

A Short History of What It Means to Be a Neutral, Impartial, and Unbiased Decisionmaker in Anglo-American Law

No man is allowed to be a judge in his own cause, because his interest would certainly bias his judgment, and, not improbably, corrupt his integrity.
–James Madison, *Federalist No. 10* (1787)

[T]he test of an independent judiciary is a simple one — the one you would apply in choosing an umpire for a baseball game. What do you ask of him? You do not ask that he shall never make a mistake or always agree with you, or always support the home team. You want an umpire who calls them as he sees them.
–Robert H. Jackson, Annual Bar Dinner of the American Bar Association (1951)

The History of the Right to an Impartial Criminal Jury

The modern American concept of impartiality in legal decisionmaking has its genesis in England's Magna Carta. Nearly eight centuries ago, a group of English barons met at Runnymede and watched King John affix his official seal to a document that was meant to preserve a tenuous thirteenth century peace. There is no known primary draftsman of Magna Carta of 1215, but the barons as a group sought to limit the king's power with the Great Charter. They did this because King John had plunged the English kingdom into quite a bit of turmoil during his reign. Most notably, John repeatedly went to war with France between 1202 and 1214, which led to the continual need to raise taxes to finance these military excursions. John also quarreled with Pope Innocent III from 1205 to 1213; this led to the Catholic Church placing all of England under an interdict, suspending all church services in the country, which was a tremendous burden to the medieval English people. In 1214, when John returned home after another defeat at the hands of the French and asked the barons to pay a fee in lieu of military service, the barons decided that they would rather fight the king than pay him again, and they demanded that the king provide written protections for their property rights and other liberties. Thus, Magna Carta was born on June 15, 1215. However, by this time, John and Pope Innocent were on good terms, and two months after John agreed to the terms of Magna Carta, Innocent declared that the document was null and void, thus leading to continued conflict between John and the barons. John died shortly thereafter, but Magna Carta would live on, being reissued by his son, King Henry III, in 1225, and then reissued and reconfirmed multiple times over the succeeding centuries.[1]

This retelling of Magna Carta's tale demonstrates that English nobility wanted to place limits on the power of the king. Although there were a total of sixty-three articles that limited the king's power, the one that endures the most is Article 39: "No free man shall be taken, imprisoned, disseised, outlawed, banished, or in any way destroyed, nor will We proceed against or prosecute him, except by the lawful judgment of his peers and by the law of the land."

Some observations can be made from reading Article 39 of Magna Carta. First, the barons limited the king from exercising arbitrary power and imprisoning someone without a lawful purpose. Second, if the king did imprison or otherwise interfere with the liberty or property of one of his subjects, there was a proper set of procedures — the law of the land — that had to be followed. Third, the phrase "by the lawful judgment of his peers" began the right to a jury trial in criminal cases. Overall, Article 39 was the genesis of a new idea that the executive branch cannot make the final determination of guilt. Instead, if property, liberty, or life is to be taken away, a predetermined set of procedures need to first be followed, and a jury of one's peers would eventually be required to determine if one is guilty or not. Although complete separation between the executive and judicial branches would not come to fruition for several more centuries, Article 39 ultimately was the beginning of the executive branch of government needing to let someone else, someone within the judiciary who has no conflict of interest, determine the outcome of the case.[2]

This concept of a neutral person or persons making a legal decision was only just beginning in 1215. Yet, placing it in Magna Carta helped develop the right and advance it well past what was then occurring in continental Europe, which was very much struggling with how to determine guilt and innocence. Pope Innocent III, in addition to squabbling with King John, also banned clergy from using trial by ordeal. But during that same period Innocent also changed church law into an inquisitorial system designed to punish heretics. This system included secret accusations, self-incriminations, and torture. Innocent's approach became the model for many other European countries' criminal justice systems during the Middle Ages. Although England was only beginning to move into a more enlightened system of justice with Magna Carta, the rights to due process and an impartial jury would progressively develop out of it. When

Magna Carta was reissued by King Edward I in 1297, this Article was substantially the same, with the following second sentence added: "We will sell to no man, we will not deny or defer to any man either justice or right." This addition strengthened the emphasis on impartiality.[3]

Magna Carta's command that no one shall be imprisoned "except by the lawful judgment of his peers" eventually developed into a full right to a criminal trial by an impartial jury. By the fourteenth century, Parliament began construing Magna Carta's provision requiring "lawful judgment of his peers" to mean a trial by a jury.[4] By the sixteenth century, English jurors were selected to represent a cross-section of the community, and in criminal cases they were to base their decisions only on evidence presented to them and on witnesses who testified under oath in their presence.[5] When Parliament penned the 1689 Bill of Rights, it had more fully developed this right in its declaration that "jurors ought to be duly impaneled and returned, and jurors which pass upon men in trials for high treason ought to be freeholders."[6]

Famous English jurist William Blackstone, in his treatise *Commentaries on the Laws of England*, noted in 1769 the importance in a criminal trial of "particular jurors being *omni exceptione majores*," meaning that they should be beyond all exception or above suspicion. Blackstone went on to say that jurors who are empaneled should not be *propter defectum* (incompetent because of alienage, infancy, or nonresidency), *propter affectum* (related to a party), or *propter delictum* (previously stripped of citizenship). Potential jurors who fit any of these descriptions could be challenged and removed for these causes. In addition to these challenges for cause, Blackstone also emphasized the need in criminal cases for peremptory challenges, which he described as "an arbitrary and capricious species of challenge to a certain number of jurors, without shewing any cause at all." Blackstone explained that one important reason for this right is that we are liable to have "sudden impressions and unaccountable prejudices" upon seeing someone; if that happens we should not sit on a jury in that case because a defendant should not "be tried by any one man against whom he had conceived a prejudice, even without being able to assign a reason for such his dislike."[7] Clearly, these prescriptions were aimed at ensuring that a criminal defendant received a trial by an impartial panel of jurors.

During this same era, the developing impartial criminal jury trial right came to America, where it manifested itself in colonial charters and other legal documents. For instance, the General Laws of New-Plimouth of 1671 allowed for peremptory challenges to protect the right to an impartial jury:

> And it shall be in the liberty of both Plaintiffe and Defendant or any Delinquent, that is to be tryed by a Jury, to chalenge any of the Jurors, and if the chalenge be found just and reasonable by the Bench, it shall be allowed him, and others without exception shall be impannelled in their room; And if it be in case of Life and Death, the Prisoner shall have liberty to except against six or eight of the Jury, without giving any reason for his exception.[8]

Similarly, the Concessions and Agreements of West New Jersey of 1676 required trial by jury in criminal cases by "Twelve good and lawful men," of the "Neighbourhood" of the defendant, and it offered criminal defendants the right to "except against any of the said Neighbourhood, without any Reason rendered, (not exceeding thirty-five)" potential jurors.[9] The same law went on to require that the jurors not only be lawful men, but also "honest men of the Neighbourhood."[10] The colony of New York had a similar provision in 1691, declaring that "in all cases Capital and Criminal, there shall be...Twelve Good Men of the Neighbourhood to Try the Offender; who, after his Plea to the Indictment, shall be allowed his reasonable Challenges."[11]

Once the American Revolution had commenced and independence had been declared, the states began protecting the right to an impartial jury in criminal cases in their new constitutions. Beginning in 1776, they read as follows:

- **Delaware's Declaration of Rights (1776)**: "in all prosecutions for criminal offences, every man hath a right...to a speedy trial by an impartial jury."
- **Maryland's Declaration of Rights (1776)**: "in all criminal prosecutions, every man hath a right...to a speedy trial by an impartial jury."
- **North Carolina's Declaration of Rights (1776)**: "no Freeman shall be convicted of any Crime, but by the unanimous Verdict of a Jury of good and lawful Men."
- **Pennsylvania's Constitution (1776)**: "in all prosecutions for criminal offences, a man hath a right to...a speedy public trial, by an impartial jury of the country."
- **Virginia's Declaration of Rights (1776)**: "in all capital or criminal prosecutions a man hath a right...to a speedy trial by an impartial jury of his vicinage."
- **Vermont's Constitution (1777)**: "in all Prosecutions for criminal offences, a Man hath a Right to...a speedy public Trial, by an impartial jury of the Country."[12]

These six early state constitutions evidence a similarity of verbiage on the right to impartiality. Within the group of states that demanded impartiality among its criminal juries, only North Carolina retained the old colonial language that required a jury to be composed of "good and lawful men." The other states which specified the right in their new constitutions used the word "impartial" when enumerating this right. Every other state developed a constitution during this time, and in every state a jury trial right was created in criminal cases. Even if these remaining states did not stipulate that their criminal juries act impartially, due to English legal heritage that would have been assumed by the time of the American Revolution.

Once the war was won, the new country felt for various reasons that the existing national governing document, the Articles of Confederation, was inadequate. For instance, the British government decided it would negotiate treaties with each state government, as the British government thought that the new American confederation government was too weak to enforce such documents. In addition, state erection of trade barriers and coinage of state money were combining to cause drag on the national economy. Perhaps most importantly, the American confederation government appeared powerless in 1786-87 to put down Shays's Rebellion, a mob of farmers in western Massachusetts who tried to prevent the courts from opening so as to thwart foreclosures on their debt-ridden lands. For these and other reasons, the U.S. Constitution was drafted in 1787 and ratified the next year. Among other rights, the framers of the Constitution placed the right to a trial by jury in criminal cases in Article III: "The trial of all crimes, except in cases of impeachment, shall be by jury." However, during the ratification of the Constitution there were widespread calls for a bill of rights to protect many rights, including those of the criminally accused. More specifically, several state ratifying conventions in 1787-88 proposed amendments that would protect the right to an impartial criminal jury, including New York, North Carolina, Pennsylvania, Rhode Island, and Virginia.[13]

Not satisfied with the existing constitutional language on criminal juries, James Madison introduced a bill of rights in the first Congress, including the following: "The trial of all crimes...shall be by an impartial jury."[14] Madison followed the more modern course that nearly half of the state constitutions had already adopted of specifying the need for impartiality in criminal cases. After some tinkering, Congress approved the following language, which was subsequently ratified by the states as part of the Sixth Amendment: "In all criminal prosecutions, the accused shall enjoy the right to a speedy and public trial, by an impartial jury." Thus, by 1791, Magna Carta's promise of a jury trial had become firmly rooted within the United States, and the emphasis on impartiality would now be an explicit part of that guarantee.[15]

As initially interpreted by the U.S. Supreme Court, however, in *Barron v. Baltimore* (1833), the Bill of Rights only limited the powers of the federal government.[16] This left state governments free to set their own procedures and liberty protections via their respective state constitutions, which many of them ultimately did. However, *Barron* also meant that constitutional rights were protected better against some state governments than against others, as some states were more vigilant than others in protecting these rights (this point will become clear in the chapters that follow). The ratification of the Fourteenth Amendment in 1868 would eventually pave the way for most of the Bill of Rights to apply to the states. The provision in that amendment that the Court would use to limit state power in this respect was the Due Process Clause, "nor shall any State deprive any person of life, liberty, or property, without due process of law," something which will be elaborated on in more detail below. One hundred years after the Fourteenth Amendment was ratified, the Court held in *Duncan v. Louisiana* (1968) that the Due Process Clause protected the right to an impartial jury trial in state criminal cases.[17] Thus, by 1968, every jurisdiction in the United States had to ensure in criminal prosecutions that the accused would be tried by an impartial jury. As we will also see below, one important piece of impartiality became the requirement that juries include a proper cross-section of the community, which would ultimately touch on issues of jury unanimity[18] and jury size.[19] In addition, the Fourteenth Amendment's Equal Protection Clause has come into play and been used by the Court to invalidate discrimination against potential jurors; in effect, the reach of the Sixth Amendment has extended to the Fourteenth Amendment in cases where juror discrimination occurred on the basis of race and sex.

The History of the Right to Due Process

This leads us to the other constitutional right protecting neutrality in decisionmaking: due process. Not only did the Fourteenth Amendment incorporate the Sixth Amendment's right to an impartial jury in criminal cases; it also includes a due process provision that is similar to the one in the Fifth Amendment. The right to due process, in either the Fifth Amendment or the Fourteenth Amendment, has been interpreted by the U.S. Supreme Court to protect the right to an impartial jury in civil cases (when read with the Seventh Amendment) as well as to a neutral judge and a neutral decisionmaker in other contexts.

The modern concept of "due process" arose from the same language in Magna Carta that eventually led to the right to an impartial jury in criminal cases. Recall that document's 1215 command in Article 39: "No free man shall be taken, imprisoned, disseised, outlawed, banished, or in any way destroyed, nor will We proceed against or prosecute him, except by the lawful judgment of his peers and by the law of the land." The key language concerning due process is "by the law of the land." By the fourteenth century, this phrase was a major part of English law.

The vitality of the guarantee to be treated according to the law of the land, and its relation to having a neutral decisionmaker, was directly at issue in *Dr. Bonham's Case* (1610). In the sixteenth and early seventeenth centuries, the Royal College of Physicians in London was empowered by the English Parliament to regulate the local practice of medicine, and it issued certificates to this effect. The college had power not only to accuse persons of practicing medicine poorly or without a license; it also had authority to act as a court to hear such cases, and sanctions included fines and indefinite imprisonment.[20]

Thomas Bonham, a Doctor of Physic from the University of Cambridge, was charged by the College of Physicians for practicing medicine in London without a license issued by the college. He was tried in the college's own court. Bonham claimed that he did not need a license from the college, as he was a doctor of medicine at the University of Cambridge, and thus the College of Physicians had no jurisdiction over him. The college court disagreed, finding him guilty of practicing without a license and being "less sufficient and unskillful to administer physic." He was fined and imprisoned. As allowed by its corporate charter, the college proposed to keep one half of the fine imposed.[21]

Bonham appealed this case to the Court of Common Pleas, which found that the College was not empowered to imprison Bonham for unlicensed practice. Furthermore, the court found fault with the college for fining Bonham and then collecting a portion of the fine.[22] In a decision written by Sir Edward Coke, the chief justice of the court, it was declared that this was an unjust practice:

> The censors cannot be judges, ministers, and parties; judges to give sentence or judgment; ministers to make summons; and parties to have the moiety of the forfeiture, *quia aliquis non debet esse Judex in propria causa, imo iniquum est aliquem suae rei esse judicem* and one cannot be judge and attorney for any of the parties...And it appears in our books, that in many cases, the common law will controul acts of parliament, and sometimes adjudge them to be utterly void: for when an act of parliament is against common right and reason, or repugnant, or impossible to be performed, the common law will controul it, and adjudge such act to be void.[23]

The Latin phrase above is translated as follows: "because someone ought not to be a judge in his own cause, for it is unfair for someone to be a judge in his own affairs."[24] Coke was making two important points in this passage from *Dr. Bonham's Case*. First, very obviously, Coke believed that self-interest is too strong a motivator to allow one who is a party to a case to also preside over the case, as was the case with the college. Second, Coke believed that if the law is against "common right and reason," or if it is "repugnant," then even if the law that is duly passed by Parliament is still void. This was confirmed by Coke's further assertion that "some statutes are made against law and right, which those who made them perceiving, would not put them in execution."[25] The common right and the law which Coke was referring to is "the law of the land." Thus, even though the college was empowered by law to sit in judgment of Bonham and then keep one half of the fine imposed, that authorization itself violated the law of the land, in part, because the college could not possibly be neutral in any real sense of the term.

Dr. Bonham's Case would eventually be the inspiration for judicial review in the United States.[26] Before that occurred, however, the right was strengthened in England and then in the American colonies. One of the more notable moments involving due process was when the right to be protected by the "law of the land" was written into the 1628 Petition of Right. The Petition was passed by Parliament in response to King Charles I's arbitrary imprisonment of five knights who had failed to pay loans to the king; the knights were not formally charged with any crime, nor were they given the opportunity for bail.[27] In effect, the King tried to act as both the prosecutor and the judge. This action, taken in violation of the "law of the land" guarantee, led Parliament to reaffirm that the right to be protected by the law of the land in Magna Carta was not simply an act of monarchical grace. Rather, the Petition reminded Charles that his attempt at exercising this type of power would be met in a way similar to how the barons met the actions of his predecessor John — with strong resistance.[28]

With this as a backdrop, the right migrated to the other side of the Atlantic Ocean. During the seventeenth century, the language "law of the land" was maintained by the colonial legal texts. For instance, the 1639 Maryland Act for the Liberties of the People affirmed that its inhabitants "Shall not be imprisoned nor disseissed or disposed of their freehold goods or Chattels or be out Lawed Exiled or otherwise destroyed fore judged or punished then according to the Laws of this province."[29] In addition, the Massachusetts 1641 Body of Liberties declared that "No mans life shall be taken away, no mans honor or good name shall be stayned, no mans person shall be arrested, restrayed, banished, dismembred, nor any ways punished...unless it be by vertue or equitie of some express law of the Country wanting the same."[30] New York's "Act Declaring...Rights and Privileges" of 1691 stated that "no Free-man shall be taken or imprisoned, or be deprived of his Free-hold or Liberty...but by the lawful Judgment of his Peers, and by the Laws of this Province."[31] Other colonies employed similar phraseology. Although this colonial language differed slightly from Magna Carta's "law of the land" terminology, the evolving concept of due process had taken root.

Much like the guarantee to an impartial criminal jury, the right to due process took more shape once independence had been declared and states began writing their own constitutions in 1776. They include the following protections:

- **Connecticut's Declaration of Rights (1776)**: "no Man's Life shall be taken away: No Man's Honor or good Name shall be stained: No Man's Person shall be arrested, restrained, banished, dismembered, nor any ways punished: No Man shall be deprived of his Wife or Children: No Man's Goods or Estate shall be taken away from him, nor any ways indamaged under the colour of Law, or countenance of Authority; unless clearly warranted by the Laws of this State."
- **Maryland's Declaration of Rights (1776)**: "no freeman ought to be taken or imprisoned, or disseized of his freehold, liberties or privileges, or outlawed, or exiled, or in any manner destroyed, or deprived of his life, liberty, or property, but by the judgment of his peers, or by the law of the land."
- **North Carolina's Declaration of Rights (1776)**: "no Freeman ought to be taken, imprisoned or dississed of his Freehold, Liberties, or Privileges, or outlawed or exiled, or in any manner destroyed or deprived of his Life, Liberty, or Property, but by the Law of the Land."
- **Pennsylvania's Constitution (1776)**: "nor can any man be justly deprived of his liberty except by the laws of the land, or the judgment of his peers."
- **Virginia's Declaration of Rights (1776)**: "no man [shall] be deprived of his liberty except by the law of the land, or the judgment of his peers."

- **New York's Constitution (1777)**: "no Member of this State shall be disfranchised, or deprived of any of the Rights or Privileges secured to the Subjects of this State by this Constitution, unless by the Law of the Land, of the Judgment of his Peers."
- **Vermont's Declaration of Rights (1777)**: "nor can any man be justly deprived of his Liberty, except by the Laws of the Land, or the Judgment of his Peers."
- **South Carolina's Constitution (1778)**: "no Freeman of this State [shall] be taken, or imprisoned, or disseized of his Freehold, Liberties, or Privileges, or out-lawed, or exiled, or in any Manner destroyed, or deprived of his Life, Liberty, or Property, but by the Judgment of his Peers, or by the Law of the Land."
- **Massachusetts' Constitution (1780)**: "no subject shall be arrested, imprisoned, despoiled, or deprived of his property, immunities, or privileges, put out of the protection of the law, exiled, or deprived of his life, liberty, or estate, but by the judgment of his peers, or the law of the land."
- **New Hampshire's Constitution (1783)**: "no subject shall be arrested, imprisoned, despoiled, or deprived of his property, immunities, or privileges, put out of the protection of the law, exiled, or deprived of his life, liberty, or estate, but by the judgment of his peers, or the law of the land."[32]

Some conclusions are readily apparent from looking over this list. First, shortly after the Revolution began, nearly every state had some sort of explicit due process provision (unlike the impartial criminal jury trial guarantee, which in over half of the states was not explicitly listed in the state constitution). Second, a wide variety of rights were protected by "the law of the land" in these new state constitutions, although they could eventually be easily summarized by the phrase "life, liberty, or property" that found its way into the U.S. Constitution's Fifth Amendment. Third, some states used the same language. In particular, Massachusetts and New Hampshire had identical provisions, and the protections in Pennsylvania and Virginia differed only stylistically. Part of this similarity is, no doubt, due to a copying in some states of phraseology from the relevant provision in Magna Carta, which then led to later states copying the language from earlier states.

Finally, some states were using, or would soon begin to use, the "life, liberty, or property" and "due process of law" phrases. Most notably, New York, which used the older "law of the land" phrase in its 1777 constitution (listed above), later rewrote the highest law of the state in a 1787 state bill of rights. In that latter document, New York declared in four separate provisions that there was a right to "due Process of Law" when various rights were at stake.[33] In another example, Pennsylvania's 1776 constitution (listed above) declared that "liberty" was protected by the law of the land. When rewritten in 1790, that state's constitution stated that one could not be deprived of "life, liberty, or property," except by the law of the land.[34] South Carolina's 1778 constitution (listed above) as well as its 1790 rewrite both used the "life, liberty, or property" language.

All of this state constitutional language gave James Madison plenty to work with when he drafted the relevant portion of the U.S. Bill of Rights in 1789. His proposal was that "No person shall...be deprived of life, liberty, or property without due process of law."[35] Madison used the newer phrase "due process," instead of the older "law of the land." The language of the Fifth Amendment, when ratified in 1791, was precisely what Madison proposed: "No person shall...be deprived of life, liberty, or property without due process of law." Madison did this to place a stronger limit on executive power than the vaguer "law of the land" phrase could.[36] Madison also chose to use the word "shall" when stating what the right protected, which is language that is markedly stronger than some of the states' requirements that persons "ought" to not be deprived of this right. Proof that impartiality of decisionmakers was on his mind at this time was evidenced not only in Madison's drafting of the impartial jury right, but also in his Coke-like statement in *Federalist No. 10* that "[n]o man is allowed to be a judge in his own cause, because his interest would certainly bias his judgment, and, not improbably, corrupt his integrity."[37]

The U.S. Supreme Court has long held that the Fifth Amendment's Due Process Clause protects the rights identified in Magna Carta. This has been recognized since Justice Benjamin Curtis penned the following words when speaking for the Court in *Murray's Lessee v. Hoboken Land & Improvement Co.* (1856), explaining why the Framers used "due process of law" instead of the older phrasing from Magna Carta:

> The words, "due process of law" were undoubtedly intended to convey the same meaning as the words "by the law of the land," in Magna Charta. Lord Coke, in his commentary on those words, says they mean due process of law. The Constitutions which had been adopted by the several States before the formation of the federal Constitution, following the language of the great charter more closely, generally contained the words, "but by the judgment of his peers, or the law of the land"...To have followed, as in the state constitutions, and in the ordinance of 1787, the words of Magna Charta, and declared that no person shall be deprived of his life, liberty, or property but by the judgment of his peers or the law of the land, would have been in part superfluous and inappropriate. To have taken the clause, "law of the land," without its immediate context, might possibly have given rise to doubts, which would be effectually dispelled by using those words which the great commentator on Magna Charta had declared to be the true meaning of the phrase, "law of the land," in that instrument, and which were undoubtedly then received as their true meaning.[38]

Thus, largely for the sake of clarity, over time the phrasing from Magna Carta was replaced with "due process of law" in the Fifth Amendment. Similar language was used when the Fourteenth Amendment was ratified in 1868, thus placing all state governments under this restriction as well: "nor shall any state deprive any person of life, liberty, or property, without due process of law."

Decades later, Robert H. Jackson, a U.S. Supreme Court justice who believed that the "right to fair trial is the right that stands guardian over all other rights,"[39] famously dissected the meaning of procedural due process and the tie between this right and an impartial judge: "Procedural fairness, if not all that originally was meant by due process of law, is at least what it most uncompromisingly requires. Procedural due process…must be a specialized responsibility within the competence of the judiciary on which they do not bend before political branches of the Government."[40] Justice Jackson then went on to note the following:

> Only the untaught layman or the charlatan lawyer can answer that procedures matter not. Procedural fairness and regularity are of the indispensable essence of liberty. Severe substantive laws can be endured if they are fairly and impartially applied. Indeed, if put to the choice, one might well prefer to live under Soviet substantive law applied in good faith by our common-law procedures than under our substantive law enforced by Soviet procedural practices.[41]

Justice Jackson here was drawing the connection between due process and an impartial arbiter. The best written laws are nothing without a fair and impartial application and procedural fairness. Jackson also elaborated on this point by analogizing to America's pastime during a speech to the American Bar Association honoring Judge Learned Hand and Judge Augustus Hand:

> [T]he test of an independent judiciary is a simple one — the one you would apply in choosing an umpire for a baseball game. What do you ask of him? You do not ask that he shall never make a mistake or always agree with you, or always support the home team. You want an umpire who calls them as he sees them.[42]

Thus, Jackson rightfully ties together an independent judiciary to the notion of procedural fairness. The decisionmaker's impartiality is closely connected to being free from undue influence. Just as we would not want an umpire in a baseball game to be selected by the home team, we want to make sure that neither of the parties has power over the legal decisionmaker, whether that person is a jury, a judge, or someone else. This impartiality is a key part of understanding the Due Process Clauses of the Fifth and Fourteenth Amendments.

Eventually, the U.S Supreme Court would use these two due process clauses to protect not only the right to an impartial criminal jury trial (via incorporation), but also the right to an impartial civil jury, the right to a neutral judge, and the right to a neutral decisionmaker in many other contexts, including hearing officers and boards that hold proceedings regarding prisoner discipline, parole, mental health commitments, license reviews, and enemy combatants. Some key examples of how this right came before the Supreme Court for interpretation are examined in the chapters that follow.

Defining Our Terms: Neutral, Impartial, and Unbiased

Before moving on to the real world cases about neutrality, impartiality, and being unbiased, it is important to offer some preliminary definitions of these terms. Although these definitions will become fuller and clearer throughout the book when examining the cases that follow, it is first necessary to make sure that the general idea of these concepts is clear.

As a starting point, *Black's Law Dictionary* defines "neutrality" as the "state or quality of being impartial or unbiased." It further defines the adjective "neutral" in three different ways: (1) "Indifferent;" (2) "(Of a judge, mediator, arbitrator, or actor) refraining from taking sides in a dispute;" and (3) "Impartial; Unbiased." *Black's Law Dictionary* also defines "impartial" as "Unbiased; disinterested." Although "unbiased" is not defined in the dictionary, the term "bias" is described as "[i]nclination; prejudice; predilection." Finally, an "impartial jury" is one that "has no opinion about the case at the start of the trial and that bases its verdict on competent legal evidence."[43]

A few points are discernible from these definitions. First, it is clear that these three terms — neutral, impartial, and unbiased — can generally be used interchangeably. Second, there is either an implicit or explicit emphasis with all three terms on the decisionmaker not making up its mind before hearing evidence, instead coming to conclusions after hearing only evidence that it is supposed to hear.

Third, all of these terms are defined in ways quite similar to the ways in which those outside of the legal community tend to understand them. *Merriam-Webster's Collegiate Dictionary* offers the primary definition of the adjective "neutral" as "not engaged on either side," and it later lists "indifferent" under the definitions. The dictionary defines "impartial" as meaning "not partial or biased: treating or affecting all equally." Merriam-Webster describes "unbiased" as "free from bias; *esp*: free from all prejudice and favoritism."[44] Thus, these legal terms should not be thought of as legalese, as they are meant generally to convey the same meaning as when used by the average citizen in similar contexts.

The U.S. Supreme Court has offered its opinion as to what these terms mean as well. In particular, the Court noted the following in *United States v. Wood* (1936) when determining the meaning of the right to an impartial jury under the Sixth Amendment: "Impartiality is not a technical conception. It is a state of mind. For the ascertainment of this mental attitude of appropriate indifference, the Constitution lays down no particular tests and procedure is not chained to any ancient and artificial formula."[45] However, this does little to describe anything specific about this right, save to say that to a certain degree it defies specification.

The Supreme Court was more precise a few decades later when deciding *Irvin v. Dowd* (1961). *Irvin* involved a case where the defendant, after being convicted of murder, claimed that he was denied a fair trial by impartial jurors because of prejudicial pretrial publicity (a topic explored in more detail in chapter one). Of particular note was the fact that eight of the twelve jurors admitted during jury selection that they thought Irvin was guilty. The Supreme Court eventually vacated the decision, finding that Irvin was denied his impartial jury right.[46]

In the course of its *Irvin* decision, the Court spelled out in more detail what it means to have an impartial jury. According to the Court, "[i]n essence, the right to jury trial guarantees to the criminally accused a fair trial by a panel of impartial, "indifferent" jurors. The failure to accord an accused a fair hearing violates even the minimal standards of due process... In the language of Lord Coke, a juror must be as "indifferent as he stands unsworne." His verdict must be based upon the evidence developed at the trial."[47]

There is no question that an impartial juror must be indifferent to the outcome before trial, basing his or her vote of "guilty" or "not guilty" on the evidence entered into the trial record. But how far does this concept of indifference extend? The Court in *Irvin* proposed a limit, finding that a juror can know a few things about a case and still be able to sit in judgment of a criminal defendant:

> It is not required, however, that the jurors be totally ignorant of the facts and issues involved. In these days of swift, widespread and diverse methods of communication, an important case can be expected to arouse the interest of the public in the vicinity, and scarcely any of those best qualified to serve as jurors will not have formed some impression or opinion as to the merits of the case. This is particularly true in criminal cases. To hold that the mere existence of any preconceived notion as to the guilt or innocence of an accused, without more, is sufficient to rebut the presumption of a prospective juror's impartiality would be to establish an impossible standard. It is sufficient if the juror can lay aside his impression or opinion and render a verdict based on the evidence presented in court.[48]

Given the advances in communications technology by the early 1960s, the Court found that in some cases it might be nearly impossible to find a jury of persons completely ignorant of all facts in a case (something which is certainly even more true more than one half century later). Thus, a juror can learn some facts about a case before being empaneled and still be indifferent to the extent of being impartial if he or she is willing to set aside any "preconceived notion as to the guilt or innocence of the accused." Again, the key is that the juror *considers* only the evidence presented at trial.

This need for impartiality or neutrality, with the help of due process, extends well beyond the jury box to other decisionmakers. Most notable here are judges. According to the ABA's *Model Code of Judicial Conduct*, a judge is "impartial" if he or she possesses "absence of bias or prejudice in favor of, or against, particular parties or classes of parties, as well as maintenance of an open mind in considering issues that may come before a judge."[49] In a case that did not involve a judge presiding over any particular case, *Republican Party of Minnesota v. White* (2002) dealt with the issue of free speech for judges running for office. At issue was a 1974 Minnesota judicial ethics rule that prohibited judicial candidates, including incumbent judges, from announcing their views on disputed legal or political issues. Sitting judges who violated this rule could be disciplined, with penalties including removal from office or suspension without pay, while attorneys running for judicial office who violated the rule could be suspended from the practice of law or disbarred. When Gregory Wersal ran for the Minnesota Supreme Court in 1996 and 1998, he wished to distribute literature criticizing the court's decisions on various issues, including crime, welfare, and abortion. The legal uncertainty here for Wersal led him to file a lawsuit, alleging that the rule violated his First Amendment right to free speech. In response, Minnesota claimed that this rule was necessary to preserve the *actual* impartiality of the state's judiciary and to preserve the *appearance* of impartiality of the state's judiciary. A majority on the U.S. Supreme Court sided with Wersal, holding that the ethics rule violated the First Amendment and that Minnesota's purported justifications for the law that emphasized impartiality did not survive scrutiny.[50]

In the course of its *White* decision, the Court majority, through the pen of Justice Antonin Scalia, waxed in great detail about the meaning of judicial impartiality. Justice Scalia began with a basic premise:

> One meaning of "impartiality" in the judicial context — and of course its root meaning — is the lack of bias for or against either *party* to the proceeding. Impartiality in this sense assures equal application of the law. That is, it guarantees a party that the judge who hears his case will apply the law to him in the same way he applies it to any other party. This is the traditional sense in which the term is used.[51]

This understanding of impartiality reflects the basic definitions cited above. Scalia would go on to add a second possible definition of "impartial" when interpreting the judicial role: "It is perhaps possible to use the term 'impartiality' in the judicial context (though this is certainly not a common usage) to mean lack of preconception in favor of or against a particular *legal view*," with Scalia elaborating that this "sort of impartiality would be concerned, not with guaranteeing litigants equal application of the law, but rather with guaranteeing them an equal chance to persuade the court on the legal points in their case." However, Scalia rejected this as a possible definition, as "it is virtually impossible to find a judge who does not have preconceptions about the law," and such a judge would be so ignorant as to be unqualified.[52]

Justice Scalia noted one remaining conceivable meaning of impartiality:

> A third possible meaning of "impartiality" (again not a common one) might be described as openmindedness. This quality in a judge demands, not that he have no preconceptions on legal issues, but that he be willing to consider views that oppose his preconceptions, and remain open to persuasion, when the issues arise in a pending case. This sort of impartiality seeks to guarantee each litigant, not an *equal* chance to win the legal points in the case, but at least *some*

chance of doing so. It may well be that impartiality in this sense, and the appearance of it, are desirable in the judiciary.[53]

Regardless of the different potential meanings of impartiality, there is no question that the Court in *White* did not think the threat to judicial impartiality or the appearance of it was great enough to overcome the First Amendment rights of judicial candidates in Minnesota. Yet, the case did not completely clarify the meaning of impartiality, nor did every justice on the Court agree with Scalia's interpretation of that word. For instance, in a concurring opinion Justice Sandra Day O'Connor noted that "[w]e of course want judges to be impartial, in the sense of being free from any personal stake in the outcome of the cases to which they are assigned. But if judges are subject to regular elections they are likely to feel that they have at least some personal stake in the outcome of every publicized case."[54] Thus, O'Connor called into the question the impartiality of elected judges generally. For O'Connor, the solution is not to restrict the free speech rights of judicial candidates; instead, she suggested that the state should adopt a merit selection system, where judges do not run against challengers in contested elections.

In his dissent, Justice John Paul Stevens was very clear that a judicial candidate who makes something other than general legal statements during the course of a campaign to solicit votes "demonstrates either a lack of impartiality or a lack of understanding of the importance of maintaining public confidence in the impartiality of the judiciary."[55] Thus, Stevens believed that a judge who makes any specific statements about the meaning of the law during a judicial campaign cannot possibly be neutral on those questions when later sitting on the bench: "the judicial reputation for impartiality and openmindedness is compromised by electioneering that emphasizes the candidate's personal predilections rather than his qualifications for judicial office."[56] Overall, then, the *White* case demonstrates that although Supreme Court justices share no well-settled definition of judicial impartiality, they generally see it as important and as related to open-mindedness and being unbiased.

Finally, impartiality arises in a third context among a different class of decisionmakers beyond jurors and judges. Among some other government officials and hearing officers, due process demands that they act with a degree of neutrality. The Court most particularly stated this requirement in *Goldberg v. Kelly* (1970), a case which held that a fair hearing was required prior to the termination of welfare benefits.[57] Writing for the Court, Justice Brennan noted the following about the need for these hearing officers to be impartial:

> [T]he decisionmaker's conclusion as to a recipient's eligibility must rest solely on the legal rules and evidence adduced at the hearing. To demonstrate compliance with this elementary requirement, the decision maker should state the reasons for his determination and indicate the evidence he relied on, though his statement need not amount to a full opinion or even formal findings of fact and conclusions of law. And, of course, an impartial decision maker is essential.

> We agree with the District Court that prior involvement in some aspects of a case will not necessarily bar a welfare official from acting as a decision maker. He should not, however, have participated in making the determination under review.[58]

Like the definitions we have seen for jurors and judges, administrative hearing officers must also rely on the evidence presented in accordance with prior established legal rules. They should also state the reasons for their decisions to prove that they have reached reasoned conclusions based on that evidence presented. Yet, beyond requiring this type of decisionmaker to base decisions on evidence presented, be "impartial," and state the reasons for the decision, the Court in *Goldberg* allowed for much more flexibility under this definition of impartiality, including some prior involvement in the case. For jurors and judges, that type of prior involvement might meet the very definition of partiality. But in the administrative hearing context, as we will see in more detail when we reach Part Three, the notion of neutrality and impartiality becomes more fluid.

Of course, these definitions here are only a start. The following cases will provide flesh to the relatively bare bones legal phrases "impartial jury" and "due process of law" in the context of understanding what it means to have a neutral decisionmaker. The subsequent real world cases, with actual facts, help to demonstrate what these powerful legal concepts were meant to guarantee and what they were meant to prevent.

Notes

1. Nick Barratt, "The Revenues of John and Phillip Augustus Revisited," in S.D. Church, ed., *King John: New Interpretations* (Woodbridge: The Boydell Press, 1999), 86-90; Danny Danziger and John Gillingham, *1215: The Year of Magna Carta* (New York: Simon and Schuster, 2003), 132; A.E. Dick Howard, *Magna Carta: Text and Commentary* (Charlottesville: University of Virginia Press, 1998), 3; F. Donald Logan, *A History of the Church in the Middle Ages* (New York: Routledge, 2002), 188; Samuel Dash, *Intruders: Unreasonable Searches and Seizures from King John to John Ashcroft* (New Brunswick, NJ: Rutgers University Press, 2004), 15.
2. Eric T. Kasper, "The Influence of Magna Carta in Limiting Executive Power in the War on Terror," *Political Science Quarterly* 126 (2011-12): 547-78, 554.
3. David J. Bodenhamer, *Fair Trial: Rights of the Accused in American History* (New York: Oxford, 1992), 12-13; Kasper, "The Influence of Magna Carta."
4. A.E. Dick Howard, *The Road from Runnymede: Magna Carta and Constitutionalism in America* (Charlottesville: University Press of Virginia, 1968), 8.
5. Thomas Buckles, *Laws of Evidence* (Clifton Park, NY: Thomas Delmar Learning, 2003), 10.
6. Leonard W. Levy, *Origins of the Bill of Rights* (New Haven: Yale University Press, 1999), 271.
7. William Blackstone, *Commentaries on the Laws of England, Volume 4* (Chicago: University of Chicago Press, 1769 (1979), 346-47.
8. Neil H. Cogan, ed., *The Complete Bill of Rights: The Drafts, Debates, Sources, & Origins* (New York: Oxford University Press, 1997), 404.

9. Cogan, *Complete Bill of Rights*, 405.
10. Cogan, *Complete Bill of Rights*, 407.
11. Cogan, *Complete Bill of Rights*, 409.
12. Cogan, *Complete Bill of Rights*, 402-413.
13. Cogan, *Complete Bill of Rights*, 401-02; David Brian Robertson, "Madison's Opponents and Constitutional Design," *The American Political Science Review* 99 (2005): 225-243, 226; Benjamin Ginsberg, Theodore J. Lowi, and Margaret Weir, *We the People: An Introduction to American Politics* (New York: Norton, 2011), 43-44.
14. Annals of Congress, Volume 1, 452 (1789).
15. The Seventh Amendment also protected the right to a jury trial in civil cases: "In suits at common law, where the value in controversy shall exceed twenty dollars, the right of trial by jury shall be preserved."
16. *Barron v. Baltimore*, 32 U.S. 243 (1833).
17. *Duncan v. Louisiana*, 391 U.S. 145 (1968).
18. *Johnson v. Louisiana*, 406 U.S. 356 (1972); *Apodoca v. Oregon*, 406 U.S. 404 (1972).
19. *Williams v. Florida*, 399 U.S. 78 (1970); *Ballew v. Georgia*, 435 U.S. 223 (1978).
20. Mary Sarah Bilder, "The Corporate Origins of Judicial Review," *Yale Law Journal* 116 (2006): 502-566, 531; Samuel Edmund Thorne, *Essays in English Legal History* (London: Hambledon Press, 1985), 269.
21. Bilder, "Corporate Origins," 531; Thorne, *English Legal History*, 269; John V. Orth, *Due Process of Law: A Brief History* (Lawrence, KS: University Press of Kansas, 2003), 18.
22. Orth, *Due Process of Law*, 18.
23. *Dr. Bonham's Case*, 8 Co. Rep. 107a, 118a, 77 Eng. Rep. 638, 652 (C.P. 1610).
24. Orth, *Due Process of Law*, 19.
25. *Dr. Bonham's Case*, 8 Co, Rep. at 118a, 77 Eng. Rep. at 652.
26. Bilder, "Corporate Origins," 505; Allen Dillard Boyer, "'Understanding, Authority, and Will': Sir Edward Coke and the Elizabethan Origins of Judicial Review," *Boston College Law Review* 39 (1997): 43-93.
27. Mark Kishlansky, "Tyranny Denied: Charles I, Attorney General Heath, and the Five Knights' Case," *The Historical Journal* 42 (March 1999): 59-60.
28. Kasper, 559-60.
29. Cogan, *Complete Bill of Rights*, 350.
30. Cogan, *Complete Bill of Rights*, 350.
31. Cogan, *Complete Bill of Rights*, 352.
32. Cogan, *Complete Bill of Rights*, 349-355.
33. Cogan, *Complete Bill of Rights*, 353.
34. Cogan, *Complete Bill of Rights*, 353-54.
35. Annals of Congress, Volume 1, 452.
36. Bernard Schwartz, *The Great Rights of Mankind: A History of the American Bill of Rights* (Madison: Madison House, 1992), 151-52.
37. *The Federalist No. 10*, at 162 (James Madison) (Jack N. Rakove, ed., 1999).
38. *Murray's Lessee v. Hoboken Land & Improvement Co.*, 59 U.S. 272, 276 (1856) (internal citations omitted).
39. *Dennis v. United States*, 339 U.S. 162, 173 (1950) (Jackson, J., concurring).
40. *Shaughnessy v. Mezei*, 345 U.S. 206, 224 (1953) (Jackson, J., dissenting).
41. *Shaughnessy v. Mezel*, 345 U.S. at 224.

42. Robert H. Jackson, "Why Learned and Augustus Hand Became Great," Annual Bar Dinner, American Bar Association, Waldorf-Astoria Hotel, New York, New York, December 13, 1951.

43. Bryan A. Garner, ed., *Black's Law Dictionary* (St. Paul, MN: West, 2009), 183, 820, 934, 1140.

44. Frederick C. Mish, ed., *Merriam-Webster's Collegiate Dictionary* (Springfield, MA: Merriam-Webster, 2009), 622, 834, 1360.

45. *United States v. Wood*, 299 U.S. 123, 145-46 (1936).

46. *Irvin v. Dowd*, 366 U.S. 717 (1961).

47. *Irvin*, 366 U.S. at 722.

48. *Irvin*, 366 U.S. at 722-23.

49. American Bar Association, *ABA Model Code of Judicial Conduct*, Terminology, http://www.americanbar.org/content/dam/aba/administrative/professional_responsibility/2010_mcjc_final_for_website.authcheckdam.pdf, adopted February 2007 and amended August 2010 (accessed June 7, 2012).

50. *Republican Party of Minnesota v. White*, 536 U.S. 765 (2002).

51. *White*, 536 U.S. at 775-76 (emphasis in original).

52. *White*, 536 U.S. at 777-78 (emphasis in original).

53. *White*, 536 U.S. at 778 (emphasis in original).

54. *White*, 536 U.S. at 788-89 (O'Connor, J., concurring).

55. *White*, 536 U.S. at 800 (Stevens, J., dissenting).

56. *White*, 536 U.S. at 802.

57. *Goldberg v. Kelly*, 397 U.S. 254 (1970).

58. *Goldberg*, 397 U.S. at 271.

Part One:

An Impartial Jury Trial in Criminal Cases

~ 1 ~

Prejudicial Pretrial Publicity: *Sheppard v. Maxwell* (1966)

Due process requires that the accused receive a trial by an
impartial jury free from outside influences.
– *Sheppard v. Maxwell*, 384 U.S. 333, 362 (1966)

As noted in the Introduction, the right to a trial by jury has an eight century history in Anglo-American law. It was enshrined in the U.S. Constitution, and it is a major part of the American legal system today. The importance of this right cannot be underestimated. Thomas Jefferson was particularly fond of the right, once noting that "trial by jury is part of a bright constellation which leads to peace, liberty, and safety." An even more insightful comment by Jefferson was as follows: "I consider trial by jury as the only anchor ever yet imagined by man, by which a government can be held to the principles of its constitution." Although not every American gives as much responsibility to this right, there is no question that it remains a popular right to this day.[1]

Yet, for this right to be meaningful, jurors need to be impartial. They must be selected in a manner that discards anyone with prior involvement in the case, they must be allowed to hear only evidence that is admissible, and they must not be influenced by outside sources during the trial. Anything short of this could create bias on the jury.

Even to modern observers who have witnessed the spectacles that were the criminal trials of O.J. Simpson and Casey Anthony, the trial of Dr. Samuel Sheppard remains perhaps the greatest media circus in American legal history. The trial captivated the public, it was covered extensively by the press, and it is believed to have inspired the popular 1960s television program, *The Fugitive*, as well as the blockbuster and critically acclaimed 1993 movie of the same name. This saga would also eventually land in the U.S. Supreme Court.

As will be described in more detail, the main issue before the U.S. Supreme Court in *Sheppard v. Maxwell* (1966) was whether or not Sam Sheppard received a fair trial before an impartial jury under cloud of prejudicial pretrial publicity that existed in his case. In its review of Sheppard's case, the Court had to strike a balance between two of the Constitution's commands: the right of a criminal defendant under the Sixth Amendment and Fourteenth Amendment's Due Process Clause to receive a fair and impartial jury trial was pitted against the First and Fourteenth Amendment right to the freedom of the press.

Sam Sheppard's saga began on the evening of July 3, 1954. He and his wife, Marilyn Sheppard, were entertaining neighborhood friends, the Aherns, at their lakeshore home in Bay Villiage, Ohio, a suburb of Cleveland on Lake Erie. At the time, Sheppard was a rather successful thirty-year-old osteopath, and his wife was pregnant. After dinner, the group retired to the Sheppard living room to watch television. Subsequently, Sam Sheppard fell asleep on the couch. Sheppard claims that later in the evening after their guests left, Marilyn partially woke him to tell him that she was going off to bed.[2]

According to Sheppard, he was awoken at some point in the pre-dawn hours of July 4 by a moan or scream, which he assumed was from his wife. Sheppard claimed that he immediately ran upstairs, where he saw "a white form" with bushy hair standing beside his and Marilyn's bed. Sheppard claimed to have then struggled with the "form" until he was struck on the back of the neck, which caused him to pass out. When he regained consciousness, Sheppard checked his wife's pulse, finding her dead. After checking on his son, Sheppard heard a noise downstairs. When he investigated the sound, he claimed that he discovered this same bushy haired man leaving by the backdoor. Sheppard caught up with the man on the beach, where he again fought with him until losing consciousness. Sheppard awoke partially in the water, at which time he was alone. Sheppard then phoned the city's mayor, Spencer Houk, a neighbor whom he knew personally, for help. Shortly after the mayor and his wife arrived at the house, the mayor called the police.[3]

When police arrived, they found Marilyn's body half-nude, in a pool of blood, with her head severely beaten. Dr. Sam Gerber, the Coroner, was reported to have remarked that morning, "Well, it is evident the doctor did this, so let's go get the confession out of him." After Sheppard initially received treatment for his injuries rather than be questioned by authorities, Gerber did eventually interrogate Sheppard later that morning while the widower was sedated.[4] On the afternoon of July 4, Sheppard was interrogated at length by Bay Village Police Chief John Eaton and two other officers. Over the next few weeks, Sheppard was interrogated multiple times and given a lie detector test, all without having an attorney present.[5] Clearly, Sheppard had quickly become the primary suspect in his wife's homicide.

Given the intriguing story, as well as the relatively high profile of the successful Dr. Sheppard, the local media began covering the investigation vigorously. On July 7, the day of Marilyn's funeral, Assistant Cuyahoga County Attorney John Mahon sharply criticized the Sheppard family in a local newspaper story for Sheppard not immediately taking questions from authorities. This began a series of newspaper stories that attacked Sheppard for not cooperating, implicated Sheppard in his wife's death, or criticized authorities for not acting quickly enough to arrest Sheppard. Headlines over the following weeks and months from the three Cleveland newspapers included the following samples, many of which were on the front pages of their respective papers:

- Why Isn't Sam Sheppard in Jail?
- Quit Stalling — Bring Him In
- Gerber Tells of Surgery Tool Imprint on Marilyn's Pillow
- Coroner Says Dr. Sam Had Normal Pulse
- Why No Inquest? Do It Now, Dr. Gerber
- Getting Away With Murder
- Kerr Urges Sheppard's Arrest
- Why Don't Police Quiz Top Suspect?
- Dr. Sam Faces Quiz At Jail On Marilyn's Fear Of Him
- Sam Called A "Jekyll-Hyde" By Marilyn, Cousin To Testify
- Says Dr. Sam Talked Divorce
- Link 5 Women to Doctor
- Patient Tells About Dates
- But Who Will Speak for Marilyn?[6]

One of the headlines from this list, "Why No Inquest? Do It Now, Dr. Gerber," was run on July 21. A coroner's inquest is a hearing to determine facts when there has been a death, including the identity of the deceased and how, when, and where the deceased died. The day that the headline ran, Coroner Gerber called for an inquest to be held the following day,[7] probably as a reaction to the publicity. The atmosphere at the inquest was like that of a carnival. It was held in a crowded gymnasium to help accommodate the press, and it was attended by innumerable reporters and photographers. Before the inquest began, Sheppard was searched in front of the press and other spectators. His attorneys were allowed to be present, but they were prohibited from participating in the inquest in any way. Sheppard was interrogated for over five hours over the three-day inquest, which was broadcast live on television.[8]

The extensive media coverage continued as the investigation carried on. For instance, a cartoon of the body of a sphinx with Sheppard's head appeared in a newspaper with this caption below it: "'I Will Do Everything In My Power to Help Solve This Terrible Murder.' — Dr. Sam Sheppard." In total, five volumes were later filled with newspaper clippings related to the case. By one count, *The Cleveland Press* alone ran 399 stories on the case over a six month period. The case was also covered on local radio and television stations.[9]

When the case was set for trial, seventy-five prospective jurors were called for duty. In what can be characterized as nothing short of incredible, all three Cleveland newspapers published their names and addresses. Due to this, every prospective juror received some or all of the following about the case: anonymous letters, anonymous telephone calls, and/or contacts from friends.[10]

Eleven of the twelve jurors chosen for jury duty testified to having read about the case in the Cleveland newspapers or having heard broadcasts about it before the trial began. A majority of the jury had at least one Cleveland newspaper delivered to their home. When the jury was being selected, individual pictures of prospective jurors appeared daily in the newspaper. While jury selection was occurring, a local radio station ran a live broadcast where local newspaper reporters tried to argue that Sheppard's hiring of a prominent defense attorney was a concession of guilt.[11]

By the time Dr. Sheppard's murder trial was scheduled to start in mid-October 1954, there was barely a soul in the local area who had not heard a substantial amount about the case. The politics of the November elections also threatened the impartiality of the trial: the chief prosecutor, John Mahon, was a candidate for a judgeship, and the presiding judge in the case, Edward Blythin, was up for reelection.[12] In many ways, the well had already been poisoned, ensuring that the trier of fact would be far from impartial in Sheppard's trial.

When the case proceedings began, the media did more than simply report on the trial — they became a part of the background and even the foreground. A long temporary press table was set up on the courtroom directly behind the counsel tables. Numerous newspapers, as well as television and radio reporters, were present throughout the trial at this table or seated elsewhere in the gallery. The courtroom was more than full each day of the trial. Outside of the courthouse, the jury and judge were filmed and interviewed by numerous crews as they entered and exited the building. Cameras were also prominent in the courthouse corridors, filming and photographing all persons associated with the trial. Photographs were likewise taken in the courtroom during recess periods.[13]

As the trial went on, media attention remained high, including with regard to the jurors. By one count, during the trial, pictures of the jury appeared over forty times in the three Cleveland newspapers. Pictures of the jurors at the Sheppard home, when they toured the house as evidence, appeared in one newspaper. Another newspaper did a feature story on the home life of an alternate juror. The day before the jury rendered a verdict in the case, they posed for pictures which then ran in area newspapers.[14]

While the trial was occurring, jurors also heard out-of-court information about Sheppard that was damaging to the defense. For instance, during the trial, the Cleveland radio station WHK broadcast a program two days after a Cleveland police officer testified. The police officer's testimony contradicted a written statement that Sheppard previously gave to police. The radio broadcast characterized Sheppard as a perjurer and compared him to well-known convicted perjurer Alger Hiss. When Sheppard's attorney asked the judge to question the jury to learn if they heard the broadcast, the judge refused to do so and overruled a motion for a continuance by stating the following: "we can't stop people, in any event, [from] listening to it. It is a matter of free speech, and the court can't control everybody...We are not going to harass the jury every morning... I have confidence in this jury."[15]

On another occasion during trial, WXEL television and WJW radio each broadcast a story that Carole Beasley, who was under arrest in New York City for robbery, had stated that she had given birth to Sheppard's child, which was a result of their extramarital affair together. The next day, Sheppard's attorney asked the judge to question the jury about the broadcast. This time judge complied, and two jurors admitted they had heard the broadcast. The judge then asked each juror if this would have any effect on their judgment. Each juror answered "no," and the judge found this to be adequate, denying the defense motion for a mistrial.[16] This allegation, like others about numerous parts of the investigation or that Sheppard had an affair, was reported in the media but never produced as evidence at trial by the prosecution.

Although the jury was not sequestered during the trial, the court sequestered them in an area hotel when the trial ended and the jury deliberated. During this period, jurors were allowed to make telephone calls every day. Not surprisingly, the jury returned a verdict of guilty against Sheppard for second-degree murder on December 21, 1954. He was sentenced to life in prison. The decision was later affirmed by an Ohio appellate court and the Ohio Supreme Court.[17]

Sheppard spent a decade in prison before his case was reviewed by the U.S. Supreme Court. During that period, a young F. Lee Bailey took over as Sheppard's counsel. After several motions to reopen the case failed, Bailey ultimately was able to appeal to the Supreme Court. This was due in part to Bailey coming across a witness who claimed that the presiding judge in Sheppard's trial, Judge Blythin, remarked early in the trial that "Sheppard is as guilty as hell."[18] Armed also with the record of inadmissible information that the jurors heard during the case, Bailey now had the ammunition to demonstrate that neither the judge nor the jury were impartial.

The U.S. Supreme Court sided with Sheppard by a vote of 8-1. Justice Tom C. Clark, writing for the majority, began by noting the important role that the media has in a free society in covering trials and the proceedings of the criminal justice system: "The principle that justice cannot survive behind walls of silence has long been reflected in the Anglo-American distrust for secret trials," because the "press does not simply publish information about trials but guards against the miscarriage of justice by subjecting the police, prosecutors, and judicial processes to extensive public scrutiny and criticism."[19] Thus, the Court correctly recognized that the press generally helps to protect the rights of the accused under the theory that sunshine is the best disinfectant for corruption and injustice in the legal system.

Clark then explained that there are limits to press coverage of legal trials. He said that criminal proceedings should not be likened to elections, which can be won or lost in the press. Rather, trials should be fair and free from prejudice. Furthermore, "the jury's verdict [should] be based on evidence received in open court, not from outside sources."[20] Of course, this was a major problem in Sheppard's trial, as a substantial amount of inadmissible information was reported in the media as well as seen and heard by the jury. This was compounded by the fact that the trial judge, Edward Blythin, was up for reelection, thus making it more likely that he would want to appeal to the majority of the electorate in his statements and actions reported by the media.

Clark went on to chastise Judge Blythin for not taking measures to protect the jurors and, ultimately Sheppard, from the media onslaught. According to Clark, Judge Blythin did not take these threats to impartiality very seriously, finding wholly inadequate Judge Blythin's suggestions and requests that the jurors try to ignore the newspaper, radio, and television reports. Justice Clark concluded as follows: "The fact is that bedlam reigned at the courthouse during the trial and newsmen took over practically the entire courtroom, hounding most of the participants in the trial, especially Sheppard."[21]

Speaking for the Court, Justice Clark warned that "the presence of the press at judicial proceedings must be limited when it is apparent that the accused might otherwise be prejudiced or disadvantaged."[22] For Clark, there is no question that this is a command of the Constitution: "Due process requires that the accused receive a trial by an impartial jury free from outside influences."[23] Since modern communications (even as of the 1950s and 1960s) are so pervasive, creating the threat of "prejudicial publicity [in] the minds of the jurors," due process requires trial courts to "take strong measures to ensure that the balance is never weighed against the accused."[24]

When, then, are these measures? Throughout his opinion, Clark compiled a long list of potential methods for a trial judge to ensure that a jury remains impartial when there is prejudicial pretrial publicity. The Supreme Court characterized Shepard's trial as being a "carnival atmosphere" and suggested that the following things could have been done to prevent such a miscarriage of justice:

- Ordering a change of venue;
- Sequestering the jury;
- Holding a short continuance until after the upcoming judicial elections;
- Limiting the number of reporters in the courtroom;
- Placing reporters farther away from counsel tables, witnesses, and jurors;
- Prohibiting the media from interviewing witnesses before and during the trial;
- Placing a gag order on the police, witnesses, and counsel for both sides;
- Warning the media to check the accuracy of their accounts; and
- Declaring a mistrial and ordering a new trial.[25]

Thus, Judge Blythin had a multitude of options to ensure impartiality for Sheppard. However, he did none of the above. According to Justice Clark, "courts must take such steps by rule and regulation that will protect their processes from prejudicial outside interferences."[26] According to these standards of due process, Blythin "did not fulfill his duty to protect Sheppard from the inherently prejudicial publicity which saturated the community and to control disruptive influences in the courtroom."[27]

Indeed, it is difficult to imagine that the jurors could have been impartial in Sheppard's first trial. They were laypersons, untrained in the law, who were inundated by the press for weeks and months with half-truths, innuendo, and many uncorroborated statements that were either inadmissible in court or were never presented by the prosecution. It is difficult, if not impossible, to defend oneself against such accusations. Dr. Sheppard did not have a fighting chance.

The second time around, Sheppard did have a fairer opportunity, this time represented by the very capable F. Lee Bailey, who characterized the prosecution's case as "ten pounds of hogwash in a five-pound bag." Sheppard was found not guilty at his 1966 trial. Of course, this time around, media attention was not quite a great as it was in 1954, and the trial judge, Francis J. Talty, took steps to ensure that it would not again be a media circus.[28] The media was allowed to cover the trial in a limited manner that still met the First Amendment goal of allowing the press to expose government action to the public. Sam Sheppard's right to a fair trial and his due process guarantee of an impartial jury were also guaranteed. The U.S. Supreme Court ensured that a proper balance would be struck the second time around.

As for Sheppard, his new found freedom was short-lived and less than fruitful. Things started out relatively well. After he was acquitted in 1966, Dr. Sheppard went back to practicing medicine. He also married a wealthy German divorcee, Ariane Tebbenjohanns. However, Sheppard subsequently committed gross errors while performing two different surgeries, resulting in the deaths of two patients. The hospital that employed Sheppard was sued for malpractice, and Sheppard was released. Unable to find work within the medical community, Sheppard became a professional wrestler in 1969. He took the unfortunate name "Killer" Sheppard. He also divorced Tebbenjohanns, who claimed that Sheppard had threatened her with a gun. A few months later Sheppard, then in his mid-forties, married twenty-year-old Colleen Strickland, the daughter of his wrestling promoter. He died in April 1970 of a liver disease that was likely brought about by alcoholism. In 2000, Sheppard's son, Sam Reese Sheppard unsuccessfully sued the State of Ohio for wrongful imprisonment, in an attempt to prove that his father was innocent in the murder of his late mother. The jury, however, unanimously found for the State of Ohio.[29]

We may never know what actually happened in the Sheppard home on July 3-4, 1954. Whether Dr. Sam Sheppard was guilty or innocent of murdering his wife will likely remain a mystery forever. There is no question, though, that the way his 1954 trial was conducted violated Sheppard's constitutional rights. The jury in his case could not possibly have been impartial under those circumstances. Although solace came years too late, the U.S. Supreme Court eventually corrected this egregious error.

Notes

1. Michael Burg, "A Message from the President," *The Trial Lawyer: A Magazine for Trial Lawyers & a Voice for Justice*, 2010, http://www.thetriallawyermagazine.com/about (accessed September 18, 2011).

2. *Sheppard v. Maxwell*, 384 U.S. 333, 335-36 (1966); Colin Evans, "Samuel Sheppard Trials: 1954 and 1966," *Great American Trials: From Salem Witchcraft to Rodney King*, ed. Edward W. Knappman, (Canton, MI: Visible Ink Press, 2003), 471.

3. *Sheppard*, 384 U.S. at 336; Evans, "Samuel Sheppard Trials," 471-72.

4. Robert Hardaway and Douglas B. Tumminello, "Pretrial Publicity in Criminal Cases of National Notoriety: Constructing a Remedy for the Remediless Wrong," *American University Law Review* 46 (1996): 39-90, 56.

5. *Sheppard*, 384 U.S. at 337-38; Evans, "Samuel Sheppard Trials," 472.

6. *Sheppard*, 384 U.S. at 338-48; Cynthia L. Cooper and Sam Reese Sheppard, *Mockery of Justice: The True Story of the Sheppard Murder Case* (Boston: Northeastern University Press, 1995).

7. *Sheppard*, 384 U.S. at 339.

8. Joseph F. Flynn, "Prejudicial Publicity in Criminal Trials: Bringing *Sheppard v. Maxwell* into the Nineties," *New England Law Review* 27 (1993): 857-882, 863.

9. *Sheppard*, 384 U.S. at 342; Cooper and Sheppard, *Mockery of Justice*.

10. Robert S. Stephen, "Prejudicial Publicity Surrounding a Criminal Trial: What a Trial Court Can Do to Ensure a Fair Trial in the Face of a 'Media Circus,'" *Suffolk University Law Review* 26 (1992):1063-1106, 1072.

11. *Sheppard*, 384 U.S. at 342, 346.

12. *Sheppard*, 384 U.S. at 346.

13. *Sheppard*, 384 U.S. at 342-44; Flynn, "Prejudicial Publicity in Criminal Trials," 865.

14. *Sheppard*, 384 U.S. at 345.

15. *Sheppard*, 384 U.S. at 347.

16. *Sheppard*, 384 U.S. at 348.

17. *Sheppard*, 384 U.S. at 349; Stephen, "Prejudicial Publicity Surrounding a Criminal Trial," 1073; Cooper and Sheppard, *Mockery of Justice*.

18. Evans, "Samuel Sheppard Trials," 473.

19. *Sheppard*, 384 U.S. at 349-50 (internal citations and quotations omitted).

20. *Sheppard*, 384 U.S. at 351.

21. *Sheppard*, 384 U.S. at 355.

22. *Sheppard*, 384 U.S. at 358.

23. *Sheppard*, 384 U.S. at 362.

24. *Sheppard*, 384 U.S. at 362.

25. *Sheppard*, 384 U.S. at 352-63.

26. *Sheppard*, 384 U.S. at 363.

27. *Sheppard*, 384 U.S. at 363.

28. Evans, "Samuel Sheppard Trials," 474.

29. Jack P. DeSario and William D. Mason, *Dr. Sam Sheppard on Trial: The Prosecutors and the Marilyn Sheppard Murder* (Kent, OH: Kent State University Press, 2003), vii, 78-79, 324.

~2~

Avoiding Mob Justice: *Frank v. Mangum* (1915) and *Moore v. Dempsey* (1923)

Whatever disagreement there may be as to the scope of the phrase "due process of law," there can be no doubt that it embraces the fundamental conception of a fair trial, with opportunity to be heard. Mob law does not become due process of law by securing the assent of a terrorized jury.
– *Frank v. Mangum*, 237 U.S. 309, 347 (1915) (Justice Holmes, Dissenting)

If in fact a trial is dominated by a mob so that there is an actual interference with the course of justice, there is a departure from due process of law.
– *Moore v. Dempsey*, 261 U.S. 86, 90-91 (1923)

Some stories have happy endings; others don't. *Moore v. Dempsey* is an example of the former; *Frank v. Mangum* is an example of the latter. Each case involved a murder trial in a southern state where prejudice led to mob justice taking control over the legal proceedings and making an impartial jury impossible.

The story of Leo Frank is one of epic tragedy. Frank was convicted in an anti-Semitic atmosphere, and his untimely death was at the hands of a lynch mob. It was such an infamous affair that it led to both the creation of the B'nai B'rith Anti-Defamation League and to a resurgence of the Ku Klux Klan.[1] The case even spawned a murder ballad.

Leo Max Frank was born in Paris, Texas on April 17, 1884, but his family moved to Brooklyn when he was only a few months old. He had a Jewish upbringing, attended public schools as a child, and graduated from Cornell University in 1906. Shortly thereafter, he accepted a job offer from his uncle, Moses Frank, to move to Atlanta and help establish the National Pencil Factory. In 1910, he married Lucille Selig, and two years later he was elected president of the local chapter of the B'nai B'rith. Things seemed to be going quite well for Frank. All of this would change in 1913 with the death of a young girl at the factory that Frank managed. Mary Phagan, who was thirteen years old at the time, worked at the National Pencil Factory. As a child laborer, she attached the copper caps that held erasers at the end of pencils.[2]

On Saturday, April 26, 1913, Phagan arrived shortly after noon to pick up her paycheck from Frank, who was at work most of the day. Besides leaving for lunch from around 1:00 p.m. to approximately 3:00 p.m., Frank was at work until about 6:00 p.m. At 4:00 p.m., Frank told the watchman, Newt Lee, to take a few hours off, and Lee obliged. Between 6:25 p.m. and 7:00 p.m., Frank phoned Lee multiple times. Frank finally reached Lee on the last attempt at around 7:00 p.m. Apparently, Frank was phoning Lee because a disgruntled fired employee, John Gantt, had visited Frank shortly after Mary Phagan did that day. Gantt arrived at the factory to recover a pair of his shoes. Frank was nervous about Gantt's presence at the factory not only because Frank had fired him for stealing, but also because Gantt had a reputation as a drunkard. Thus, it is not surprising that Frank phoned Lee during the evening to see if everything was alright at the factory.[3]

When Lee was making his rounds at approximately 3:30 a.m. on Sunday morning, he discovered in the factory cellar the body of young Mary Phagan. Sawdust, wood shavings, and grime covered her bloodied corpse. She was bruised and had been cut. She had also been hit with a blunt object and strangled by a length of rope that remained at the scene. Some of her fingers were ripped out of their joints, and her clothing was torn. Lee called the police, who arrived with newspaper reporter Britt Craig. Craig uncovered two scraps of paper. One of the slips of paper read "he said he wood love me and land down play like night witch did it but that long tall black negro did buy his sef;" the other one stated "mam, that negro hire doun here did this i went to make water and he push me doun that hole a long tall negro black that hoo it was long sleam tall negro i wright while play with me." Craig believed that these notes were written by Phagan to identify her attacker, and police began to focus their investigation on watchman Newt Lee, who was a tall African American man. Although Lee was the one who called the police and appeared to be honest in response to their questioning, he was jailed and held without charges for months.[4]

Even with Lee in custody, the police went to Frank's house to make further inquiries, since he had seen Phagan the day before and he had made the now seemingly suspicious phone calls to Lee. Police officer John Starnes would later describe Frank as nervous when Starnes picked him up on the morning of April 27 for questioning. The police eventually centered on Frank as a suspect, and in the face of mounting pressure from local newspapers, he was arrested on April 29.[5]

In the meantime, there was mounting evidence that the factory's African American janitor, Jim Conley, was Phagan's murderer. Statements by some of the women who worked at the factory implicated Conley in the homicide. Conley had a prior record of arrests for theft and disorderly conduct. He had been seen by a factory foreman washing blood from his shirt the day that Phagan was murdered. That morning, Conley had also been seen drinking beer and whiskey. Police, even after Frank had been indicted for Phagan's murder, questioned Conley, who gave conflicting statements about what happened on the day of Phagan's death. These conflicts led police to interrogate Conley on multiple occasions, which ultimately provoked Conley to offer the following story: Frank killed Phagan, Frank directed Conley to write the note that was found on Phagan's body, and Frank had Conley help him move Phagan's body to the factory cellar. According to Conley, Frank even promised him $200 for all of this. Each time he was interrogated by police, Conley's story changed. It was later alleged that the police coached Conley until he weaved together a believable story against Frank.[6]

Armed with Frank's nervousness, Conley's statements, and Mary Phagan's body, lead prosecutor Hugh Mason Dorsey decided to proceed to trial against Frank on July 28, 1913. According to some accounts, Dorsey said he wanted to prosecute the "Yankee Jew" Frank rather than the "nigger" Conley because it would help sensationalize the case. This prejudice against Frank for being an educated outsider quickly became widespread, with even the pastor of the Phagan family's church publicly referring to Frank as a "Yankee Jew." Although one might expect that a prejudiced public in early twentieth century Georgia would be looking to target an African American rather than a white Jewish man, the specifics of this case made the Jewish Frank the easier target of prejudice. The crime appeared to have involved some elaborate planning. Apparently, those involved in Frank's prosecution, as well as many members of the general public, thought it more logical to pin this complicated scheme on a well-educated Northern Jew than on a barely literate African American. Thus, Southern prejudice worked in Conley's favor and against Frank.[7]

At trial, the prosecution put Officer Starnes on the witness stand to testify as to Frank's nervousness on the morning when he was shown Phagan's body and questioned about her murder. Prosecutors also put Conley on the stand, who told his previous story about Frank committing the murder, and Conley testified that Frank had confessed the murder to him on the day it happened. Conley also testified that he had "watched for" Frank on previous occasions that the superintendent entertained women in his office. The mob-like atmosphere that existed in the courtroom was confirmed by what happened after defense counsel objected to this last line of questioning: when the judge overruled the objection, the spectators applauded. According to one account, those in the courtroom "broke out in a wild uproar like a bloodthirsty mob at a bull fight." It was difficult for the judge to calm to crowd.[8]

This was but one example of the anti-Semitic prejudice that had developed over the case. Frank's defense attorneys and the trial judge, Leonard Roan, received threats during the trial that they would not leave the courtroom alive if the "damned Jew" were to be acquitted. Evidence exists that jurors received similar threats. When lead prosecutor Dorsey left the courtroom each day, he was met with crowds which gave him ovations. These same outside crowds chanted "Hang the Jew" during the trial, and catcalls of this phrase were made periodically in the courtroom. This prejudicial flame was something that Dorsey was more than willing to fan in his closing statement, when he referenced activities of convicted criminals who were Jewish, before opining that Jews "rise to heights sublime, but they also sink to the lowest depths of degradation!"[9]

Given the death threats and the mob chants during the trial, Judge Roan obviously knew that this poisonous environment threatened the jury's impartiality. This is evidenced by the actions and statements of the judge at the time and later. Indeed, Judge Roan advised Frank and his attorneys to be absent from the courtroom when the jury delivered its verdict, out of the fear that a "not guilty" verdict would result in Frank and his attorneys immediately being kidnapped by the mob and lynched. This notwithstanding, Judge Roan was personally convinced that Frank was innocent of the crime. Attorney Arthur Powell (who would later become an appellate judge) was asked by Judge Roan to do research for him during the trial. According to Powell, Judge Roan remarked to him that Frank's "innocence [was] proved to a mathematical certainty." Anti-Semitism won the day, however, and Frank was convicted of Phagan's murder by the jury on September 26, 1913. When the verdict was announced by the jury foreman, the roar of applause was so loud that the judge could not hear the jurors when he polled them. Judge Roan, even though convinced of Frank's innocence, appeared to be intimidated by the mob too. The judge denied Frank's motion for a new trial, and he sentenced Frank to die by hanging on October 10, 1913. Apparently, Judge Roan, not wanting to take the heat for ordering a new trial or a sentence other than death, hoped to pass his thoughts along to the governor in the hopes of a commutation or pardon at a later date, after the anti-Semitism surrounding the trial had died down.[10]

Frank's attorneys were convinced that he had been denied due process of law under the Fourteenth Amendment by virtue of both the judge and jury being intimidated by the mob inside and outside of the courtroom. They appealed his conviction, which was upheld by a split vote of the Georgia Supreme Court. Next was an appeal to the U.S. Supreme Court. The vote there was again split, with a 7-2 decision upholding Frank's conviction.[11]

Writing for the Court, Justice Mahlon Pitney found no violation of due process because of juror or judicial partiality. According to Pitney,

> As to the "due process of law" that is required by the Fourteenth Amendment, it is perfectly well settled that a criminal prosecution in the courts of a State, based upon a law not in itself repugnant to the Federal Constitution, and conducted according to the settled course of judicial proceedings as established by the law of the State, so long as it includes notice, and a hearing, or an opportunity to be heard, before a court of competent jurisdiction, according to established modes of procedure, is "due process" in the constitutional sense.[12]

Accordingly, Pitney stated that the Court would not be reviewing much of the particulars of the case: "we may not review irregularities or erroneous rulings upon the trial, however serious...the writ of habeas corpus will lie only in case the judgment under which the prisoner is detained is shown to be absolutely void for want of jurisdiction in the court that pronounced it."[13] Noting that Georgia allowed Frank to appeal his conviction to the state supreme court on various grounds, Pitney found that most questions of due process should be decided by the state courts. Couching his opinion in the language of federalism, Pitney declared that due process

> [D]oes not mean that the operations of the state government shall be conducted without error or fault in any particular case, nor that the Federal courts may substitute their judgment for that of the state courts, or exercise any general review over their proceedings, but only that the fundamental rights of the prisoner shall not be taken from him arbitrarily or without the right to be heard according to the usual course of law in such cases.[14]

Pitney did not say that federalism prevented the federal courts from intervening under any circumstances. According to the justice, "if a trial is in fact dominated by a mob, so that the jury is intimidated and the trial judge yields, and so that there is an actual interference with the course of justice, there is, in that court, a departure from due process of law in the proper sense of that term."[15] Since this is seemingly what happened in Frank's case, one may wonder why the U.S. Supreme Court would fail to intervene. Pitney, though, found that federal interference was only necessary if the state fails to supply "corrective process" and subsequently executes a defendant who was found guilty at a mob-dominated trial.[16] According to Pitney, such state corrective processes include a "familiar procedure of a motion for a new trial followed by an appeal to its Supreme Court."[17] Pitney concluded that since bad trials had been remedied by these processes in Georgia in the past, there was no reason to doubt them now. Given that Pitney framed the case as one of federal deference to the states, it is no surprise that the majority of the Court found no violation of due process.

What Pitney failed to understand was the past practice of a court system is not necessarily determinate of present or future performance. Mob domination clearly occurred in this case, which biased the jury to find Frank guilty and scared the judge into allowing the conviction to stand and into sentencing Frank to death. The "corrective process" was an appeal to the supreme court of the same state, a court which sat in Atlanta, in the same general vicinity of the trial. The justices of the Georgia Supreme Court may have felt the same sort of intimidation that was experienced by the trial judge and jury. Thus, there was no guarantee that they would have given Frank an unbiased review to guarantee him due process. The justices of the U.S. Supreme Court, sitting hundreds of miles away, could certainly offer an additional check to guarantee due process. They could have chastised Judge Roan for not doing more to ensure impartiality, such as having a change of venue. In many ways, the threat to impartiality was even greater in this case than it was for Sam Sheppard. Sheppard only had to contend with a voracious media; Leo Frank's trial was enveloped within a general public wave of anti-Semitism. The Court had a duty to ensure that Frank was guaranteed due process. Unfortunately for Frank, such thinking about this right would not yet win over a majority of the Court.

That the mob atmosphere violated Frank's due process rights was an argument that did win over two of the Court's justices: Oliver Wendell Holmes, Jr. and Charles Evans Hughes. Justice Holmes began his dissent by recounting some of the facts of the case that evidenced the mob's domination of the trial. He then concluded the following about the meaning of due process:

> Whatever disagreement there may be as to the scope of the phrase 'due process of law,' there can be no doubt that it embraces the fundamental conception of a fair trial, with opportunity to be heard. Mob law does not become due process of law by securing the assent of a terrorized jury. We are not speaking of mere disorder, or more irregularities in procedure, but of a case where the processes of justice are actually subverted. In such a case, the Federal court has jurisdiction to issue the writ.[18]

Indeed, according to Holmes, barring federal court review of a case with these facts would make the right to due process under the Fourteenth Amendment "a barren one."[19] To prove his point, Holmes offered what he characterized as an extreme example:

> [I]f the trial and the later hearing before the Supreme Court had taken place in the presence of an armed force known to be ready to shoot if the result was not the one desired, we do not suppose that this Court would allow itself to be silenced by the suggestion that the record showed no flaw. To go one step further, suppose that the trial had taken place under such intimidation and that the Supreme Court of the State on writ of error had discovered no error in the record, we still imagine that this court would find a sufficient one outside of the record, and that it would not be disturbed in its conclusion by anything that the Supreme Court of the State might have said.[20]

The notion of an armed force ready to kill if they received the verdict they disliked was not far from the truth in Frank's case. According to Holmes, federalism should not be a deterrent to federal courts ensuring that due process and justice have been achieved in cases like this by guaranteeing an impartial jury and neutral judge.

Applying this interpretation of the Fourteenth Amendment to the facts of this case, Holmes declared the following:

> [W]hen we find the judgment of the expert on the spot, of the judge whose business it was to preserve not only form but substance, to have been that if one juryman yielded to the reasonable doubt that he himself later expressed in court as the result of most anxious deliberation, neither prisoner nor counsel would be safe from the rage of the crowd, we

think the presumption overwhelming that the jury responded to the passions of the mob.[21]

Accordingly, Holmes called upon his brethren to right this wrong: "it is our duty to act upon them now and to declare lynch law as little valid when practiced by a regularly drawn jury as when administered by one elected by a mob intent on death."[22] For Holmes, only a reversed judgment and a new trial would be just in Frank's case.

Unfortunately for Leo Frank, Justice Holmes's arguments largely fell on deaf ears on the Supreme Court. Frank's last refuge was the office of Georgia's governor, John Slaton. Judge Roan, who had since been diagnosed with cancer, wrote a note that stated, among other things, that he doubted Frank's guilt and he declared the following: "I wish to say that at the proper time I shall ask the prison commission to recommend and the governor to commute Frank's sentence to life imprisonment."[23] The Georgia Prison Commission heard Frank's appeal for executive commutation on May 31, 1915. Nine days later, on June 9, the commission voted 2-1 against recommending commutation of Frank's death sentence. However, Governor Slaton, claiming that he was following his conscience, commuted Frank's sentence to life imprisonment on June 21, 1915.[24]

Even if Governor Slaton had seen the injustice in the mob law that was Frank's trial, many others did not. Slaton was hanged in effigy outside of Atlanta with a sign that read "John M. Slaton: The King of the Jews." The "Ballad of Leo Frank and Mary Phagan," a twenty stanza song, was written after Frank's commutation to describe Mary's murder and announce to the world how Frank was guilty. Ultimately, these angry agitators got what they wanted. A lynch mob from Phagan's hometown of Marietta, Georgia drove to the prison where Frank was being held on August 16, 1915. Seven automobiles arrived at the penitentiary armed with shotguns and pistols. They abducted Frank from the guards on duty and drove him back to Marietta, a seven hour trip. Shortly after 7:00 a.m. on August 17, Frank was lynched from a tree in the Cobb County countryside. The lynching helped revive the Ku Klux Klan in the South, as the rallying cry of "Vindication of Mary Phagan" was used to spread the group's hateful message and recruit new members.[25]

The mob, both at trial and after commutation, drove the outcome of the proceedings more than any judge, juror, or governor. The case represents the epitome of a partial jury and biased judge, not because any jurors or the judge necessarily harbored malevolent motives toward Frank, but because they feared what the mob might also do to them. Governor Slaton showed courage in commuting Frank's sentence, but he could not guard Frank day and night to ensure the man's safety.

The great tragedy of the Leo Frank case lies in not only the lack of due process and the failure of the proceedings to be impartial. The additional tragedy is that Frank was lynched for a crime he did not commit. In 1983, 85-year-old Alonzo Mann, who had worked at the National Pencil Factory as a child laborer, finally came forward to announce that he had seen Jim Conley carrying Mary Phagan's corpse shortly after noon on April 26, 1913. Conley threatened to kill Mann if he told anyone what he had seen. Mann's story corroborated a statement made by Conley's lawyer in 1914, when attorney William M. Smith publicly announced that his client had murdered Phagan. Mann's admission helped spur another effort to clear Frank's name, which was finally accomplished in 1986, when the Georgia Board of Pardons issued a posthumous pardon for Frank in the murder of Mary Phagan.[26]

As vindicating as this subsequent action was, it was seven decades too late to do Leo Frank any good. Certainly, the interpretation of the Fourteenth Amendment by a majority of the U.S. Supreme Court did not assist Frank in clearing his name or escaping his horrible fate. Given the mood of the Georgia mob, it was not clear that a Court ruling to the contrary would have stopped the lynching. What is clear, however, is that the Supreme Court did not help the matter with its decision that offered legal justification to put Frank to death.

Not long after Leo Frank was lynched, it appeared that mob justice was going to be tragically carried out again by another southern state, this time in Arkansas. Racial tensions were running high in Phillips County after World War I, as African American sharecroppers in the area were trying to form a tenant farmers' union to better seek redress against their white landlords' low payments. When a group of African Americans assembled in a church in Elaine, Arkansas on September 30, 1919, a crowd of whites fired into the building. At least some of those within the church returned fire, killing one of the white men outside. The killing of this white man in the rural South led to widespread race-based violence in the area, with whites hunting down and killing as many as 250 local African Americans. A total of seventy-nine African Americans were prosecuted for alleged acts related to this rioting; no whites had charges brought against them. In the process of the violence, a second white man, Clinton Lee, was killed. Twelve African American men were then arrested for Lee's murder.[27]

Governor Charles Hillman Brough appointed a Committee of Seven to quell the "insurrection" in the county and investigate the murders of the white men. All seven members of the committee were white men. On October 7, one member of the committee publicly announced that the violence was "a deliberately planned insurrection of the negroes against the whites, directed by an organization known as the 'Progressive Farmers' and 'Household Union of America' established for the purpose of banding negroes together for the killing of white people."[28]

During this pre-trial period, the local newspapers wrote incendiary pieces on the investigation. Shortly after the men were arrested, a lynch mob marched to the jail in an attempt to kidnap and murder the men. They were held off only by the armed National Guard troops who were surrounding the courthouse. In order to prevent further lynching attempts, some members of the Committee of Seven announced that they would make sure that the men who were arrested would be executed. The defendants were tortured until they confessed, and other African American witnesses were tortured until they implicated the defendants' guilt. Both witnesses and suspects were whipped with leather straps, they were beaten, they had formaldehyde placed in their nostrils, and they were placed naked in an electric chair. An all-white grand jury was empanelled on October 27. One of the Committee of Seven was on the grand jury, and it was alleged that some members of the white men who were engaged in the preceding violence also served on the grand jury. All twelve men were indicted on October 29.[29]

Their trial took place one week later, on November 3, before an all-white jury. The defendants were informed the day of trial that an attorney was appointed as their counsel. This attorney only met with them later that day, with clearly not enough time to prepare a murder case. The courthouse was surrounded by a threatening crowd. The trial lasted forty-five minutes, something unheard of for a complicated homicide case with multiple defendants. After deliberating for only five minutes, the jury returned verdicts of guilty of first degree murder for all men. According to affidavits that were later filed, no juror who voted for acquittal would have been safe, and any defendant who had been acquitted would have been lynched by the mob at the courthouse.[30]

Clearly, much like in Frank's case, the jury in this case was far from impartial. Some of the individual jurors were likely racially biased against these defendants and were really members of the mob itself. Other jurors may have been trying to take their duty seriously, but they were legitimately in fear that they might be the target of mob violence if they voted to acquit. In either case, the due process right was not upheld for the defendants. In addition, the systematic exclusion of African Americans from the jury (a topic we will revisit in chapter three) in a racially charged environment all but assured that the defendants would be convicted without regard to whether or not they were actually guilty. From start to finish, due process was non-existent.

The case for these twelve men was taken up by the National Association for the Advancement of Colored People (NAACP). The NAACP tried to seek redress for the wrongs that occurred at trial. They did not, however, initially meet with much success. The Arkansas Supreme Court upheld these convictions in March of 1920. The NAACP then filed for a writ of habeas corpus in state court. Meanwhile, in November of 1920 Governor Brough denied clemency to the defendants, and he set an execution date of June 10, 1921. Although an Arkansas Chancery Court issued the writ of habeas corpus and halted the executions, the Arkansas Supreme Court overturned the ruling. A new execution date was set for September 23, 1921, but that was stayed when a federal habeas corpus petition was filed on September 21 in the U.S. District Court for the Eastern District of Arkansas. Frank Moore was named as the lead defendant in the case, and the habeas petition was directed at the man who ultimately held the men, the Keeper of the Arkansas State Penitentiary E.H. Dempsey. An appeal to the U.S. Supreme Court was now imminent, and the case worked its way to the Court for oral arguments on January 9, 1923. The Court rendered a decision a little over one month later on February 19. This quick turnaround probably demonstrates that the majority greatly disliked what the lower court did, as one month is a very short time for the Court to issue a written opinion in a case.[31]

Given that the Court had decided *Frank v. Mangum*, a case with a similar mob-dominated atmosphere, less than eight years earlier, there was reason for the defendants in *Moore v. Dempsey* to be less than hopeful. After all, the *Frank* Court was very clear that due process is not violated by a mob-dominated jury trial as long as "corrective process" (i.e.: a state appellate process) is in place to remedy any trial problems. Interference in this process would run afoul of federalism. Furthermore, of the two dissenters in *Frank*, one of them, Charles Evans Hughes, had since resigned from the Court.

But the Court had new blood that was open to hearing the pleas of Moore et al. For instance, Justice Joseph Lamar died in office in 1916, and his seat on the Court was filled with Louis Brandeis. In private practice in 1915, Brandeis was an outspoken critic of the resolution of the *Frank* case. Similarly, Chief Justice Edward White died in office in 1921, and he was replaced by former U.S. President William Howard Taft. Taft was part of an Executive Committee meeting of the American Bar Association that condemned the lawlessness of Frank's lynching. These were justices who might be more concerned about due process and juror impartiality than pre-Fourteenth Amendment notions of federalism.[32]

This time, the Court's decision was 6-2, with the defendants triumphant. Justice Holmes was no longer dissenting; in *Moore* he wrote the majority opinion. Holmes began his relatively short opinion with a simple proposition: "if in fact a trial is dominated by a mob so that there is an actual interference with the course of justice, there is a departure from due process of law."[33] Holmes conceded what the Court ruled in *Frank*: that "corrective process" for these types of errors can be supplied by state appellate courts, thus leaving no role for the Court if justice is carried out at the state level. Holmes went beyond the Court's *Frank* opinion though, stating that the U.S. Supreme Court has a role if this task is not fulfilled at the state level:

> [I]f the case is that the whole proceeding is a mask — that counsel, jury and judge were swept to the fatal end by an irresistible wave of public passion, and that the State Courts failed to correct the wrong, neither perfection in the machinery for correction nor the possibility that the trial court and counsel saw no other way of avoiding an immediate outbreak of the mob can prevent this Court from securing to the petitioners their constitutional rights.[34]

The majority in *Moore* easily found that due process was violated, and that juror and judicial impartiality failed to occur in the case. The Court ordered that the habeas corpus petition could be heard in the federal district court. After some additional legal maneuvering, all defendants in the case were ultimately released in January 1925.[35]

Although justice was delayed to the *Moore* defendants, it was ultimately not denied. They were eventually freed, and the situation in Arkansas had settled to a degree that the men were not in danger of being lynched for their release, like Leo Frank was when his sentence had been commuted to life in prison. Both cases, *Frank* and *Moore*, are examples of the dangers of letting the mob predetermine guilt and innocence. Juries must be impartial for justice to be carried out. The Supreme Court's decision in the latter case went a long way to ensure that appellate courts, including federal courts, would not permit such egregious violations.

Notes

1. W. William Hodes, "What Ought to be Done—What Can Be Done—When the Wrong Person is in Jail or about to Be Executed: An Invitation to a Multi-Disciplined Inquiry, and a Detour about Law School Pedagogy," *Loyola of Los Angeles Law Review* 29 (1996): 1547-83, 1563.
2. Leonard Dinnerstein, *The Leo Frank Case, Revised Edition* (Athens, GA: University of Georgia Press, 2008), 5-6; Jim Carnes, *Us and Them: A History of Intolerance in America* (New York: Oxford University Press, 1999), 67.
3. Richard H. Underwood, "Perjury: An Anthology," *Arizona Journal of International and Comparative Law* 13 (1996): 307-79, 337; Stephen G. Christianson, "Leo Frank Trial," in *Great American Trials: From Salem Witchcraft to Rodney King*, ed. Edward W. Knappman, (Canton, MI: Visible Ink Press, 2003), 268.
4. Dinnerstein, *Leo Frank Case*, 2; Underwood, "Perjury: An Anthology," 337-38; Christianson, "Leo Frank Trial," 268.
5. Christianson, "Leo Frank Trial," 268-69.
6. Nancy MacLean, "The Leo Frank Case Reconsidered: Gender and Sexual Politics in the Making of Reactionary Populism," *The Journal of American History* 78 (1991): 917-948, 917; Underwood, "Perjury: An Anthology," 338-39; Dinnerstein, *Leo Frank Case*, 20-25.
7. Christianson, "Leo Frank Trial," 269; Dinnerstein, *Leo Frank Case*, 33, 45-46; MacLean, "Frank Case Reconsidered," 917.
8. Dinnerstein, *Leo Frank Case*, 41-47.
9. Dinnerstein, *Leo Frank Case*, 53-60; Christianson, 270.
10. Underwood, "Perjury: An Anthology," 342-43; Hodes, "What Ought to be Done," 1564; Christianson, "Leo Frank Trial," 270; *Frank v. Mangum*, 237 U.S. 309, 346 (1915) (Holmes, J., dissenting).
11. *Frank*, 237 U.S. 309 (1915).
12. *Frank*, 237 U.S. at 326.
13. *Frank*, 237 U.S. at 327.
14. *Frank*, 237 U.S. at 334-35.
15. *Frank*, 237 U.S. at 335.
16. *Frank*, 237 U.S. at 335.
17. *Frank*, 237 U.S. at 335
18. *Frank*, 237 U.S. at 347 (Holmes, J., dissenting).
19. *Frank*, 237 U.S. at 348 (Holmes, J., dissenting).
20. *Frank*, 237 U.S. at 348 (Holmes, J., dissenting).

21. *Frank*, 237 U.S. at 349 (Holmes, J., dissenting).
22. *Frank*, 237 U.S. at 350 (Holmes, J., dissenting).
23. Steve Oney, *And the Dead Shall Rise: The Murder of Mary Phagan and the Lynching of Leo Frank* (New York: Pantheon Books, 2003), 469.
24. Oney, *Dead Shall Rise*, 480-502.
25. Oney, *Dead Shall Rise*, 561-65; Christianson, "Leo Frank Trial," 271-72; Franklyn Bliss Snyder, "Leo Frank and Mary Phagan," *The Journal of American Folklore* 31 (April 1918): 264-266.
26. Oney, *Dead Shall Rise*, 644-49; Dinnerstein, *Leo Frank Case*, 114-15.
27. Michael J. Klarman, "The Racial Origins of Modern Criminal Procedure," *Michigan Law Review* 99 (2000): 48-97, 50-51; Bernard Ryan, Jr., "*Moore et al. v. Dempsey* Appeal," *Great American Trials: From Salem Witchcraft to Rodney King*, ed. Edward W. Knappman, (Canton, MI: Visible Ink Press, 2003), 300.
28. *Moore v. Dempsey*, 261 U.S. 86, 88 (1923).
29. *Moore*, 261 U.S. at 88-89; Klarman, "Racial Origins," 52; Grif Stockley, *Blood in Their Eyes: The Elaine Race Massacres Of 1919* (Fayetteville, AR: University of Arkansas Press, 2001), 197.
30. *Moore*, 261 U.S. at 89-90.
31. Stockley, *Blood in Their* Eyes, 160; Ryan, *"Moore et al.,"* 301; Eric M. Freedman, "Leo Frank Lives: Untangling the Historical Roots of Meaningful Federal Habeas Corpus Review of State Convictions," *Alabama Law Review* 51 (2000): 1467-1540, 1508-16; *Moore*.
32. Freedman, "Leo Frank Lives,"1497-98.
33. *Moore*, 261 U.S. at 90-91.
34. *Moore*, 261 U.S. at 91.
35. *Moore*, 261 U.S. at 92; Freedman, "Leo Frank Lives," 1529-30.

~3~

Racial Discrimination in Jury Selection: *Batson v. Kentucky* (1986) and *Millet-El v. Dretke* (2005)

Selection procedures that purposefully exclude black persons from juries undermine public confidence in the fairness of our system of justice.
– *Batson v. Kentucky*, 476 U.S. 79, 87 (1986)

[T]he very integrity of the courts is jeopardized when a prosecutor's discrimination invites cynicism respecting the jury's neutrality and undermines public confidence in adjudication.
– *Miller-El v. Dretke*, 545 U.S. 231, 238 (2005)

Anyone familiar with American history understands that the United States has a tortured past with respect to race. Although great strides have been made over time to promote and protect racial equality, we cannot forget that our present-day institutions were shaped by terrible past practices, including slavery, segregation, and Jim Crow, among other tragedies. As an example, the motivating factor in the prosecution in *Moore v. Dempsey* in the last chapter involved a significant amount of racism. This biased thinking has manifested itself not just in who has been charged with crime, but also in who has been allowed to serve on the juries that decide guilt and innocence. For instance, in *Strauder v. West Virginia* (1880), the U.S. Supreme Court reversed the conviction of an African American man because the state did not allow African Americans to serve as jurors.[1] The relevant West Virginia statute, which the Court found unconstitutional, stated that "[a]ll white male persons who are twenty-one years of age and who are citizens of this State shall be liable to serve as jurors, except as herein provided" (those excepted were state officials).[2] Thus, after *Strauder*, such blatant racial discrimination in jury selection would not stand. However, if juror discrimination was any more subtle than a state statute barring jury service to all persons of one race or multiple races, then the

Court would fail to find constitutional fault with the practice for several more decades.

Before the Sixth Amendment's jury trial requirement was incorporated via the Fourteenth Amendment in *Duncan v. Louisiana* (1968), the U.S. Supreme Court did not interpret the U.S. Constitution to limit state courts in the same way that it limited federal courts. Instead, before incorporation, the Supreme Court read the Fourteenth Amendment's Due Process Clause as a provision to only limit state criminal prosecutions that were arbitrary or capricious. Recall *Frank v. Mangum*, where the Court stated that due process meant "only that the fundamental rights of the prisoner shall not be taken from him arbitrarily or without the right to be heard according to the usual course of law in such cases."[3] Still, there were cases before 1968 where the U.S. Supreme Court declared jury partiality to be a violation of due process (such as *Moore v. Dempsey* and *Sheppard v. Maxwell*), and there were other requirements imposed too. For instance, in *Glasser v. United States* (1942), the U.S. Supreme Court emphasized "the concept of the jury as a cross-section of the community."[4] Indeed, fundamental to the concept of impartiality is that the jurors will embody various demographic characteristics from the community or, at the very least, that groups generally will not be systematically excluded from a jury pool. However, these examples notwithstanding, the Court largely saw itself as having nothing more than a loose advisory role over this issue before *Duncan*.

For example, one pre-1968 case where jury selection and race were at issue was *Swain v. Alabama* (1965). Robert Swain, an African American, was indicted and convicted of rape in the Circuit Court of Talladega County, Alabama. He was later sentenced to death. On appeal, Swain claimed discrimination in jury selection, as all eight African Americans on the jury venire were struck by the prosecutor upon the use of his peremptory challenges. In any jury trial, each party is given a certain number of these peremptory challenges, which they can use to strike potential jurors without giving a reason (this is different than challenges for cause, which, as the name suggests, are suggestions by each party to remove a juror only when a cause can be given; these challenges are only granted upon approval by the presiding judge). When his case reached the U.S. Supreme Court, Swain was able to demonstrate that African American males made up 26 percent of the males in Talladega County. Even though an average of six to seven African Americans were called as potential jurors in the county, incredibly, none had actually served on jury in the fifteen years prior to *Swain*! Apparently, African Americans were always struck before trial.[5]

However, since the right to an impartial jury had not yet been incorporated in 1965, Swain was unable to raise a Sixth Amendment claim in this state case, nor did he even attempt to raise a Fourteenth Amendment due process claim. Instead, Swain relied on the Fourteenth Amendment's Equal Protection Clause, which commands that no state shall "deny to any person within its jurisdiction the equal protection of the laws." Even a very liberal Warren Court failed to find an Equal Protection Clause violation in *Swain*. Instead, according to the Court, "we cannot hold that the striking of Negroes in a particular case is a denial of equal protection of the laws. In the quest for an impartial and qualified jury, Negro and white, Protestant and Catholic, are alike subject to being challenged without cause."[6] The Court further explained that "[t]o subject the prosecutor's challenge in any particular case to the demands and traditional standards of the Equal Protection Clause would entail a radical change in the nature and operation of the challenge."[7] Thus, showing racial bias in jury selection *in this case* was not enough to show a constitutional violation. Later in the opinion, the majority on the Court clarified that long term juror discrimination, whereby prosecutors in the county were systematically striking African American jurors, could be a basis for a constitutional violation. Even though not a single African American served on a jury in the county dating back to 1950, the Court ruled that this was not proven to be completely the result of prosecutorial bias. For instance, the Court identified prior cases where African American defendants in the county struck African American jurors. If a long term pattern of discrimination had been shown by Swain, the Court claimed that there would have been a constitutional violation. The Court concluded that no such pattern had been demonstrated. Accordingly, the Court affirmed Swain's conviction.[8]

After 1968, the U.S. Supreme Court continued to analyze claims of racial discrimination in jury selection under the Equal Protection Clause, but the Court used the Sixth Amendment principle of jury impartiality as a determining factor when deciding its cases. One such case where jury impartiality was analyzed under the Equal Protection Clause was *Batson v. Kentucky* (1986). James Batson, an African American man, was on trial for second degree burglary and receipt of stolen goods. During *voir dire* (jury selection), the prosecutor used his peremptory challenges to strike all four of the African Americans who were in the jury venire. The resulting jury was composed *only* of whites. Batson's attorney's objected to the prosecution's use of peremptory challenges to exclude all of the potential jurors of his race. The judge denied the defense's motion to discharge the jury, noting that the parties were able to use their peremptory challenges to "strike anybody they want to." Swain was convicted on both counts of the indictment, and his appeals eventually led him to the U.S. Supreme Court, where Batson argued that "the prosecutor's conduct violated his rights under the Sixth and Fourteenth Amendments to an impartial jury and to a jury drawn from a cross section of the community."[9]

The Court, by a vote of 7-2, found that Batson's rights were infringed on by the prosecution's practice. Writing for the majority, Justice Lewis Powell found that the prosecution's systematic exclusion of African American jurors violated the Fourteenth Amendment's Equal Protection Clause. In his majority opinion, Powell noted that "resolution of [Batson's] claim properly turns on application of equal protection principles," so the justices in the majority "express[ed] no view on the merits of any of [Batson's] Sixth Amendment arguments."[10]

However, the impartiality requirement of the Sixth Amendment certainly informed the Court's opinion. For instance, Powell penned the following with respect to racial discrimination on the basis of jury selection:

> Racial discrimination in selection of jurors harms not only the accused whose life or liberty they are summoned to try. Competence to serve as a juror ultimately depends on an assessment of individual qualifications and ability impartially to consider evidence presented at a trial. A person's race simply is unrelated to his fitness as a juror. As long ago as *Strauder*, therefore, the Court recognized that by denying a person participation in jury service on account of his race, the State unconstitutionally discriminated against the excluded juror.[11]

Thus, Powell emphasized that it was not just the right of the defendant to an impartial jury that was at stake in *Batson*. Also at issue was the discrimination against the jurors themselves when they were excluded on the basis of their race. Powell further clarified that constitutionally, a prosecutor cannot "challenge potential jurors solely on account of their race or on the assumption that black jurors as a group will be unable impartially to consider the State's case against a black defendant."[12] What Powell described was an interesting interplay between the Equal Protection Clause and the Impartial Jury Clause, whereby the Fourteenth Amendment, and its prohibition on racial discrimination, helps to protect the right to an impartial jury and vice versa. A potential juror's race is not a valid reason to determine that potential juror's impartiality and impartiality as a term cannot be defined with reference to race.

Powell went on to find a constitutional problem greater than the rights of the defendant and the potential jurors in the case: "The harm from discriminatory jury selection extends beyond that inflicted on the defendant and the excluded juror to touch the entire community. Selection procedures that purposefully exclude black persons from juries undermine public confidence in the fairness of our system of justice."[13] Justice cannot exist where the decisionmaker is partial to one of the parties. Thus, racial discrimination in jury selection, which is, in itself, corrosive of impartiality, denies justice and fairness and the public's perception that our judicial system is fair and just.

For these reasons, the majority in *Batson* set forth procedures to follow when the defense believes that jurors are being struck because of their race. The defendant must make a *prima facie* showing of discrimination in the defendant's case, such as by demonstrating a pattern of striking multiple jurors of the same race or showing a discriminatory nature to the questions that are asked of potential jurors by the prosecutor. If that is done, then the burden shifts to the prosecutor, who "must articulate a neutral explanation" why the jurors of that race were eliminated. The judge must then decide if purposeful racial discrimination was, in fact, the motivating factor of the prosecution's juror strikes. Since the trial judge in Batson's case summarily denied his claim of discrimination, the Court remanded the case so that these new procedures could be followed.[14]

Powell's opinion did not go so far as to do away with peremptory challenges though: "Nor do we think that this historic trial practice [of using peremptory challenges], which long has served the selection of an impartial jury, should be abolished because of an apprehension that prosecutors and trial judges will not perform conscientiously their respective duties under the Constitution."[15] Powell and other justices in the majority in *Batson* instead saw peremptory challenges as a way to protect jury impartiality because the practice allows either side to sweep away potentially biased jurors who do not publicly reveal their biases in ways that can be proven to a judge.

Not every member of the U.S. Supreme Court shared Powell's view of the proper resolution of the case, nor did every member of the majority share all of Powell's reasoning. For example, Justice Thurgood Marshall did not think the Court went far enough. Although he noted that Justice Powell's opinion "takes a historic step toward eliminating the shameful practice of racial discrimination in the selection of juries," Marshall also thought that the *Batson* decision would "not end the racial discrimination that peremptories inject into the jury-selection process."[16] Marshall's fear was that the *Batson* rules would still allow prosecutors to strike African Americans from juries out of the stereotypical view that they will be more sympathetic to defendants, particularly African American defendants, than white jurors would be.

Justice Marshall's alternative was the abolition of peremptory challenges altogether. He first traced the history since *Strauder* of prosecutors' "more subtle ways of keeping blacks off jury venires," including the high rates of African Americans being struck from jury venires and a historical Dallas prosecutor manual that advocated the striking of "minorities" from juries.[17] Then, Marshall observed that "[a]ny prosecutor can easily assert facially neutral reasons for striking a juror, and trial courts are ill equipped to second-guess those reasons," thus meaning that "the protection erected by the Court today may be illusory."[18] Furthermore, Marshall argued that a prosecutor's "own conscious or unconscious racism may lead him easily to the conclusion that a prospective black juror is 'sullen,' or 'distant,' a characterization that would not have come to his mind if a white juror had acted identically."[19] Since Marshall believed that peremptory challenges are "not of constitutional magnitude, and may be withheld altogether without impairing the constitutional guarantee of impartial jury and fair trial," he concluded that they should be eliminated: "The inherent potential of peremptory challenges to distort the jury process by permitting the exclusion of jurors on racial grounds should ideally lead the Court to ban them entirely from the criminal justice system."[20]

On the other side of the spectrum, Chief Justice Warren Burger and then Justice William Rehnquist disagreed with the majority's conclusion, finding no constitutional violation in *Batson*. Instead, these two justices believed that the Court's interference with the peremptory challenge system would do more harm than good:

> The effect of the Court's decision, however, will be to force the defendant to come forward and "articulate a neutral explanation," for his peremptory challenge, a burden he probably cannot meet. This example demonstrates that today's holding will produce juries that the parties do not believe are truly impartial. This will surely do more than "disconcert" litigants; it will diminish confidence in the jury system.[21]

Chief Justice Burger's concern was that it is very difficult to prove a negative. In other words, if a prosecutor were to strike an African American juror during *voir dire* and the defense objected based on *Batson*, how could the prosecutor prove that the juror was struck for a reason *other than* race? His concern was the exact opposite of Justice Marshall, who believed that a race neutral reason could be easily offered in any exercise of a peremptory challenge, even if that juror was struck because of his or her race.

Although Chief Justice Burger raised a potential for abuse with the procedures devised by the majority, the experience with *Batson* has been far from Burger's fear that *Batson* claims will be raised frequently and that the potential for such claims will reduce public confidence in the jury system. In fact, even though the Court later extended *Batson*'s requirement against jury discrimination to apply to the defense in *Georgia v. McCollum* (1992),[22] research suggests that Justice Marshall's position was correct and that *Batson* did not do enough to curb racial discrimination in jury selection. For instance, studies before and after *Batson* have shown that traditionally underrepresented racial groups in the United States, particularly African Americans, continue to be excluded from jury service at greater levels than whites.[23] Thus, it should come as no surprise that the issue of racial discrimination in jury selection, and this practice's impact on building a fair and impartial jury, again came before the U.S. Supreme Court nearly two decades after *Batson* in *Miller-El v. Dretke* (2005).

Jury selection for the criminal trial of Thomas Miller-El began before *Batson* was decided in 1986, but his saga was not heard by the U.S. Supreme Court until the twenty-first century. His case arose out of a robbery that took place at a Dallas, Texas Holiday Inn on November 16, 1985. Two men bound and gagged two hotel employees. One of the men then proceeded to shoot the two employees, killing one and severely wounding the other, rendering the second victim a paraplegic. Police came to believe that Miller-El, an African American man, was the shooter, and he was eventually put on trial for capital murder. During jury selection, 108 persons were empanelled as part of the jury venire. Of those, twenty were African Americans. Nine of the African Americans were excused for cause or by agreement of both parties. The prosecution used its peremptory challenges to strike ten of the eleven African Americans venire members who were subsequently examined. In other words, 91 percent of the eligible African Americans were struck by the prosecutors' peremptory challenges. The prosecution only used its peremptory challenges on 14 percent of the white potential jurors.[24]

Furthermore, African American potential jurors were treated differently during *voir dire* than the white potential jurors who were examined. For example, one African American on the panel, Billy Jean Fields, stated that he believed in capital punishment (death-qualified juries will be discussed in greater detail in chapter five). Fields went so far as to say that the state acts on God's behalf when it imposes the death penalty. The prosecution pressed Fields on this point, and Fields noted that the possibility of rehabilitation might be relevant to the likelihood that a defendant would commit future acts of violence. However, in response to the prosecutor's questions, Fields then went on to state that although he believed any person could be rehabilitated, this would not bar him from voting for capital punishment if the case warranted it:

> If for some reason the testimony didn't warrant death, then life imprisonment would give an individual an opportunity to rehabilitate. But, you know, you said that the jurors didn't have the opportunity to make a personal decision in the matter with reference to what I thought or felt, but it was just based on the questions according to the way the law has been handed down.

Nevertheless, prosecutor James Nelson used a peremptory strike to remove Fields, offering the following rationale:

> [W]e...have concern with reference to some of his statements as to the death penalty in that he said that he could only give death if he thought a person could not be rehabilitated and he later made the comment that any person could be rehabilitated if they find God or are introduced to God and the fact that we have a concern that his religious feelings may affect his jury service in this case.

As later described by the U.S. Supreme Court, prosecutor Nelson "mischaracterized" Field's testimony, as Fields indicated he could impose the death penalty whether a defendant could be rehabilitated or not. There was no evidence in the trial record that Fields expressed reservations about the death penalty due to a defendant finding religion.[25]

Non-black potential jurors, on the other hand, expressed concerns about the death penalty but were not struck by the prosecution. For instance, Sandra Hearn, a white juror, stated that she supported the death penalty only "if a criminal cannot be rehabilitated and continues to commit the same type of crime," and that she would not necessarily vote for the death penalty even if a defendant "would probably commit some criminal acts of violence in the future." No further questions about rehabilitation were asked of Hearn. Latino Fernando Gutierrez said that he would consider the death penalty for someone who could not be rehabilitated, but again the prosecution asked no follow up questions. Still, the prosecution did not use peremptory strikes against these two potential jurors, even though their statements would make them appear to be less ideal jurors for the prosecution compared to the African American Fields.[26]

In another example, African American venireman Joe Warren was asked what he thought the death penalty accomplished. He responded, "I don't know. It's really hard to say because I know sometimes you feel that it might help to deter crime and then you feel that the person is not really suffering. You're taking the suffering away from him. So it's like I said, sometimes you have mixed feelings about whether or not this is punishment or, you know, you're relieving personal punishment."

When prosecutor Paul Macaluso was later asked why he used a peremptory challenge to strike Warren, he offered the following explanation, "I thought [Warren's statements on *voir dire*] were inconsistent responses. At one point he says, you know, on a case-by-case basis and at another point he said, well, I think – I got the impression, at least, that he suggested that the death penalty was an easy way out, that they should be made to suffer more."

As later pointed out by the U.S. Supreme Court, this explanation by the prosecution seems to make sense, but much like the case with Billy Jean Fields, the prosecution's justification fails when compared to the treatment of non-black venire members. For instance, Kevin Duke declared that "sometimes death would be better to me than – being in prison would be like dying every day and, if you were in prison for life with no hope of parole, I['d] just as soon have it over with than be in prison for the rest of your life." Similarly, Leta Girard noted that "living sometimes is a worse – is worse to me than dying would be." Even though these comment were similar to the one made by Warren, the state did not move to strike either Duke or Girard.[27]

The jury shuffle was another practice used by the prosecutors in this case that may cause one to question their motives and the impartiality of the jury that was ultimately selected. The jury shuffle is a Texas practice whereby either party may ask for the cards bearing the names of potential jurors to be shuffled, so that the order changes in which they will be seated in the jury box and questioned during *voir dire*. During jury selection for the Miller-El trial, prosecutors twice asked for this shuffle when a larger number of the jurors seated at the front of the panel were African Americans. The shuffle then increased the chances that African Americans would *not* be seated at the front of the panel, thus significantly decreasing the likelihood that they would be chosen for jury duty.[28]

By itself, the evidence above would make a strong case for prosecutorial discrimination in jury selection, demonstrating that the prosecutors in Miller-El's trial were trying to build an unconstitutionally biased jury against him. But there is more artifact to consider. The Dallas County District Attorney's Office, before *Batson*, had a history of discrimination in jury selection (remember, Miller-El's jury selection took place before *Batson* was decided by the U.S. Supreme Court). In 1963, the DA's office produced a circular that directed prosecutors to use peremptory strikes against potential jurors of minority groups. This is the same circular referenced by Justice Marshall in *Batson*. The circular ordered as follows: "Do not take Jews, Negroes, Dagos, Mexicans or a member of any minority race on a jury, no matter how rich or how well educated." In 1968, a former prosecutor wrote an article for the office's "Jury Selection in a Criminal Case" manual; this article articulated the reasons why minorities should be excluded from jury service. The manual remained in circulation in the office until at least 1976, and evidence suggests that the manual was available to at least one of the prosecutors in Miller-El's trial in 1986. A judge from Dallas County testified that during his service in the district attorney's office in the 1950s and 1960s, his superior told him that he would be fired if he allowed African-Americans to serve on a jury. Another Dallas County judge who had served in the district attorney's office in the mid- to late 1970s later testified that it was his belief that the district attorney's office had a policy of systematically excluding African-Americans from juries. That these considerations were on the minds of the prosecutors in Miller-El's trial can be shown by the fact that they kept notes as to each juror's race. If they were not concerned with the race of each juror, such notes would be irrelevant.[29]

Whatever policies may or may not have officially existed in the Dallas County District Attorney's Office in 1986, historical practices, dating back at least one quarter of a century, suggest that the backdrop of Miller-El's trial was one where the race of the jurors mattered. The history of the DA's office indicates that prosecutors in Dallas wanted to take African Americans off of juries because they thought that such jurors would vote to acquit defendants, particularly defendants who were also African Americans. Such a practice, and the stereotypical thinking that accompanies it, attacks the very heart of the right to an impartial jury. Dallas County prosecutors wanted a jury that was anything but impartial. Instead, they wanted one that was partial to the prosecution, or at least they wanted a jury that they thought, because of stereotypes, would vote to convict. It appears that the ideal juror, in their minds, was a white juror. Once one understands the history of the Dallas County District Attorney's Office, it becomes clear that the practices in Miller-El's jury selection are evidence of biased thinking.

After many appeals, including one previous hearing in front of the U.S. Supreme Court in 2003, Miller-El's case returned to the Court for a hearing in December 2004, and he received vindication from the court in June of 2005. In *Miller-El v. Dretke*, a majority of the justices held that the cumulative evidence from the case led to the conclusion that racial discrimination occurred during *voir dire*. Justice David Souter wrote the opinion for six members of the Court. In his analysis, Souter explained that "[d]efendants are harmed, of course, when racial discrimination in jury selection compromises the right of trial by impartial jury, but racial minorities are harmed more generally, for prosecutors drawing racial lines in picking juries establish state-sponsored group stereotypes rooted in, and reflective of, historical prejudice."[30] In other words, similar to Powell in *Batson*, Souter saw a constitutional violation in jury discrimination on multiple levels: (1) the immediate harm to any given case's defendant who is liable to suffer through a trial with a potentially biased jury, and (2) the greater harm caused by prosecutors continuing traditional stereotypes about non-white racial groups. According to Souter, these harms cannot be overstated because "the very integrity of the courts is jeopardized when a prosecutor's discrimination invites cynicism respecting the jury's neutrality and undermines public confidence in adjudication."[31] Indeed, if one party in a case, especially the prosecution, is, or even appears to be, tainting the neutrality of the jury, neither the defendant nor the general public can trust that the jury reaches a fair and just outcome in the case. Upon reviewing the facts of Miller-El's jury selection, Souter concluded that the "prosecutors' chosen race-neutral reasons for the strikes do not hold up and are so far at odds with the evidence that pretext is the fair conclusion, indicating the very discrimination the explanations were meant to deny."[32] Souter then used statistics to demonstrate that it was much more than mere coincidence that explained who was struck in this jury selection and who was not:

> At least two of the jury shuffles conducted by the State make no sense except as efforts to delay consideration of black jury panelists to the end of the week, when they might not even be reached. The State has in fact never offered any other explanation. Nor has the State denied that disparate lines of questioning were pursued: 53 percent of black panelists but only 3 percent of nonblacks were questioned with a graphic script meant to induce qualms about applying the death penalty (and thus explain a strike), and 100 percent of blacks but only 27 percent of nonblacks were subjected to a trick question about the minimum acceptable penalty for murder, meant to induce a disqualifying answer. The State's attempts to explain the prosecutors' questioning of particular witnesses on nonracial grounds fit the evidence less well than the racially discriminatory hypothesis...By the time a jury was chosen, the State had peremptorily challenged 12 percent of qualified nonblack panel members, but eliminated 91 percent of the black ones.[33]

Souter's recitation of the math confirms what the qualitative data indicated: race was a major consideration of the prosecutors in Miller-El's jury selection, and this was done to produce what prosecutors thought would be a partial jury. Indeed, Souter concluded that any other interpretation would be "unreasonable as well as erroneous."[34]

Not everyone on the Court agreed with Souter, however. Justice Stephen Breyer, although he joined the Court's opinion, wrote separately in a concurring opinion. Breyer harkened back to Justice Marshall's concurrence in *Batson*, and he called for an end to the peremptory challenge system: "despite *Batson*, the discriminatory use of peremptory challenges remains a problem."[35] Much like Souter's use of numerical data, Breyer used math to prove his point about the ineffectiveness of the *Batson* system: "Miller-El's challenge has resulted in seventeen years of largely unsuccessful and protracted litigation – including eight different judicial proceedings and eight different judicial opinions, and involving twenty-three judges, of whom six found the *Batson* standard violated and sixteen the contrary."[36] He followed this with citations to multiple studies showing bias in juror selection as well as several contemporary jury selection guides that use racial stereotypes. Breyer went on to explain that "[i]f used to express stereotypical judgments about race, gender, religion, or national origin, peremptory challenges betray the jury's democratic origins and undermine its representative function."[37] Because Breyer thought that such discriminatory practices are inevitable in a system with peremptory challenges, he concluded that "I believe it necessary to reconsider *Batson*'s test and the peremptory challenge system as a whole."[38]

Although Justice Breyer emphasized the dangers of the peremptory challenge system, Justice Clarence Thomas, in dissent, emphasized how this practice can protect jury impartiality: "The very purpose of peremptory strikes is to allow parties to remove potential jurors whom they suspect, but cannot prove, may exhibit a particular bias."[39] For Thomas and the other two dissenters, one could conclude that the African Americans on the venire were struck for race-neutral reasons, and that there was no racial discrimination that took place. Indeed, Thomas pointed out that on the jury of twelve, an African American, a Filipino, and a Hispanic served and voted to convict Miller-El. Given that a majority of jurors (seven) were women, Thomas found that there was a representative cross-section of the community on Miller-El's jury. He also claimed that there was no direct evidence of the prosecutors in Miller-El's trial engaging in racial discrimination in the jury selection of this, or any other, case. Thomas did not find the prosecution's jury shuffling to be indicative of discrimination, as there is no proof that it was done for that purpose and because Miller-El's attorneys also asked for the potential jurors to be shuffled. Finally, Thomas found some of the evidence considered by the Court to be inappropriate, because some of it was not raised in the Texas court system.[40]

One of the benefits of a dissenting opinion is that it keeps the majority opinion honest. Indeed, Thomas made sure that some of the details that may have been overlooked by the majority were brought to the fore. Justice Thomas's points notwithstanding, the logical conclusion that one can draw from *Miller-El* is that prosecutors were engaging in racial discrimination in an attempt to play on stereotypes to produce a jury biased toward their case. Thomas's emphasis on the need for these issues of federal constitutional analysis to be worked out in the Texas court system is reminiscent of the majority's view in *Frank v. Mangum*, where the majority left the matter up to the Georgia court system. The majority in *Miller-El*, luckily, did not take that approach.

Both the majority and Justice Thomas were in relative agreement over one issue – the use of peremptory strikes. Here, both Justice Souter and Justice Thomas were correct in that peremptory challenges are an important part of our legal system, and they can serve the end of jury impartiality. Indeed, peremptory challenges allow each party to eliminate potential jurors whom each side thinks are biased, but the party cannot conclusively prove are biased. Granted, a party with fewer scruples will play off of stereotypes to eliminate impartial jurors and create a jury biased in its favor. When carried out in this fashion, peremptory challenges help to further racist thinking and reduce the chance that an impartial jury will hear the case. However, the elimination of peremptory challenges altogether is worse, as it can put defendants at a major disadvantage. As long as the process prescribed in *Batson* is honored, race-based peremptories can be remedied while also leaving non-racial peremptories in place to do their job.

While there is a way that one can argue peremptory challenges further the end of jury impartiality, it is much more difficult to make that argument with the jury shuffle. Yes, under Texas's system each side can shuffle the jury pool, and Miller-El's attorneys had the jury shuffled too. But given that the prosecution was doing the same thing, that was Miller-El's only recourse to try and rebalance what was otherwise becoming a partial jury. It is one matter to use peremptory strikes against particular jurors after they have been questioned and a party may be able to put their finger on some type of bias in that person. It is quite a different matter to glance at a group of people who have not been questioned, as they sit in a row, with nothing more to go on than their physical appearance. The practice of juror shuffling does not just fail to further impartiality, it actively works against it. If the shuffle is done before any questioning of particular persons, and it is based solely on appearance, then the race of the potential jurors will become a factor in the forefront of the prosecutors' (and defendants') minds. Again, this not only works to create a jury of partial decisionmakers, but it also furthers racial stereotypes in a way that is harmful to other goals of the U.S. Constitution.

Selective racism that tries to minimize but not completely exclude non-whites can easily occur during jury selection. Allowing for one African American on the jury, while excluding the rest of the potential jurors who are African Americans, subtly tries to produce an almost all-white jury and increases the chances that bias will occur. Courts need to be aware of this and prevent it if those are the prosecutors' motives. Shuffling potential jurors makes this easier. Peremptory challenges, if managed carefully, do not have to lead to this same result. If there is any question about the use of peremptory challenges for this purpose, it is better to reselect the jury. Indeed, it is better to ensure that the jury is impartial and free from bias in its selection, rather than to continue to wonder under these types of circumstances. There is a cost to ensuring impartiality, but that is the price of justice.

The U.S. Supreme Court sided with both James Batson and Thomas Miller-El. Neither man's saga ended with a Supreme Court opinion, however. When the Court decided Batson's case in 1986, he was a few years into a twenty year sentence for burglary and receiving stolen property. Rather than risk another conviction at a retrial, Batson accepted a plea bargain for a five year prison sentence. Batson was in and out of trouble for many years thereafter, being subsequently convicted of burglary, theft, and receiving stolen property. Upon his release in 2003, Batson turned his life around, gaining employment as a construction worker in Louisville, Kentucky. The prosecutor in his case, Joe Gutmann, the man who used peremptory challenges to strike every African

American on the venire, has characterized the Court's decision in *Batson* as "a good one" that rightly prevents racial discrimination in jury selection. Gutmann claimed that he did not strike the venire members for their race but for another reason affecting the jury's impartiality; instead, Gutman claims that he struck the jurors he did because they were young and might sympathize with Batson (another type of stereotype). As for James Batson, he has stated of the *voir dire* at his trial that "I don't *think* it was unfair. It was unfair." Still Batson also maintained of the case that bears his name, "[i]t's so old, they ought to let it go."[41]

As for Miller-El, after the Supreme Court determined that discrimination occurred in his jury selection, he eventually accepted a plea as well. Unlike Batson, however, it is unlikely that Miller-El will ever see the outside of his prison walls. In 2008, Miller-El pleaded guilty to murder and aggravated robbery, and the judge sentenced Miller-El to life in prison. According to Miller-El's attorney, Doug Parks, "There has been, over time, a change in attitude...The attitude currently in the DA's office is not conducive to the tone that existed back when Mr. Miller-El's case was tried."[42]

Hopefully, Miller-El's attorney is correct, not just for the Dallas County District Attorney's Office, but in many other D.A. offices as well. Hopefully, most prosecutors (and lawyers generally) are beyond the crabbed notions of racial stereotypes that the U.S. Supreme Court found to be in existence in *Batson* and *Miller-El*. Even though both men were likely guilty of what they were charged (both men ultimately pleaded guilty to what they were charged), the Court's vigilance in preventing jury discrimination in furtherance of jury impartiality ensured that neither man's fate was determined by a biased jury.

Notes

1. *Strauder v. West Virginia*, 100 U.S. 303 (1880).
2. *Strauder*, 100 U.S. at 305.
3. *Frank v. Mangum*, 237 U.S. 309, 334-35 (1915).
4. *Glasser v. United States*, 315 U.S. 60, 86 (1942).
5. *Swain v. Alabama*, 380 U.S. 202, 203-05 (1965).
6. *Swain*, 380 U.S. at 221.
7. *Swain*, 380 U.S. at 221-22.
8. *Swain*, 380 U.S. at 224-25.
9. *Batson v. Kentucky*, 476 U.S. 79, 82-84 & n.4 (1986).
10. *Batson*, 476 U.S. at 84 n.4.
11. *Batson*, 476 U.S. at 87 (internal citations and quotations omitted).
12. *Batson*, 476 U.S. at 89.
13. *Batson*, 476 U.S. at 87.
14. *Batson*, 476 U.S. at 95-98, 100.
15. *Batson*, 476 U.S. at 99 n.22.
16. *Batson*, 476 U.S. at 102-03 (Marshall, J., concurring).

17. *Batson*, 476 U.S. at 103-04 (Marshall, J., concurring).
18. *Batson*, 476 U.S. at 106 (Marshall, J., concurring).
19. *Batson*, 476 U.S. at 106 (Marshall, J., concurring).
20. *Batson*, 476 U.S. at 107-08 (Marshall, J., concurring).
21. *Batson*, 476 U.S. at 129 (Burger, C.J., dissenting) (internal citations omitted).
22. *Georgia McCollum*, 505 U.S. 42 (1992).
23. Hiroshi Fukurai, Edgar W. Butler, and Richard Krooth, "Where Did Black Jurors Go? A Theoretical Synthesis of Racial Disenfranchisement in the Jury System and Jury Selection," *Journal of Black Studies* 22 (1991): 196-215.
24. *Miller-El v. Dretke*, 545 U.S. 231, 235-36, 240-41, 274 (2005); Edward Lazarus, "A Death Penalty Case the Supreme Court May Review Shows the Dysfunction of the Federal Judiciary When It Comes to Capital Punishment," *FindLaw*, June 24, 2004, http://writ.news.findlaw.com/lazarus/20040624.html (accessed April 29, 2012).
25. *Miller-El*, 545 U.S. at 242-44.
26. *Miller-El*, 545 U.S. at 244-45.
27. *Miller-El*, 545 U.S. at 247-48.
28. Mikal C. Watts and Emily C. Jeffcott, "A Primer on *Batson*, Including Discussion of *Johnson v. California*, *Miller-El v. Dretke*, *Rice v. Collins*, & *Snyder v. Louisiana*," *St. Mary's Law Journal* 42 (2011): 337-410, 352-53; John Gibeaut, "Issues that Don't Go Away: High Court's Agenda Features Batson Challenge and Alleged Prosecutor Misconduct," *ABA Journal* 88 (Nov. 2002): 40-41; Lazarus, "Death Penalty Case."
29. *Miller-El v. Cockrell*, 537 U.S. 322, 334-335 (2003); *Miller-El*, 545 U.S. at 266.
30. *Miller-El*, 545 U.S. at 237-38 (internal citations and quotations omitted).
31. *Miller-El*, 545 U.S. at 238 (internal citations and quotations omitted).
32. *Miller-El*, 545 U.S. at 265.
33. *Miller-El*, 545 U.S. at 265-66.
34. *Miller-El*, 545 U.S. at 266.
35. *Miller-El*, 545 U.S. at 268 (Breyer, J., concurring).
36. *Miller-El*, 545 U.S. at 267 (Breyer, J., concurring).
37. *Miller-El*, 545 U.S. at 272 (Breyer, J., concurring).
38. *Miller-El*, 545 U.S. at 273 (Breyer, J., concurring).
39. *Miller-El*, 545 U.S. at 292-93 (Thomas, J., dissenting).
40. *Miller-El*, 545 U.S. at 274-76, 279-85, 304-05 (Thomas, J., dissenting).
41. Kay Stewart, "'Good' reversal followed 'unfair' trial," *Louisville Courier-Journal*, November 6, 2005, http://www.courier-journal.com/article/20051106/NEWS01/511060406/-Good-reversal-followed-unfair-trial (accessed May 3, 2012) (emphasis in original).
42. "Man Pleads Guilty after Verdict Tossed," *USA Today*, March 20, 2008, http://www.usatoday.com/news/nation/2008-03-20-3755575938_x.htm (accessed May 3, 2012).

~ 4 ~

Sex Discrimination in Jury Selection: *Hoyt v. Florida* (1961) and *Taylor v. Louisiana* (1975)

[T]he exclusion of women from jury venires deprives a criminal defendant of his Sixth Amendment right to trial by an impartial jury drawn from a fair cross section of the community.
– *Taylor v. Louisiana*, 419 U.S. 522, 535-36 (1975)

Much like racial discrimination, American history cannot be fully told without referencing the long battles that have been, and still are being, fought to work toward ending sex discrimination. Many Americans today are familiar with the most visible types of sex discrimination that the law has begun to remedy, including those involving the right to vote, equal pay for equal work, domestic violence, sexual harassment in the workplace, gender equity in hiring and college admissions, and the shattering of the proverbial glass ceiling in various other contexts.

Within the legal profession, this type of discrimination historically extended to bar admission. In a famous nineteenth century case, Myra Bradwell applied to admission to the State Bar of Illinois. Bradwell passed the Illinois Bar Exam with highest honors, but the Supreme Court of Illinois denied Bradwell bar admission. At the time in Illinois (and many other states), a married women was not allowed to enter into a contract without the consent and signature of her husband. The Illinois Supreme Court thus reasoned that Bradwell, who was married, could not independently practice law, because the profession necessarily involved entering into legal contracts. The state supreme court stated that allowing women the right to practice law was not a step the justices were willing to take because it would mean that "every civil office in this State may be filled by women," and they refused to admit that such a decision would be "in harmony with the spirit of our constitution" because it would imply "that women should be made governors, judges and sheriffs."[1] Incredibly, the Illinois Supreme Court opinion wondered whether "to engage in the hot strifes of the bar, in the presence of the public, and with momentous verdicts the prizes of the struggle, would not tend to destroy the deference and delicacy with which it is the pride of our ruder sex to treat her."[2] Bradwell appealed the decision to the U.S. Supreme Court, where she argued that the Privileges and Immunities Clause of the Fourteenth Amendment prohibited this type of discrimination and protected her right to practice law. Much like the Illinois State Supreme Court, the U.S. Supreme Court disagreed with Bradwell. Justice Samuel Miller's Opinion of the Court in *Bradwell v. Illinois* (1873) denied her this right based on a narrow reading of the Privileges and Immunities Clause, finding no power by the Court to regulate state law license requirements. Although this decision appeared on its face to be gender neutral, there was more below the surface. Miller did not even bother to elaborate on the reasons for the Court's decision, instead referencing the recently decided *Slaughterhouse Cases* (1873) and stating that it "is unnecessary to repeat the argument on which the judgment in those cases is founded. It is sufficient to say they are conclusive of the present case."[3]

Furthermore, in a concurring opinion, Justice Joseph Bradley did not hide his religiously-based views on roles for men and women:

> Man is, or should be, woman's protector and defender. The natural and proper timidity and delicacy which belongs to the female sex evidently unfits it for many of the occupations of civil life. The constitution of the family organization, which is founded in the divine ordinance, as well as in the nature of things, indicates the domestic sphere as that which properly belongs to the domain and functions of womanhood. The harmony, not to say identity, of interests and views which belong, or should belong, to the family institution is repugnant to the idea of a woman adopting a distinct and independent career from that of her husband...The paramount destiny and mission of woman are to fulfill the noble and benign offices of wife and mother. This is the law of the Creator.[4]

According to Bradley, who was joined in his opinion by Justice Noah Swayne and Justice Stephen Field, this view of women led to the logical conclusion that "a married woman is incapable, without her husband's consent, of making contracts which shall be binding on her or him. This very incapacity was one circumstance which the Supreme Court of Illinois deemed important in rendering a married woman incompetent fully to perform the duties and trusts that belong to the office of an attorney and counselor."[5]

Shortly after the *Bradwell* decisions by the Illinois Supreme Court and the U.S. Supreme Court, the Supreme Court of Wisconsin denied bar admission to Lavinia Goodell in 1875. Chief Justice Edward Ryan, writing for the court, stated the following when defending the court's decision to prohibit women from practicing law:

> There are many employments in life not unfit for female character. The profession of the law is surely not one of these. The peculiar qualities of womanhood,

> its gentle graces, its quick sensibility, its tender susceptibility, its parity, its delicacy, its emotional impulses, its subordination of hard reason to sympathetic feeling, are surely not qualifications for forensic strife. Nature has tempered woman as little for the juridical conflicts of the court room, as for the physical conflicts of the battle field. Womanhood is moulded [*sic*] for gentler and better things. And it is not the saints of the world who chiefly give employment to our profession. It has essentially and habitually to do with all that is selfish and malicious, knavish and criminal, coarse and brutal, repulsive and obscene, in human life. It would be revolting to all female sense of the innocence and sanctity of their sex, shocking to man's reverence for womanhood and faith in woman, on which hinge all the better affections and humanities of life, that woman should be permitted to mix professionally in all the nastiness of the world which finds its way into courts of justice; all the unclean issues, all the collateral questions of sodomy, incest, rape, seduction, fornication, adultery, pregnancy, bastardy, legitimacy, prostitution, lascivious cohabitation, abortion, infanticide, obscene publications, libel and slander of sex, impotence, divorce: all the nameless catalogue of indecencies, *la chronique scandaleuse* of all the vices and all the infirmities of all society, with which the profession has to deal, and which go towards filling judicial reports which must be read for accurate knowledge of the law.[6]

Much like the courts that decided Bradwell's case, the Wisconsin Supreme Court in *Goodell* noted that given their nature, women could not handle what happens in court. For that reason, Chief Justice Ryan and the rest of the court believed that women should be excluded from the bar. Even though the Wisconsin and Illinois courts held this view of women, their respective legislatures had more progressive attitudes and soon permitted women to practice law: Illinois did so in 1872 as did Wisconsin in 1877. Even so, the growth of women in the legal profession was slow. A year after Myra Bradwell's 1869 application for bar admission, there were only five women lawyers in the country. By 1880, there were seventy-five women lawyers in the United States, but this still stood in stark contrast to the 64,000 lawyers in the country who were men (this means that in 1880, women made up 0.12 percent of all attorneys). These numbers for women took a very long time to increase. It did not help that well into the twentieth century many law schools barred women from admission. Harvard Law School did not begin admitting women students until 1950. In 1951, only 2.5 percent of attorneys in the United States were women. In 1984, although it was on the increase, only 13 percent of attorneys were women. And although their numbers are still climbing, according to the American Bar Association, as of 2011, women still only comprised 31 percent of attorneys and 19 percent of law firm partners in the United States.[7]

The *Bradwell* and *Goodell* decisions, and the glacially slow advance of women in the legal profession, help to demonstrate that sexism within the American legal profession and court system has an extensive past that affected bar membership into the twentieth and twenty-first centuries. These denials to women practicing law in the nineteenth century went further than issues of what types of employment women were deemed fit to do. These court decisions also attacked the notion of women being present in court at all, out of the stereotype-based fear that women would be harmed by being exposed to the criminal actions and unscrupulous practices that will inevitably be brought up in legal proceedings. These notions of women's capabilities continued to hold strong in many aspects of the legal profession, which continued (and continues) to be stratified by gender. Eventually, this began to give way a bit, as women were able to practice law in every state by 1900, and women were taking on other courtroom roles, such as court clerks. However, well into the twentieth century it was common for states, to varying degrees, to deny women the ultimate power to determine legal guilt or innocence by serving on juries. This was ultimately a continuation of the notions expressed in those nineteenth century bar admission cases.[8]

Even though *Strauder v. West Virginia* (discussed in the last chapter) outlawed the exclusion of African Americans from jury pools in 1880, in that same case the U.S. Supreme Court allowed states to prohibit women from serving on juries: "We do not say that within the limits from which it is not excluded by the [Fourteenth Amendment] a State may not prescribe the qualifications of its jurors, and in so doing make discriminations. It may confine the selection to males."[9] Of course, at this time, the notion of women attorneys was also relatively novel among most judges. But even as women were being admitted to law school and to the bar in every state, jury service for women was still being denied.

Evidence suggests that women were completely excluded from serving on juries in the United States until 1870, when it was permitted in the Wyoming Territory. That equity in jury service was ended shortly thereafter and long before Wyoming achieved statehood. No states permitted women to serve on juries until Utah established the practice in 1898. Still, women were limited in their jury service well into the twentieth century. In 1931, over a decade after achieving suffrage, women were still excluded from jury service in a majority of states. And although more states were progressively ending total exclusion of women from juries during the middle third of the twentieth century, in 1961 in *Hoyt v. Florida*, the U.S. Supreme Court gave its stamp of approval to states that wanted to bar women from juries.[10]

The case began with police accusing Gwendolyn Hoyt of killing her husband, Clarence Hoyt. Mr. Hoyt had been cheating on Mrs. Hoyt for some time, which led to what the Florida Supreme Court characterized as "prolonged marital discord." The two were married in 1942, but they divorced a few years later when Mrs. Hoyt found Mr. Hoyt with another woman. After some reconciliation, the two remarried in 1947. During this same period, Mrs. Hoyt was diagnosed with epilepsy, which became progressively worse in the 1950s, resulting in her becoming dizzy, fainting, having hallucinations, experiencing paralysis, and stuttering. Her doctor surmised that Mrs. Hoyt's attacks were a result of emotional disturbances and nervous tension. By the mid-1950s, Mr. Hoyt was rarely home; when he was home he frequently received phone calls from strange women, and he frequently would fly into fits of rage and batter Mrs. Hoyt. Even so, Mrs. Hoyt made a final attempt to salvage their marriage on September 18, 1957 by calling him home in the middle of the day, falsely claiming that their young son had been injured. Mrs. Hoyt then offered to forgive him and take him back, but Mr. Hoyt refused her efforts at reconciliation this time, including her sexual advances. Later that day, while he was lying down, Mrs. Hoyt took a broken baseball bat that she had intended to throw away and hit Mr. Hoyt repeatedly, including in the head. Mrs. Hoyt later claimed that if the bat had not been there, she probably would not have done anything more than slap him. She also claimed that she only intended to hit her husband in the shoulders. Mrs. Hoyt called the family doctor, who refused to go to their residence, and after some time she was finally able to have an ambulance dispatched to the home. In the meantime, Mrs. Hoyt covered her husband with a blanket, offered him water, and tried to stop the bleeding. However, the head wounds were extensive, leading to Mr. Hoyt's death two days later. Mrs. Hoyt claimed temporary insanity, but she was convicted at trial of second degree murder in 1957. Her husband's violence against her was not mentioned at the trial. After the close of evidence, the jury deliberated for only twenty-five minutes. The judge sentenced Hoyt to thirty years imprisonment.[11]

What makes Hoyt's trial relevant for present purposes is that her six-person jury was comprised solely of men. Although women were allowed to serve on juries in Florida at the time, they were not automatically placed into the jury pool. According to the relevant Florida statute, "male and female" citizens were allowed to serve on juries, but the statute went on to state that "the name of no female person shall be taken for jury service unless said person has registered with the clerk of the circuit court her desire to be placed on the jury list." No similar requirement existed for men, as all adult male citizens had their names placed on the master jury list. Unlike women, who were absolutely exempted from jury duty unless they petitioned to have their names placed on the jury list, men had their names placed on the list and had to petition to have their names taken off if they thought they qualified for an exemption. This practice meant that very few women served on Florida juries at this time. For instance, in Hillsborough County, Florida (where Hoyt's trial took place), there were 46,000 registered women voters in the county in 1957, but only 220 women were registered for jury service. This also led to a great disparity in the proportion of potential jurors who were men versus women. Of the ten thousand names on the qualified jury list in Hillsborough County 1957, only ten were women. Thus, it should come as no surprise that zero women were on Hoyt's jury. Hoyt, however, objected to this state law, claiming that it violated her rights under the Fourteenth Amendment.[12]

Even though Hoyt's case went before the U.S. Supreme Court in the early 1960s, during a period when the Warren Court was dominated by liberals, the justices unanimously found against her. This was probably due, in part, to *Hoyt* being decided before *Duncan v. Louisiana*, the case which incorporated the Sixth Amendment's right to an impartial jury to apply to the states. Still, in *Hoyt*, Justice John Marshall Harlan began with an important proposition, that "the right to an impartially selected jury [is] assured by the Fourteenth Amendment."[13] Justice Harlan then elaborated on this statement:

> That right does not entitle one accused of crime to a jury tailored to the circumstances of the particular case, whether relating to the sex or other condition of the defendant, or to the nature of the charges to be tried. It requires only that the jury be indiscriminately drawn from among those eligible in the community for jury service, untrammelled [*sic*] by any arbitrary and systematic exclusions.[14]

In other words, the right to an impartial jury does not guarantee a jury of persons who share all of the demographic characteristics of the defendant, only that there is no arbitrary, systematic discrimination in how the jury is chosen. At first blush, this seems to point toward Hoyt's favor. After all, if men were automatically placed in the jury pool, but women had to go out of their way to have their names placed in the jury pool, it would appear that an arbitrary criterion (sex) was being used to systematically exclude women. Although women could serve on juries, this additional burden, coupled with cultural gender norms in the 1950s, would likely result in few women ever serving on Florida juries.

The Supreme Court, however, analyzed this Florida law a bit differently. According to Harlan, the Florida statute "does not purport to exclude women from state jury service. Rather, the statute gives to women the privilege to serve but does not impose service as a duty."[15] Harlan then went on to make a statement that, astonishingly, harkened back to the Court's nineteenth century jurisprudence on women and the law:

> Despite the enlightened emancipation of women from the restrictions and protections of bygone years, and their entry into many parts of community life formerly considered to be reserved to men, woman is still regarded as the center of home and family life. We cannot say that it is constitutionally impermissible for a State, acting in pursuit of the general welfare, to conclude that a woman should be relieved from the civic duty of jury service unless she herself determines that such service is consistent with her own special responsibilities.[16]

One can now see the relevance in *Hoyt* of cases dating back to *Bradwell*: they constitute an unbroken string of legal opinions by American courts, including the U.S. Supreme Court, giving women a second class status in the legal world. Even though the Court would have clearly declared unconstitutional in 1961 a state statute that barred *all* women from serving on juries, a statute that accomplished the same goal, save a few exceptions, was constitutional.

There was more to the Court's opinion. Harlan went on to note that although women were allowed to serve on juries in forty-seven states in 1961 (Alabama, Mississippi, and South Carolina still prohibited women from serving on juries under any circumstances), seventeen states besides Florida and the District of Columbia created an absolute exemption for women.[17] As for the low number of women who served on juries in Hillsborough County, Harlan concluded as follows: "It is true of course that the proportion of women on the jury list (ten) to the total of those registered for such duty (some 220) was less than 5 percent...But when those listed are compared with the thirty or thirty-five women who had registered since 1952…the proportion rises to around 33 percent, hardly suggestive of an arbitrary, systematic exclusionary purpose."[18]

Thus, through a short-sighted viewing of the relevant statistics, the Court concluded that there had been no violation of the right to an impartial jury under the Fourteenth Amendment, and Hoyt's conviction stood.

And so it continued, in a fair number of states, that women would be effectively exempted from jury duty. During this same period something was going on across the country, though. The Women's Liberation Movement was growing in strength throughout the 1960s and especially in the 1970s. By 1972, the Equal Rights Amendment was introduced in Congress, and that same year Title IX became law. In 1972, Billy J. Taylor was indicted for aggravated kidnapping in the St. Tammany Parish, Louisiana. Taylor had abducted a woman with a butcher knife, and he kidnapped her, her daughter, and her grandson. He made the woman drive them all to a deserted area, where he raped her and robbed all three of them.[19]

Much like in *Hoyt*, Taylor's jury was comprised only of men. Louisiana in the 1970s had a similar rule as Florida did in the 1950s regarding women and jury service. In Louisiana at the time, women were excluded from jury service unless they wrote a letter to government officials specifically declaring their willingness to serve on juries. Much like the case in Florida, few Louisiana women wrote such letters and were not eligible to be called for jury service. In St. Tammany Parish from December 1971 through November 1972, 1,800 persons were drawn to fill jury venires, but only twelve of those persons were women. In Taylor's trial, 175 persons were chosen in April 1972 as potential jurors. None of them were women. Thus, Taylor objected to the venire, much like Hoyt did in 1957. Since this case arose after *Duncan* incorporated the Sixth Amendment's right to an impartial jury, Taylor claimed that his Sixth Amendment right to an impartial jury, as incorporated by the Fourteenth Amendment, was being violated.[20]

When Taylor's case reached the U.S. Supreme Court in 1975, the result was that the justices reversed his conviction by a vote of 8-1. At first glance, this may seem a bit odd. After all, *Hoyt* had been decided only fourteen years earlier, and both cases dealt with remarkably similar laws regarding women's eligibility for jury service. Furthermore, the Court was more conservative in 1975 than it had been in 1961, with four appointees by President Richard Nixon. Still, the nation's attitudes toward women had transformed in the intervening years, and the opinions of the justices were, apparently, in line with this national change of attitude. Indeed, by the mid-1970s, the Women's Liberation Movement was in full swing, making the Court's decision in *Hoyt* seem all the more out of the mainstream.

Justice Byron White wrote the majority opinion in *Taylor v. Louisiana* (1975). Justice White began by discussing the real world implications of Louisiana's rule on women's jury eligibility: "The Louisiana jury-selection system does not disqualify women from jury service, but in operation its conceded systematic impact is that only a very few women, grossly disproportionate to the number of eligible women in the community, are called for jury service."[21] White then noted that women made up 53 percent of the persons eligible for jury service, yet none were called for the venire in Taylor's trial, and very few were called for other trials during the time.

Next, Justice White dealt with an important argument from the attorneys for the State of Louisiana. They argued that because Billy J. Taylor was a man, and thus not a member of a protected class, he had no right to raise a claim about women being excluded from jury service. Essentially, Louisiana was arguing that only women defendants could raise objections to other women being excluded from jury service. Justice White made quick work of this argument. According to the justice, "Taylor's claim is that he was constitutionally entitled to a jury drawn from a venire constituting a fair cross section of the community and that the jury that tried him was not such a jury by reason of the exclusion of women."[22] In other words, White confirmed that there is no constitutional rule that such claims could only be brought by defendants who shared the characteristics of the class excluded from jury duty. What matters is whether a state is infringing on the right to a jury with a fair cross-section of the community, not what the defendant's sex might be.

White then launched into the heart of his opinion, explaining why the right to an impartial jury was violated in Taylor's trial. He began by noting that something else (besides the Women's Liberation Movement) was new since *Hoyt* in 1961 — the Court had decided *Duncan v. Louisiana*, which made the Sixth Amendment's right to a jury trial binding on the states via the Fourteenth Amendment's Due Process Clause: "The background against which this case must be decided includes our holding in *Duncan v. Louisiana*, that the Sixth Amendment's provision for jury trial is made binding on the States by virtue of the Fourteenth Amendment."[23] According to Justice White, "the American concept of the jury trial contemplates a jury drawn from a fair cross section of the community,"[24] by which White was confirming that the inquiry would examine the make-up of the jury pool, not the demographic characteristics of the defendant. After reviewing the relevant case law on this point, White concluded that "the selection of a petit jury from a representative cross section of the community is an essential component of the Sixth Amendment right to a jury trial."[25]

According to Justice White, the cross-section requirement was a key part of the right, making it something that also was subject to incorporation under the Fourteenth Amendment: "We accept the fair-cross-section requirement as fundamental to the jury trial guaranteed by the Sixth Amendment and are convinced that the requirement has solid foundation."[26] White then explained that this is so because the "purpose of a jury is to guard against the exercise of arbitrary power — to make available the commonsense judgment of the community as a hedge against the overzealous or mistaken prosecutor and in preference to the professional or perhaps overconditioned or biased response of a judge."[27] The problem with Louisiana's law was that it ensured that "the jury pool [was] made up of only special segments of the populace" and that a "large, distinctive" group was excluded from that pool.[28] It is broad-based, community participation which is "critical to public confidence in the fairness of the criminal justice system."[29] According to White,

> Restricting jury service to only special groups or excluding identifiable segments playing major roles in the community cannot be squared with the constitutional concept of jury trial. Trial by jury presupposes a jury drawn from a pool broadly representative of the community as well as impartial in a specific case...[The] broad representative character of the jury should be maintained, partly as assurance of a diffused impartiality and partly because sharing in the administration of justice is a phase of civic responsibility.[30]

What did all of this mean for Taylor and the Louisiana law? Applying this reasoning, White and the majority found that "the fair-cross-section requirement is violated by the systematic exclusion of women, who in the judicial district involved here amounted to 53 percent of the citizens eligible for jury service."[31] This violates the constitution because "women are sufficiently numerous and distinct from men" and "if they are systematically eliminated from jury panels, the Sixth Amendment's fair-cross-section requirement cannot be satisfied."[32]

Justice White then turned to the history of women and jury service: "until today no case had squarely held that the exclusion of women from jury venires deprives a criminal defendant of his Sixth Amendment right to trial by an impartial jury drawn from a fair cross section of the community."[33] Justice White traced the history of jury service back to the Judiciary Act of 1789, which set federal juror qualifications to be the same as the state in which the federal court was sitting; since no state allowed women jurors in 1789, this was evidence that the same Congress which drafted the Sixth Amendment did not imply by its language, "[i]n all criminal prosecutions, the accused shall enjoy the right to a speedy and public trial, by an impartial jury," that women needed to be included. However, Justice White then declared that times had changed. Indeed, Justice White repudiated more than a century of U.S. Supreme Court reasoning on the role and place of women in the law:

> [W]e think it is no longer tenable to hold that women as a class may be excluded or given automatic exemptions based solely on sex if the consequence is that criminal jury venires are almost totally male. To this extent we cannot follow the contrary implications of the prior cases, including *Hoyt v. Florida*. If it was ever the case that women were unqualified to sit on juries or were so situated that none of them should be required to perform jury service, that time has long

> since passed. If at one time it could be held that Sixth Amendment juries must be drawn from a fair cross section of the community but that this requirement permitted the almost total exclusion of women, this is not the case today. Communities differ at different times and places. What is a fair cross section at one time or place is not necessarily a fair cross section at another time or a different place. Nothing persuasive has been presented to us in this case suggesting that all-male venires in the parishes involved here are fairly representative of the local population otherwise eligible for jury service.[34]

Thus, *Hoyt*'s notion that women could be systematically excluded from jury service was overruled. The Court would no longer accept the outdated notions of women's place in the courtroom or on a jury. Beginning with *Taylor*, an impartial jury must be drawn from a jury pool that fairly allows access to women.

There was, however, a lone dissenter in *Taylor*. Justice William Rehnquist lodged his displeasure with the majority's decision, claiming that past cases led to the conclusion only that "due process and equal protection prohibit jury-selection systems which are likely to result in biased or partial juries."[35] Justice Rehnquist then contemplated the *Hoyt* decision, and claimed that nothing changed since that time to warrant the Court's decision in *Taylor*. Furthermore, even with the decision in *Duncan*, for Rehnquist there was nothing to merit overturning Taylor's conviction, because Taylor "makes no claims of prejudice or bias."[36] For Rehnquist, Louisiana's jury system was in conformance with the Sixth and Fourteenth Amendments, even though women were largely barred from participating. Rehnquist believed that there was not a constitutional violation of the right to an impartial jury "if either sex is excluded" because "presumably doctors, lawyers, and other groups, whose frequent exemption from jury service is endorsed by the majority, also offer qualities as distinct and important as those at issue here."[37] In other words, Rehnquist believed that if people can be constitutionally excluded from jury service due to their professional responsibilities, then excluding women should not pose a constitutional problem either.

Rehnquist makes an interesting point here, in that doctors and lawyers may also have something of value to add to jury pools, but they were also constitutionally excluded. There are problems with Rehnquist using these examples to justify Louisiana's exclusion of women, however. First, the percentage of the population that is comprised of doctors or lawyers is relatively small when compared to women, who make up a majority of the public. Second, these exemptions on jury service for persons fulfilling certain occupations are different from the exclusion of women. No one would argue that doctors or lawyers are somehow unqualified for jury service in the way that historical arguments were made that women should not be in the courtroom. In addition, the implication from Rehnquist seemed to be that housewives should not be considered as a protected class any more than lawyers or judges: "surely constitutional adjudication is a more canalized function than enforcing as against the States this Court's perception of modern life."[38] For Rehnquist, the majority was enforcing its notions of "modern life," but Rehnquist's idea of legally equating women with being housewives was an idea rendered outmoded by the ratification of the Fourteenth Amendment. Even if this was not Rehnquist's intent — if instead he meant to imply that housewives should not be required to serve on juries because it would be difficult for them to be in court with their family and household responsibilities — Rehnquist still missed the mark. Obviously, not all women are housewives; equally obvious, some men do not work outside of the home.

Putting aside the bitter irony that Taylor, a man who committed crimes against women, benefitted from a constitutional rule promoting women's equality, there is no doubt that the Court came to the correct legal conclusion in *Taylor*. The days of claiming that women had no place in the courtroom, either as attorneys or jurors, were finally over. Perhaps Gwendolyn Hoyt's trial would have been different if women had been on it. Perhaps her experiences in an abusive relationship and the obstacles she faced would have been better understood in a jury deliberation room that included women. Indeed, if we analogize to race, one of the problems with some of the all-white juries described in the previous chapters was that race was an issue in these trials, making all-white juries problematic from the perspective of impartiality. In Hoyt's case, the fact that it was a woman accused of killing a man made it difficult to see how a jury of only men would be as impartial as a jury of men and women. Perhaps this would have led to a conviction on lesser charges or an acquittal. This was not a consideration of the U.S. Supreme Court, however, in *Hoyt*.

Of course, it is also possible that had there been a real chance for women to be on the jury, Hoyt would have been convicted. The point is not what the outcome might have been. The point was whether or not procedural justice was achieved by protecting the right to an impartial jury. In Hoyt's trial, that was not the case. After *Taylor*, however, it has been increasingly so. Indeed, two decades later, the Supreme Court applied the logic of *Taylor* and *Batson v. Kentucky* in *J.E.B. v. Alabama* (1994), where the Court ruled that peremptory challenges could not be used to exclude jurors solely because of their gender.[39] That decision occurred because of the right choice made by the Court in *Taylor*.

Notes

1. *In the Matter of the Application of Mrs. Myra Bradwell, for a License to Practice Law*, 55 Ill. 535, 540 (1876).
2. *Application of Mrs. Myra Bradwell*, 55 Ill. at 542.
3. *Bradwell v. Illinois*, 83 U.S. 130, 139 (1873).
4. *Bradwell v. Illinois*, 83 U.S. at 141 (Bradley, J., concurring).
5. *Bradwell v. Illinois*, 83 U.S. at 141(Bradley, J., concurring).
6. *In the Matter of the Motion to Admit Miss Lavinia Goodell to the Bar of this Court*, 39 Wis. 232, 245-46 (1875).
7. Audrey Wolfson Latourette, "Sex Discrimination in the Legal Profession: Historical and Contemporary Perspectives," *Valparaiso University Law Review* 39 (2005):

859-909, 863-69, 877; Stephen J. Spurr, "Sex Discrimination in the Legal Profession: A Study of Promotion," *Industrial and Labor Relations Review* 43 (1990): 406-17, 406; American Bar Association Commission on Women in the Profession, "A Current Glance at Women in the Law 2011," 2011, http://www.americanbar.org/content/dam/aba/marketing/women/current_glance_statistics_2011.authcheckdam.pdf (accessed May 6, 2012).

8. Latourette, "Sex Discrimination," 880; Joanna L. Grossman, "Women's Jury Service: Right of Citizenship or Privilege of Difference?," *Standford Law Review* 46 (1994): 1115-1160, 1129-39.

9. *Strauder v. West Virginia*, 100 U.S. 310 (1880).

10. Grossman, "Women's Jury Service," 1133-38.

11. *Hoyt v. State*, 119 So. 2d 691, 692-93 (Fla. 1959); *Hoyt v. Florida*, 368 U.S. 57, 64 (1961).; Leslie Friedman Goldstein, "Hoyt v. Florida," in *The Oxford Companion to the Supreme Court of the United States*, Kermit L. Hall, ed., (New York: Oxford University Press, 2005), 477; Linda K. Kerber, *No Constitutional Right to Be Ladies: Women and the Obligations of Citizenship* (New York: Hill and Wang, 1998), 124-28, 163; "Baseball Bat Slayer of Husband Sentenced to 30 Years in Prison," *Ocala Star-Banner* January 20, 1958, 5.

12. *Hoyt*, 368 U.S. at 58, 64-65.

13. *Hoyt*, 368 U.S. at 59.

14. *Hoyt*, 368 U.S. at 59.

15. *Hoyt*, 368 U.S. at 60 (internal quotations omitted).

16. *Hoyt*, 368 U.S. at 61-62.

17. *Hoyt*, 368 U.S. at 62.

18. *Hoyt*, 368 U.S. at 67-68.

19. Kerber, *No Constitutional Right*, 209; *Taylor v. Louisiana*, 419 U.S. 522, 524 (1975).

20. *Taylor*, 419 U.S. at 524-25; David L. Hudson, Jr., *The Rehnquist Court: Understanding Its Impact and Legacy* (Westport, CT: Praeger, 2007), 16.

21. *Taylor*, 419 U.S. at 525.

22. *Taylor*, 419 U.S. at 526.

23. *Taylor*, 419 U.S. at 526 (internal citation omitted).

24. *Taylor*, 419 U.S. at 527.

25. *Taylor*, 419 U.S. at 528.

26. *Taylor*, 419 U.S. at 530.

27. *Taylor*, 419 U.S. at 530.

28. *Taylor*, 419 U.S. at 530.

29. *Taylor*, 419 U.S. at 530.

30. *Taylor*, 419 U.S. at 530-31 (internal quotations and citations omitted).

31. *Taylor*, 419 U.S. at 531.

32. *Taylor*, 419 U.S. at 531.

33. *Taylor*, 419 U.S. at 535-36.

34. *Taylor*, 419 U.S. at 537.

35. *Taylor*, 419 U.S. at 539 (Rehnquist, J., dissenting).

36. *Taylor*, 419 U.S. at 541 (Rehnquist, J., dissenting).

37. *Taylor*, 419 U.S. at 542 (Rehnquist, J., dissenting).

38. *Taylor*, 419 U.S. at 542 (Rehnquist, J., dissenting).

39. *J.E.B. v. Alabama*, 511 U.S. 127 (1994).

~ 5 ~

Death-Qualified Juries: *Witherspoon v. Illinois* (1968) and *Lockhart v. McCree* (1986)

A sentence of death cannot be carried out if the jury that imposed or recommended it was chosen by excluding veniremen for cause simply because they voiced general objections to the death penalty or expressed conscientious or religious scruples against its infliction.
– *Witherspoon v. Illinois*, 391 U.S. 510, 522 (1968)

[T]he evidence is sufficient to establish that death qualification constitutes a substantial threat to a defendant's Sixth and Fourteenth Amendment right to a fair jury trial.
– *Lockhart v. McCree*, 476 U.S. 162, 202 (1986) (Justice Marshall, dissenting)

As was described in greater detail in chapters three and four, the Sixth Amendment's command of an impartial jury in criminal cases includes a requirement that the jury represents a fair cross-section of the community. There is no question that exclusion of jurors based on their race and sex violates this requirement. Of course, there are limits to this command when other characteristics are at issue. Federal courts classify the following groups of people as unqualified for jury service: non-citizens, persons under eighteen years of age, non-residents of the district where the trial is occurring, persons who are not "adequately proficient" in English, persons with a "disqualifying mental or physical condition," persons who are currently charged with a felony, and those who have been convicted of a felony.[1] Most states have similar exclusions. Although some of these exclusions are controversial, many of them make a great deal of sense. After all, we would not want a four-year-old to serve on a jury, nor would we want someone with a severe casc of schizophrenia to serve on a jury. Within this context, a fair cross-section of the community does not require perfect representation of all possible groups who exist in the world.

If certain classes of people can be excluded from jury service because of their age, their citizenship status, and their status as a felon, what about excluding people based on their personal beliefs? Usually, personal beliefs will not be grounds for jury exclusion, as a diverse set of views is an important part of ensuring a fair cross-section of the community. A diverse set of personal beliefs usually furthers the notion of a "jury of one's peers" and serves the greater end of impartiality. In one area, though, the U.S. Supreme Court has found that certain personal views or convictions can be systematically excluded from the jury: persons who would refuse, under any circumstances, to impose the death penalty in capital cases.

Witherspoon v. Illinois (1968) began when William C. Witherspoon was arrested for the murder of police officer Mitchell Stone. Witherspoon was struggling with a woman on the street one evening in April 1959. The woman subsequently broke free and ran to a nearby police car. There, she told police that Witherspoon had a gun. Witherspoon fled the police to a nearby parking lot, where he hid in a tractor-trailer. When Officer Stone came upon Witherspoon, Witherspoon shot him. Before he died, Stone identified Witherspoon as the shooter. Witherspoon, however, claimed that his gun went off by accident when he was handing it over to officer Stone.[2]

Witherspoon was charged with capital murder in April 1960. At the time, Illinois had a statute which stated that "[i]n trials for murder it shall be a cause for challenge of any juror who shall, on being examined, state that he has conscientious scruples against capital punishment, or that he is opposed to the same." Due to this statute, the trial judge noted during *voir dire*, "[l]et's get these conscientious objectors out of the way, without wasting any time on them." Prosecutors, following the judge's lead, eliminated almost half of the venire — forty-seven persons — by challenging them for cause on the basis of their views on the death penalty. Only five of these excluded potential jurors stated that they could not support the death penalty under any circumstances. All of the others who were struck for this cause simply expressed some doubt about the death penalty, and little or no effort was made by prosecutors to clarify what this meant. The resulting jury convicted Witherspoon of Stone's homicide, and that same jury sentenced Witherspoon on April 22, 1960 to death in the electric chair. After appealing his conviction and holding off the imposition of his sentence for eight years, Witherspoon finally had his appeal heard by the U.S. Supreme Court in 1968.[3]

The basis of Witherspoon's objection to the Illinois law was that the state was trying to stack the deck in its own favor. Witherspoon saw this as a threat to the jury's impartiality, as he argued that the practice took out of the jury pool persons who were not just against the death penalty, but also jurors who were more predisposed to side with defendants generally. For Witherspoon, this threatened the Sixth Amendment's requirement of impartiality that manifests itself in the need for a cross-section of the community to serve on the jury. In support of his argument, Witherspoon cited two unpublished surveys of college students and one unpublished survey of former jurors.[4]

Writing for the Court majority, Justice Potter Stewart began his analysis by entertaining this point from Witherspoon but rejecting the studies behind it. According to Justice Stewart, such unpublished studies were "too tentative and fragmentary to establish that jurors not opposed to the death penalty tend to favor the prosecution in the determination of guilt."[5] Instead, Stewart declared that "[w]e simply cannot conclude, either on the basis of the record now before us or as a matter of judicial notice, that the exclusion of jurors opposed to capital punishment results in an unrepresentative jury on the issue of guilt or substantially increases the risk of conviction," and that in "light of the presently available information, we are not prepared to announce a *per se* constitutional rule requiring the reversal of every conviction returned by a jury selected as this one was."[6]

Still, Justice Stewart went on to find the following: "it is self-evident that, in its role as arbiter of the punishment to be imposed, this jury fell woefully short of that impartiality to which the petitioner was entitled under the Sixth and Fourteenth Amendments."[7] Stewart came to this decision because a person "who opposes the death penalty, no less than one who favors it, can make the discretionary judgment entrusted to him by the State and can thus obey the oath he takes as a juror."[8] But a jury where all persons with concerns about the death penalty have been excluded creates a constitutional problem because it no longer represents a cross-section of the community: "Culled of all who harbor doubts about the wisdom of capital punishment — of all who would be reluctant to pronounce the extreme penalty — such a jury can speak only for a distinct and dwindling minority."[9] Therefore, Stewart concluded that Illinois could have excluded prospective jurors who stated that they would *never* consider a verdict of death (as that would have been "neutral" with respect to the death penalty), but by excluding all those who expressed *any* conscientious or religious scruples against capital punishment, "the State produced a jury uncommonly willing to condemn a man to die."[10] Thus, the majority of the Court held that "a sentence of death cannot be carried out if the jury that imposed or recommended it was chosen by excluding veniremen for cause simply because they voiced general objections to the death penalty or expressed conscientious or religious scruples against its infliction."[11] In other words, the prosecution cannot expect potential jurors to state, before the trial has occurred, that they will make, or will fail to make, certain sentencing choices as jurors. Instead, they can only be asked to be open to all potential penalties and then choose the one that, in their opinion, best conforms to the evidence. According to Stewart, "[w]hatever else might be said of capital punishment, it is at least clear that its imposition by a hanging jury cannot be squared with the Constitution."[12] In this case, Stewart found that prosecutors "stacked the deck" against the defendant in violation of the Constitution, and so to "execute this death sentence would deprive [Witherspoon] of his life without due process of law."[13]

That said, Stewart did confirm that there is no constitutional violation if a state wishes to exclude jurors who state that they would automatically vote against the imposition of the death penalty in all cases or if a state wishes to exclude jurors whose opposition to the death penalty would keep them from acting impartially to determine a defendant's guilt. Furthermore, Stewart's decision was a narrow one, in that he noted that juries chosen in the manner prescribed by Illinois only created a constitutional violation with respect to a defendant's sentence. The Court declined to declare if excluding potential jurors who expressed doubts about the death penalty created a constitutional violation if the resulting jury decided the defendant's guilt. Thus, Stewart and the majority drew a fine line, finding that striking jurors with scruples against the death penalty violated a defendant's right to a fair sentence but not necessarily to a fair trial.[14]

Stewart's opinion represented the views of six of the Court's nine members in *Witherspoon*. Justice William Douglas wrote separately to express some anxiety he had with the majority opinion. Specifically, Douglas noted that he had a concern with the Court's decision because, "[t]he Court permits a State to eliminate from juries some of those who have conscientious scruples against the death penalty; but it allows those to serve who have no scruples against it as well as those who, having such scruples, nevertheless are deemed able to determine after a finding of guilt whether the death penalty or a lesser penalty should be imposed."[15]

For Douglas, this fell short of what the Court should have declared because the "idea that a jury should be impartially drawn from a cross-section of the community certainly should not mean a selection of only those with a predisposition to impose the severest sentence or with a predisposition to impose at least one that is possible."[16] Douglas found fault with the majority only reversing Witherspoon's sentence, leaving his underlying conviction in place. According to Douglas, "the absence of those opposed to capital punishment...rob[s] the jury of certain peculiar qualities of human nature," and in such a case there is no cross-section of the community, creating a less than impartial jury.[17] Douglas would have gone farther than the other five justices in the majority and reversed Witherspoon's conviction.

That brings us to the dissenters in *Witherspoon*. Justice Hugo Black, in an opinion joined by Justices John Marshall Harlan and Byron White, believed that the majority mischaracterized the prosecution as stacking the deck against the defendant. Instead, Black believed that the majority was trying to indirectly abolish capital punishment by making it easier to choose juries that would not impose the death penalty. Black noted that Witherspoon had distinguished attorneys to represent him, yet those attorneys did nothing to demonstrate that the jurors struck for their scruples against the death penalty were otherwise competent, and those attorneys still had three peremptory challenges remaining when the jury was chosen. Black then showed in his opinion how Witherspoon went through multiple appeals without raising the issue of jury impartiality.[18]

Black subsequently emphasized the need for impartiality for both sides: "the people as a whole, or as they are usually called, 'society' or 'the state,' have as much right to an impartial jury as do criminal defendants."[19] Justice Black believed that the Illinois law was promoting jury impartiality:

> As I see the issue in this case, it is a question of plain bias. A person who has conscientious or religious scruples against capital punishment will seldom if ever vote to impose the death penalty. This is just human nature, and no amount of semantic camouflage can cover it up. In the same manner, I would not dream of foisting on a criminal defendant a juror who admitted that he had conscientious or religious scruples against not inflicting the death sentence on any person convicted of murder.[20]

In other words, for Black the issue was not between having a jury with those who both favor the death penalty and those who disfavor it. For Black, the issue was about excluding those who would never vote to impose the death penalty, just as we would want to exclude from such a jury people who would impose that penalty on every convicted homicide defendant.

Justice Black made a valiant effort but ultimately fell short of the mark in his *Witherspoon* dissent. True, Witherspoon may have had good legal representation, but he was not raising an ineffective assistance of counsel claim on appeal. Instead, Witherspoon was raising a claim that the jury was partial. This is something that his attorneys might have chosen not to raise as an issue at trial, but that fact alone should not preclude Witherspoon from being able to bring the issue on appeal. Furthermore, Justice Black was correct that the goal of any trial should be a jury that is impartial toward both parties. Of course, that is the definition of impartiality — being indifferent to either side winning the case.[21] Justice Black, however, took this concept to the point of being illogical when he suggested that an impartial jury for Witherspoon may not necessarily be an impartial jury for the state. An impartial jury is impartial for both sides at the same time. And the state, with its ample resources, has much more ability to prepare a partial jury than most defendants could dream to have.

Black was certainly correct that a potential juror who automatically votes to impose the death penalty on anyone found guilty would be just as excludable as someone who would never impose that penalty. However, more than those who would never impose the death penalty were being excluded under the Illinois statute, and the statute did not specifically exclude those who expressed that they favored the death penalty. Thus, Black's point, although quite valid, did not reach the ultimate issue that was being debated in *Witherspoon*.

The argument between Justice Stewart and Justice Douglas — whether or not Witherspoon's jury was impartial with respect to his guilt — also raised some interesting points. Is it the case, as Douglas was implying, that excluding those who express doubt from serving on juries would produce juries more likely to convict, not just more likely to impose the death penalty? If that is the case, then such a jury would introduce serious concerns regarding its ability to remain impartial. Justice Stewart and four other members of the majority did not find a constitutional problem in this regard, nor did the three dissenters.

There were some preliminary studies on this issue, cited but dismissed by Stewart as too "tentative and fragmentary," which concluded that such juries were biased with respect to guilt. Similar legal and social scientific studies continued to be researched and ultimately published in the 1970s and 1980s though. For instance, a 1973 law review article found that jurors chosen in the way approved in *Witherspoon* were more likely to be prosecution prone. The same article found that such exclusions eliminated close to one fourth of the jury pool, and that they disproportionately exclude women and people of color (recall from chapters three and four the constitutional defects with such juries and their resulting failure to represent a cross-section of the community). Over the next decade, additional studies showed that death-qualified jury selection had a greater chance of producing pro-prosecution juries and that they were more likely to create homogenized juries which were prone to groupthink. With such studies in place by the mid-1980s, the U.S. Supreme Court was prepared to rule on the issue left open in *Witherspoon* — whether or not death-qualified juries are impartial with respect to deciding a defendant's guilt — in *Lockhart v. McCree* (1986).[22]

The *Lockhart* case began on Valentine's Day of 1978 in Camden, Arkansas. That morning, Evelyn Boughton, the owner of a combination gift shop and service station, was shot and killed. Later that afternoon in Hot Springs (over eighty miles away from Camden), a police officer observed Ardia McCree driving a vehicle which matched an eyewitness's description of the getaway car of Boughton's killer. When questioned, McCree did not deny that he had been at Boughton's shop. McCree claimed, however, that a tall African American stranger wearing an overcoat asked him for a ride that day, took McCree's rifle out of the back of his vehicle, and then used it to kill Boughton. McCree claimed that he then drove the stranger to a nearby dirt road, where the stranger got out of the vehicle and walked away with the rifle. There were some holes in this story though. Multiple eyewitnesses who saw McCree's car at the time of the homicide claimed that they only saw one person in the vehicle, although one witness initially said that he saw two people in the vehicle. Police later recovered McCree's rifle and a bank bag from Boughton's shop alongside a nearby dirt road. Ballistics tests then revealed that the bullet which killed Boughton had been fired from McCree's rifle.[23]

With a significant amount of evidence pointing toward his guilt, prosecutors charged McCree with capital felony murder. During jury selection, the trial judge removed for cause (over McCree's objections) eight prospective jurors who stated that they could not vote for the death penalty under any circumstances. The resulting jury convicted McCree of felony murder. During the penalty phase, the jury declined to impose the death penalty, instead imposing a sentence of life in prison without the possibility of parole. McCree then lost his subsequent appeal and state post-conviction proceedings before filing a federal habeas corpus petition, claiming that his "death-qualified" jury was biased in violation of the impartial jury requirements of the Sixth and Fourteenth Amendments. After having his habeas petition granted by the federal district judge, the person against whom the petition was directed, Arkansas Department of Corrections Director A.L. Lockhart, appealed until the case was heard by the U.S. Supreme Court.[24]

Associate Justice William Rehnquist, in one of his last opinions before being elevated to chief justice, wrote the Court's opinion in a case where six of the nine justices found against McCree. Justice Rehnquist began by attacking the validity of social science studies that the federal district judge relied on when granting McCree's petition. According to Rehnquist, of the fifteen studies used as evidence by McCree, only nine of them actually measured the effects on a death-qualified jury's finding of guilt or evidence. Rehnquist claimed that eight of those nine remaining studies dealt only with generalized attitudes about the death penalty and were thus not relevant to specific jury findings of guilt and innocence. The final study, dealing with the effects on prospective jurors of *voir dire* questioning on their attitudes about the death penalty, Rehnquist characterized as not enough to raise a constitutional violation. Overall, Rehnquist found flaws in just about every study that was relied upon by McCree.[25]

For the sake of argument, Justice Rehnquist assumed that the studies cited by McCree were methodologically valid and adequate to prove that death-qualified juries led to more conviction prone juries than juries not selected in this manner. Even then, Rehnquist firmly stated the Court's holding in *Lockhart*: "the Constitution does not prohibit the States from 'death qualifying' juries in capital cases."[26] According to Rehnquist, the fair cross-section requirement of jury impartiality allowed for death-qualified juries, as the U.S. Supreme Court has "never invoked the fair-cross-section principle to invalidate the use of either for-cause or peremptory challenges to prospective jurors, or to require petit juries...to reflect the composition of the community at large."[27] Instead, since no truly representative petite jury could be required by the Constitution, the majority in *Lockhart* was unwilling to extend the fair cross-section requirement in petite juries to include views on the death penalty.

Next, Rehnquist correctly pointed out that the fair cross-section requirement mandates that there be no systematic exclusion of distinctive groups. Although Rehnquist claimed that the Court has "never attempted to precisely define the term 'distinctive group,'" and that the majority would "not undertake to do so" in *Lockhart*, Rehnquist then proceeded to identify that distinctiveness is linked to (1) guarding against the exercise of arbitrary power, (2) preserving public confidence in the fairness of the criminal justice system, and (3) implementing the belief that jury service is a part of civic responsibility.[28] Justice Rehnquist proceeded to explain that prior cases involving the Court finding a violation of the fair cross-section requirement "involved groups such as blacks, women, and Mexican-Americans," where the "wholesale exclusion of these large groups from jury service clearly contravened all three of the aforementioned purposes of the fair-cross-section requirement."[29] Indeed, as examined in previous chapters, exclusion of potential jurors because of race or sex is constitutionally defective because there is no connection between one of these immutable characteristics and the ability to be an impartial juror, thus making such practices both arbitrary and unfair, and such practices deny essential civic responsibilities from people in these groups.

However, for Rehnquist the "*Witherspoon*-excludables" who are struck to create death-qualified juries do not create such constitutional dangers. First, according to Rehnquist, a death-qualified jury serves "the State's concededly legitimate interest in obtaining a single jury that can properly and impartially apply the law to the facts of the case at both the guilt and sentencing phases of a capital trial."[30] Second, Rehnquist claimed that since "*Witherspoon*-excludables" are excluded because of their beliefs, they are excluded "on the basis of an attribute that is within the individual's control."[31] Third, according to Rehnquist, the removal of "*Witherspoon*-excludables" in death penalty cases "does not prevent them from serving as jurors in other criminal cases, and thus leads to no substantial deprivation of their basic rights of citizenship."[32] Thus, Justice Rehnquist concluded that "'*Witherspoon*-excludables,' or...any other group defined solely in terms of shared attitudes that render members of the group unable to serve as jurors in a particular case, may be excluded from jury service without contravening any of the basic objectives of the fair-cross-section requirement."[33] For Rehnquist and the majority, "an impartial *jury* consists of nothing more than *jurors* who will conscientiously apply the law and find the facts."[34] In other words, judges cannot try to balance juries during *voir dire* to ensure a balanced jury; rather they can only practically watch to make sure that individual jurors are not unduly excluded because of membership in a distinctive group: "the Constitution presupposes that a jury selected from a fair cross section of the community is impartial, regardless of the mix of individual viewpoints actually represented on the jury, so long as the jurors can conscientiously and properly carry out their sworn duty to apply the law to the facts of the particular case."[35]

If Rehnquist is correct, then what does a "fair cross-section" of the community mean? It is true that a completely representative jury is impossible, given the large number of ways that one could find demographic factors to represent and given that there are only twelve persons on a jury. Still, systematic exclusion of people with a particular view on the death penalty (an issue that is directly relevant in any capital case) does leave a jury pool that will be more likely to convict. Rehnquist claimed that these "*Witherspoon*-excludables" do not raise constitutional problems because the state is aiming at an impartial jury. Of course, the state is doing no such thing when it is excluding persons with such beliefs. Just like the systematic exclusion of women and people of color in earlier eras, the goal of prosecutors who engaged in this practice was to create a *partial* jury. Furthermore, Rehnquist's notion that "*Witherspoon*-excludables" are different from groups with more visible distinctions is a curious one. Typically, a person cannot simply decide to change a strongly held belief. One wonders if

Rehnquist would uphold the exclusion of Christians or Jews from a jury, on the basis that they are only being excluded on their religious beliefs, which they could "change." Perhaps Democrats or liberals could be systematically excluded on similar grounds under Rehnquist's reasoning. Finally, the notion that excluding people who oppose the death penalty from capital cases is acceptable because they may be called to service on other juries is equally problematic. There is no guarantee that a potential juror excluded from a capital case will be called to serve on any other jury again, thus making them unable to take part in this civic responsibility.

Rehnquist also emphasized that the Sixth and Fourteenth Amendments required only impartial *jurors*, not necessarily impartial *juries*. The language of the Sixth Amendment, however, suggests that Rehnquist is wrong: "the accused shall enjoy the right to a speedy and public trial, by an impartial jury." The constitutional language asks that the jury be impartial, not just that individual jurors are. The old saying that "the whole is more than the sum of the parts" is an apt one here. Just because there is no partiality with respect to each individual juror being chosen does not mean that the jury as a whole is impartial. That is why, for instance, *Batson* claims look at the entirety of what occurs during *voir dire*, including whether or not there is a pattern of striking multiple jurors of the same race or a discriminatory nature to the questions that are asked of potential jurors by the prosecutor. What happens in isolation with individual jurors is relevant to *Batson* claims, but the aggregate result is as well. The same should be the case with respect to jurors being struck on the basis of views on capital punishment.

The Court was not unanimous behind Justice Rehnquist's reasoning in the case, however. Justice Thurgood Marshall, writing also for Justice William Brennan and Justice John Paul Stevens, penned a dissent in *Lockhart*. For Justice Marshall, the remedy for McCree was to have "the chance to have his guilt or innocence determined by a jury like those that sit in noncapital cases," which means a jury "whose composition has not been tilted in favor of the prosecution by the exclusion of a group of prospective jurors uncommonly aware of an accused's constitutional rights but quite capable of determining his culpability without favor or bias."[36] For Marshall, the problem was that the practice approved by the majority gave "the prosecution license to empanel a jury especially likely to return that very verdict" by merely announcing that it will be seeking the death penalty in these cases.[37] Indeed, if the prosecution wants to stack the deck of jurors in a case where the death penalty is possible but the prosecution does not think death would be the appropriate penalty, *Lockhart* creates an incentive for the prosecution to make clear during *voir dire* that it wants to seek the death penalty anyway, just so that it will have the benefit of striking the "*Witherspoon*-excludables."

Justice Marshall then assembled a host of articles and studies from the early 1960s into the 1980s, showing the bias that can occur in juries where persons opposing the death penalty are excluded from service. According to Marshall, the social science evidence suggests that between 11 percent and 17 percent of potential jurors who could be impartial during the guilt phase of the trial are excluded under the method used by prosecutors in McCree's trial, and a disproportionate number of these potential jurors in the studies were African Americans and women. This raises issues similar to the ones on the last two chapters, especially if striking potential jurors opposed to the death penalty is a backdoor way of excluding women and people of color.[38]

Additionally, Marshall cited studies from the district court that showed death-qualified jurors are "more likely to believe that a defendant's failure to testify is indicative of his guilt, more hostile to the insanity defense, more mistrustful of defense attorneys, and less concerned about the danger of erroneous convictions."[39] They have a "pro-prosecution bias" and hold a "greater readiness...to convict or to convict on more serious charges."[40] According to Marshall, even the process of death qualifying a jury during *voir dire* changes the perceptions of the jurors who are asked questions about the death penalty by focusing their attention on guilt and capital punishment. Examining these studies, Marshall found that they have shown that this process "predispose[s] the jurors that survive it to believe that the defendant is guilty."[41] On the other side, Marshall was able to cite studies in which "[m]embers of the excluded group have been shown to be significantly more concerned with the constitutional rights of criminal defendants and more likely to doubt the strength of the prosecution's case."[42]

Marshall referred to study after study on the biasing effects of death qualification. Numerous studies had been conducted and undertaken since *Witherspoon*, bolstering what was in 1968 only a "tentative and fragmentary" conclusion about the effects of the practice. Marshall then noted something that Rehnquist failed to mention when tearing apart these studies: there were no studies which contradicted the proposition that death qualification biases juries. In other words, every single study on the topic found that the practice created jury bias. Even if there may be some methodological concerns with some of these studies, the fact that all of them reached the same conclusion gives one pause.[43] This led Marshall and the other dissenters to conclude the following: "the evidence is sufficient to establish that death qualification constitutes a substantial threat to a defendant's Sixth and Fourteenth Amendment right to a fair jury trial."[44]

Justice Marshall's solution to this constitutional problem was to have true jury bifurcation in capital cases: select one jury to decide the defendant's guilt and select another jury to determine the convicted defendant's sentence. Potential jurors would not be asked their views on capital punishment when being chosen for the guilt phase of the trial, but potential jurors chosen for the sentencing phase of the trial could be asked such questions to sift out nullifiers. Thus process would protect against selecting a jury biased to find guilt, and it would also protect the prosecution's interest in ensuring that all jurors are impartial and would follow the law at the sentencing phase.[45] Justice Marshall's solution is the best approach, as it does protect the impartiality of the jury when deciding guilt, while also making sure that the sentencing jury properly excludes those who cannot follow the law.

Witherspoon and McCree may have both been guilty. If so, they each deserved a significant sentence. But that is not the point of their respective appeals. What neither deserved was a biased jury. The Constitution requires that each defendant has a fair trial, so that the evidence can be examined by independent jurors who come to their own conclusions. Indeed, in cases where there is a substantial amount of evidence implicating a defendant, prosecutors should not need to stack the deck against that defendant. If the practice of death qualification had not been used by prosecutors, through the luck of the draw the exact same jurors may even have been chosen in each case. But that is not the point either. The point is that one side should not have an advantage to purposely choose a jury more biased in its favor. Practices such as death qualification only lead to second guessing when defendants are convicted, which is not good for the integrity of the criminal justice system or the legitimacy of the right to an impartial jury. If the U.S Supreme Court can uphold these convictions with these juries, it causes the public to question the impartiality of juries in other contexts.

Notes

1. United States Courts, "Juror Qualifications, Exemptions and Exclusions," *Federal Courts*, http://www.uscourts.gov/FederalCourts/JuryService/JurorQualificaitons.aspx (accessed April 22, 2012).
2. *Witherspoon v. Illinois*, 391 U.S. 510, 533 (1968) (Black, J., dissenting); Kenan Heise, "William Witherspoon: Beat the Chair 15 Times," *Chicago Tribune*, March 6, 1990, http://articles.chicagotribune.com/1990-03-06/news/9001190215_1_electric-chair-william-witherspoon-killing (accessed May 26, 2012).
3. *People v. Witherspoon*, 36 Ill. 2d 471, 472 (Ill. 1967); *Witherspoon* 391 U.S. at 512-15; Heise.
4. *Witherspoon*, 391 U.S. at 516-17 & n.10.
5. *Witherspoon*, 391 U.S. at 517.
6. *Witherspoon*, 391 U.S. at 517-18.
7. *Witherspoon*, 391 U.S. at 518.
8. *Witherspoon*, 391 U.S. at 519.
9. *Witherspoon*, 391 U.S. at 520.
10. *Witherspoon*, 391 U.S. at 520-21.
11. *Witherspoon*, 391 U.S. at 522.
12. *Witherspoon*, 391 U.S. at 523.
13. *Witherspoon*, 391 U.S. at 523.
14. *Witherspoon*, 391 U.S. at 522 n.21.
15. *Witherspoon*, 391 U.S. at 523-24 (Douglas, J., concurring).
16. *Witherspoon*, 5391 U.S. at 24-25 (Douglas, J., concurring) (internal citations and quotations omitted).
17. *Witherspoon*, 391 U.S. at 532 (Douglas, J., concurring).
18. *Witherspoon*, 391 U.S. at 533-35 (Black, J., dissenting).

19. *Witherspoon*, 391 U.S. at 535 (Black, J., dissenting).
20. *Witherspoons*, 391 U.S. at 35-36 (Black, J., dissenting).
21. *Irvin v. Dowd*, 366 U.S. 717, 722 (1961).
22. Susan D. Rozelle, "The Principled Executioner: Capital Juries' Bias and the Benefits of True Bifurcation," *Arizona State Law Journal* 38 (2006): 769-807, 779-81. Rozelle cited a host of research on this point, including Welsh S. White, "The Constitutional Invalidity of Convictions Imposed by Death-Qualified Juries," *Cornell Law Review* 58 (1973): 1176; Claudia L. Cowan *et al.*, "The Effects of Death Qualification on Jurors' Predisposition to Convict and on the Quality of Deliberation, *Law and Human Behavior* 8 (1984): 53; Edward J. Bronson, "Does the Exclusion of Scrupled Jurors in Capital Cases Make the Jury More Likely to Convict? Some Evidence from California," *Woodrow Wilson Journal of Law* 3 (1980): 11; Robert Fitzgerald and Phoebe C. Ellsworth, "Due Process vs. Crime Control: Death Qualification and Jury Attitudes," *Law and Human Behavior* 8 (1984): 31.
23. *McCree v. State*, 585 S.W.2d 938, 939-41 (Ark. 1979); *Lockhart v. McCree*, 476 U.S. 162, 165-66 (1986).
24. *Lockhart*, 476 U.S. at 166-68.
25. *Lockhart*, 476 U.S. at 168-73.
26. *Lockhart*, 476 U.S. at 173.
27. *Lockhart*, 476 U.S. at 173.
28. *Lockhart*, 476 U.S. at 174-75.
29. *Lockhart*, 476 U.S. at 175 (internal citations omitted).
30. *Lockhart*, 476 U.S. at 175-76.
31. *Lockhart*, 476 U.S. at 176.
32. *Lockhart*, 476 U.S. at 176.
33. *Lockhart*, 476 U.S. at 176-77.
34. *Lockhart*, 476 U.S. at 178 (internal quotations omitted) (emphasis in original).
35. *Lockhart*, 476 U.S. at 184.
36. *Lockhart*, 476 U.S. at 185 (Marshall, J., dissenting).
37. *Lockhart*, 476 U.S. at 185 (Marshall, J., dissenting).
38. *Lockhart*, 476 U.S. at 185-87 (Marshall, J., dissenting).
39. *Lockhart*, 476 U.S. at 188 (Marshall, J., dissenting).
40. *Lockhart*, 476 U.S. at 188 (Marshall, J., dissenting).
41. *Lockhart*, 476 U.S. at 188 (Marshall, J., dissenting).
42. *Lockhart*, 476 U.S. at 199-200 (Marshall, J., dissenting).
43. *Lockhart*, 476 U.S. at 189-90 (Marshall, J., dissenting).
44. *Lockhart*, 476 U.S. at 202 (Marshall, J., dissenting).
45. *Lockhart*, 476 U.S. at 203-06 (Marshall, J., dissenting); Rozelle, "The Principled Executioner," 794-806.

Part Two:

Due Process and the Right to an Impartial Judge

~ 6 ~

Mayor-Judges with a Financial Stake in the Outcome: *Tumey v. Ohio* (1927) and *Ward v. Village of Monroeville* (1972)

It certainly violates the Fourteenth Amendment, and deprives a defendant in a criminal case of due process of law, to subject his liberty or property to the judgment of a court the judge of which has a direct, personal, substantial, pecuniary interest in reaching a conclusion against him in his case.
– *Tumey v. Ohio*, 273 U.S. 510, 523 (1927)

Petitioner is entitled to a neutral and detached judge in the first instance.
– *Ward v. Village of Monroeville*, 409 U.S. 57, 62 (1972)

The state of Ohio has a long tradition of allowing mayors to simultaneously serve as judges, with the practice originating in the middle of the nineteenth century. Although not completely without parallel, Ohio's system of giving mayors the authority to sit as judges is fairly rare in the United States today, as only Louisiana and Ohio make use of the practice in the twenty-first century. In Ohio, if a municipality has more than 100 people but does not have municipal court, a mayor's court may hear cases involving alleged violations of local ordinances and state traffic laws. According to the 2010 Mayor's Court summary report by the Ohio Supreme Court, the state has 320 mayor's courts, mainly in smaller communities. To this day, the courts remain controversial because some see them as little more than revenue generators for their respective municipalities, and the state legislature has tried to abolish them in recent years.[1]

According to the website for the Supreme Court of Ohio, mayor's courts are not a part of the judicial branch of Ohio. That statement notwithstanding, mayor's courts in Ohio effectively function as courts. Mayor's courts hear cases like any other court, and they must file statistics with the state supreme court. In addition, the Ohio Supreme Court has adopted rules for mayor's court procedures, and it sets basic legal education requirements for mayors who preside over these courts. A person convicted in a mayor's court may appeal the conviction to a municipal or county court that has jurisdiction over the municipality. Mayors who preside over these courts in Ohio are not required to be attorneys (an issue we will revisit in chapter eight). If mayors do not wish to preside over one of these courts, they may appoint a magistrate to serve in this capacity. That magistrate must be an attorney who has practiced law for at least three years.[2]

On two occasions these mayor's courts have been challenged in the U.S. Supreme Court as violating the due process rights of defendants. More particularly, the questions raised have been whether a mayor can be an impartial judge if he or she has a direct financial stake in the outcome or if the forfeitures and fines make up a substantial portion of the municipality's finances. In each case, separated by nearly one half century, the U.S. Supreme Court has held that these situations violate due process.

Tumey v. Ohio (1927) involved a public official, acting in a judicial capacity, who also served in the executive branch. The case demonstrates the problems of partiality that can result when the separation of powers is not properly honored and when judicial compensation is tied to case outcomes.

American Prohibition (1919-1933) was the result of federal statutes (including the Volstead Act) as well as the Eighteenth Amendment to the U.S. Constitution. The amendment prohibited "the manufacture, sale, or transportation of intoxicating liquors" in the United States. Ohio, which already had mayors serving in a judicial capacity in many jurisdictions, enforced prohibition within its borders via the Crabbe Act. This state law compensated mayors, some non-mayor-judges, and certain law enforcement officials with additional money beyond their normal pay whenever they arrested, convicted, and/or fined violators of the Eighteenth Amendment. During this time, these officials often tried to extend their jurisdiction into nearby cities to arrest and prosecute more violators and to enhance the mayor-judges' paychecks.[3]

North College Hill, Ohio is a small city just north of Cincinnati. In 1923, the mayor of North College Hill was A.R. Pugh. He presided over a mayor's court that included not only that city but also nearby White Oak, Ohio. When the creation of this mayor's court was being publicly debated, Mayor Pugh advocated for establishing the court, noting that if the village was in need of finances, he was in favor of, and would serve on, "the liquor court," as it was popularly called. After the court was created, Mayor Pugh personally led a raid on the residence of Ed Tumey, where alcohol was allegedly discovered, leading to Tumey's arrest. Tumey was charged with possession of alcohol in violation of Ohio's prohibition law.[4]

It must have been quite a shock to Ed Tumey when he later walked into the courtroom to find that the man presiding over his case was the man who led the raid against him and effectively ordered his prosecution! This alone would be enough to raise serious doubt as to Pugh's impartiality. However, that was not all. After finding Tumey guilty, Pugh fined him $100 and ordered Tumey imprisoned until he paid the fine. Furthermore, for a $100 fine such as this, Pugh collected $12 above and beyond his mayoral salary (This $12 might not appear to be very significant. However, according to the inflation calculator maintained by the U.S. Bureau of Labor Statistics, $12 in 1923 would be the equivalent of $161 in 2012,[5] far from an insignificant sum.). The village marshal also collected a portion of the fine. Neither Mayor Pugh nor any other public official would collect any money if a defendant such as Tumey were found not guilty. In other words, if a defendant was not convicted, the mayor received nothing for his judicial service.[6]

Tumey, understandably, smelled a rat with this system and appealed the decision. Tumey claimed that this mayor's court did not afford him an impartial judge and thus violated due process. On appeal, Hamilton County Court of Common Pleas Judge Stanley Struble likened Pugh's court to a kangaroo court and overturned the conviction. However, Tumey's conviction was subsequently upheld by an Ohio appeals court and the Supreme Court of Ohio, before Tumey finally appealed to the U.S. Supreme Court.[7]

The U.S. Supreme Court justices unanimously found fault with this Ohio practice. Chief Justice William Howard Taft, a man with executive experience as a former U.S. President, wrote the Court's opinion. Taft began by not only noting that Mayor Pugh earned $12 from Tumey's case; during a roughly six month period catalogued in 1923, Pugh received $696.35 (approximately $9,350 in 2012 dollars) from the fines in these liquor cases.[8]

Taft then described for the Court why this was a violation of due process. He began by stating the following: "That officers acting in a judicial or quasi-judicial capacity are disqualified by their interest in the controversy to be decided is, of course, the general rule."[9] Taft went on to explain that this only applies if there is a real interest in the case by the decisionmaker, and he gave examples, such as a judge's capacity as a taxpayer, that did not raise issues of impartiality. However, Taft clearly identified situations in which a judge would be partial: "it certainly violates the Fourteenth Amendment, and deprives a defendant in a criminal case of due process of law, to subject his liberty or property to the judgment of a court the judge of which has a direct, personal, substantial, pecuniary interest in reaching a conclusion against him in his case."[10] According to Taft, Tumey was in such a situation because of Mayor Pugh's role: "The Mayor of the Village of North College Hill, Ohio, had a direct, personal, pecuniary interest in convicting the defendant who came before him for trial, in the twelve dollars of costs imposed in his behalf, which he would not have received if the defendant had been acquitted."[11] Although this practice was used in various places in Ohio, Taft could find no historical examples in English or U.S. federal courts where a judge was rewarded financially for finding defendants guilty, and in American states he only found a handful of examples of the practice in the past.

After this review, Taft concluded the following: "A system by which an inferior judge is paid for his service only when he convicts the defendant has not become so embedded by custom in the general practice either at common law or in this country that it can be regarded as due process of law, unless the costs usually imposed are so small that they may be properly ignored as within the maxim *de minimis non curat lex*."[12]

The $12 in this case (remember, that is roughly $161 in 2012 dollars) and the average amount Pugh earned per month from convictions, was not, in the court's opinion, "a minute, remote, trifling or insignificant interest," nor was it a minor matter for defendants such as Tumey.[13] Taft then opined that "[t]here are doubtless mayors who would not allow such a consideration as $12 costs in each case to affect their judgment in it; but the requirement of due process of law in judicial procedure is not satisfied by the argument that men of the highest honor and the greatest self-sacrifice could carry it on without danger of injustice."[14] Although some mayors might be able to carry out their functions in a way fair to defendants with such a direct financial benefit available, that was not enough for Taft or the rest of the Court. That amount of financial incentive was too tempting to the average judge.

Yet, there was something more going on here, according to Taft, than just individual self-interested judicial officers. One of Taft's concerns was the lack of separated powers that occurred when the executive branch and the judicial branch combined like they were in these mayor's courts:

> The mayor is the chief executive of the village. He supervises all the other executive officers. He is charged with the business of looking after the finances of the village. It appears from the evidence in this case, and would be plain if the evidence did not show it, that the law is calculated to awaken the interest of all those in the village charged with the responsibility of raising the public money and expending it, in the pecuniarily successful conduct of such a court. The mayor represents the village and can not [*sic*] escape his representative capacity. On the other hand, he is given the judicial duty, first, of determining whether the defendant is guilty at all, and second, having found his guilt, to measure his punishment...With his interest, as mayor, in the financial condition of the village, and his responsibility therefor, might not a defendant with reason say that he feared he could not get a fair trial or a fair sentence from one who would have so strong a motive to help his village by conviction and a heavy fine?[15]

Thus, in addition to thinking about his self-interest in convicting defendants to earn additional take-home pay, Taft feared that Mayor Pugh would be thinking about his municipality's finances. Taft did not go so far as to say that any mere union of executive and judicial functions violated due process. However, too much overlap in the same office did raise questions about a judge's impartiality, as at a certain point, there could be a "temptation to the average man as a judge to forget the burden of proof required to convict the defendant, or which might lead him not to hold the balance nice, clear and true between the State and the accused."[16] For Taft, the level of overlap in this case resulted in a constitutional violation: "A situation in which an official perforce occupies two practically and seriously inconsistent positions, one partisan and the other judicial, necessarily involves a lack of due process of law in the trial of defendants charged with crimes before him."[17] Since Tumey raised an objection to Pugh sitting as his judge, Taft found that he was entitled to relief. The rest of the U.S. Supreme Court agreed, as the justices unanimously reversed Tumey's conviction.[18]

Tumey stands for the proposition that a judge should not financially benefit from convicting defendants over acquitting them; doing this would amount to having a partial decisionmaker. It also held that too much of a connection between an official's executive and judicial duties posed a serious due process problem for neutrality. Thus, it seemed as though these Ohio mayor's courts might be on their way out in 1927. Yet, over forty years later a decision in one of these mayor's courts was appealed to the U.S. Supreme Court for reasons quite similar to those raised in *Tumey*.

The Village of Monroeville, Ohio is in the northern part of the state. It is one county south of Lake Erie, and it is about halfway between Cleveland and Toledo. In the late 1960s, the mayor of the village had a wide variety of executive duties, including serving as president of the village council, presiding at all council meetings, voting in case of a council tie, reporting village finances to the council, filling vacancies in village offices, and having general supervision of village affairs. On the issue of village finances, a major portion of the municipality's finances were derived from the fines, forfeitures, costs, and fees imposed in the village mayor's court. In fact, during the five calendar years from 1964 to 1968, each year between one third and one half of the village income came from the court's citation revenue.[19]

Ward v. Village of Monroeville (1972) involved the case of Clarence Ward, who was charged with failing to comply with a lawful order of a police officer, and for refusing to produce his driver's license upon request by a police officer. The charges arose out of the same incident during a traffic stop. His case was heard in the mayor's court of Monroeville. Ward, similar to Tumey before him, objected to a mayor sitting as the judge in his case, claiming that a mayor "could not sit as a disinterested and impartial tribunal."[20] His motions to dismiss and to have the trial moved to a different court were denied. Ward was found guilty by the mayor, and he was sentenced to pay $50 on each of the two offenses.[21]

One of the more egregious errors present in *Tumey*, paying the judge an additional sum for convicting a defendant, was not present in *Ward*. However, comparable to the situation in *Tumey*, Ward's objection was that the mayor could not be impartial in his case because, as mayor, he had the municipality's financial obligations on his mind. Also true in both cases was that the mayor had responsibility for oversight of law enforcement. This related to Chief Justice Taft's argument in *Tumey* that a significant merging of judicial and executive functions in the same official was a separation of powers violation that necessarily would lead to partiality in a judge. The mayor disagreed and thought that he could be neutral. The Ohio Court of Appeals and the Ohio Supreme Court agreed with the mayor. The U.S. Supreme Court did not.[22]

Writing for a seven member majority, Justice William Brennan found fault with Ohio's continued use of mayor's courts. He began by reminding the reader of a proposition stated by Taft in *Tumey*, that due process is not violated simply by the mere union of executive and judicial powers. Brennan found too much overlap between the mayor's executive and judicial duties in this case, which was only magnified by the substantial portion of village funds that were raised by the court. The justice was particularly disturbed because from the period of 1964 to 1968, between 37 percent and 51 percent of the village's annual revenues were derived from the fines, forfeitures, costs and fees imposed by the mayor's court.[23] Brennan's fear was just what Ward himself suspected: a mayor in these situations would be thinking more about the city's bottom line than individualized justice in each case. Furthermore, that this problem might be corrected by having the case reviewed in a higher court was not enough: "Nor, in any event, may the State's trial court procedure be deemed constitutionally acceptable simply because the State eventually offers a defendant an impartial adjudication. Petitioner is entitled to a neutral and detached judge in the first instance."[24] For these reasons, the Court found that Ward's conviction was unjust, and the justices reversed that decision.

Writing for the Court, Brennan did not go so far as to declare unconstitutional all of Ohio's mayor's courts. Instead, he referenced favorably *Dugan v. Ohio* (1928), in which the Court gave its stamp of approval to a mayor's court where the city manager, not the mayor, exercised most of the city's executive powers, including powers related to city finances. In *Ward*, however, the mayor's substantial control over, and supervision of, the municipality's finances meant that the mayor could not be impartial.[25]

Unlike *Tumey*, however, *Ward* was not a unanimous decision. Justice Byron White wrote a dissenting opinion, which Justice William Rehnquist joined. According to these two justices, *Tumey* was decided the way it was solely because the judge there had a direct financial stake in the outcome. They took their brethren to task for invalidating a conviction simply because the judge was also mayor who dealt with the city's finances: "the Court must assume either that every mayor-judge in every case will disregard his oath and administer justice contrary to constitutional commands or that this will happen often enough to warrant the prophylactic...I can make neither assumption with respect to Ohio mayors."[26]

Granted, the constitutional violation in *Ward* was not as serious and deep as was the case in *Tumey*, but it was a violation nevertheless. A direct financial benefit that occurs when a judge finds a defendant guilty is clearly a violation of due process, as it introduces an unconscionable level of partiality into the court. But Justice White failed to see that a mayor, when he or she is the person primarily responsible for a municipality's finances, can be consumed by the need to balance the budget, especially during unfavorable economic times. Even though the mayor in *Ward* received no direct financial benefit, his reelection chances were strongly tied to the fiscal success of the village. This is not true of the vast majority of judges, nor should it be. Justice should be blind not just to personal judicial gain; it should also be blind to any need for a judge to have to raise money for others. It is for this reason that my state of Wisconsin, like many other states, has strict rules on judges' ability to raise money for other candidates for public office. The same should be the case when raising money for a municipality — a judge should have no direct involvement in the process. Anything less risks the impartiality that is due to each defendant.

Luckily, the Court made the right decisions in *Tumey* and in *Ward*. Because of this, the overwhelming majority of these limited jurisdiction courts are not mayor's courts today. Instead, the *Tumey* and *Ward* decisions forced many localities, even in Ohio, to choose a local judge who is not the mayor.[27] At the very least, these cases have required mayor-judges in mayor's courts to be far less involved in the finances of their respective municipalities. They have also required that judges are not paid a bounty for convicting defendants. Due process requires nothing less.

Notes

1. The Supreme Court of Ohio, "Judicial System Structure," http://supremecourt.ohio.gov/JudSystem/ (accessed August 27, 2011); Paul Revelson, "Nothing But Trouble: The Ohio Legislature's Failed Attempts to Abolish Mayor's Courts," *University of Dayton Law Review* 35 (2010): 223; Michael Cooper, "Mayor's Courts Lucrative — and Controversial," *Springfield News-Sun*, June 23, 2012, http://www.springfieldnewssun.com/news/crime/mayors-courts-lucrative-and-controversial-1395602.html (accessed July 15, 2012).
2. The Supreme Court of Ohio.
3. Ohio Historical Society, "*Tumey v. Ohio*," *Ohio History Central: An Online Encyclopedia of Ohio History*, 1999-2011, http://www.ohiohistorycentral.org/entry.php?rec=563 (accessed August 28, 2011).
4. Ohio Historical Society, "*Tumey v. Ohio*,"; Jim Blount, "U.S. Supreme Court Decision Stopped Crusading Village Mayors," *Journal-News*, February 12, 2003, http://www.lanepl.org/Blount/JBCOLS/documents/5665992053CD8DE5256873837D2697C0BAE3169E.html (accessed August 28, 2011); *Tumey v. Ohio*, 273 U.S. 510, 521 (1927).
5. U.S. Bureau of Labor Statistics, "CPI Inflation Calculator," 2011, http://www.bls.gov/data/inflation_calculator.htm (accessed April 16, 2012).
6. *Tumey v. Ohio*, 273 U.S. 510, 520, 531-32 (1927).
7. Jerry Hurter, "Don Quixote Judge and Case Celebre: Kangaroo Court Tyranny K.O.'d Sixty-One Years Ago," *Cincinnati Magazine*, March 1988: 43-44.
8. *Tumey*, 273 U.S. at 522.
9. *Tumey*, 273 U.S. at 522.

10. *Tumey*, 273 U.S. at 523.
11. *Tumey*, 273 U.S. at 523.
12. *Tumey*, 273 U.S. at 531.
13. *Tumey*, 273 U.S. at 532.
14. *Tumey*, 273 U.S. at 532.
15. *Tumey*, 273 U.S. at 533.
16. *Tumey*, 273 U.S. at 532.
17. *Tumey*, 273 U.S. at 534.
18. *Tumey*, 273 U.S. at 535.
19. *Ward v. Village of Monroeville*, 409 U.S. 57, 58 (1972).
20. *Village of Monroeville v. Ward*, 21 Ohio App. 2d 17, 17 (1969).
21. *Village of Monroeville*, 409 U.S. 57; *Ward*, 409 U.S. at 58.
22. Rowland Young, "Supreme Court Report," *American Bar Association Journal* 59 (January 1973): 72.
23. *Ward*, 409 U.S. at 58.
24. *Ward*, 409 U.S. at 61-62.
25. *Ward*, 409 U.S. at 60.
26. *Ward*, 409 U.S. at 62 (White, J., dissenting).
27. David L. Martin, *Running City Hall: Municipal Administration in America* (Tuscaloosa, AL: University of Alabama Press, 1990), 88.

~ 7 ~

A Judge Hearing a Contempt Proceeding after Being Vilified by the Defendant: *Mayberry v. Pennsylvania* (1971)

> [B]y reason of the Due Process Clause of the Fourteenth Amendment a defendant in criminal contempt proceedings should be given a public trial before a judge other than the one reviled by the contemnor.
> – *Mayberry v. Pennsylvania*, 400 U.S. 455, 466 (1971)

As a municipal judge, I understand the importance of maintaining decorum in the courtroom. If the courtroom becomes too casual, or if people appearing in court are allowed to disregard the court's authority with impunity, it threatens the very integrity of the court. This is why the judge has a gavel and why the judge can find someone in contempt of court. I am happy to say that as of this writing I have had to neither bang my gavel in court nor find anyone in contempt.

There are occasions, though, when judges have faced persons so disruptive that their conduct or comments inhibit court proceedings, interfere with the administration of justice, or impair the respect due the court. For instance, if someone refuses to follow a court order or answer a question, or if someone fails to remain quiet or stay seated during court proceedings, that could cause disruption. Failure to adequately deal with these situations could result in those present, or those who hear about it later, to lose respect for the court. The effects of this could include people not following court orders generally, which would cause serious legal problems for society. Thus, if an admonishment or a banging gavel does not cause one to stop engaging in such behavior, an adjudication of contempt is the next logical step.

But can a judge be a fair and impartial arbiter of such a dispute? After all, if the conduct or comments at issue occurred in a judge's courtroom, might that judge, as a witness to or target of the action, be more likely to convict than a judge who was not present? Generally, a judge is permitted to conduct a subsequent contempt proceeding unless he or she became emotionally involved in the prior conduct.[1] However, it is bad public policy to let judges preside over criminal contempts in these cases because the judges may confuse minor affronts to themselves with genuine obstructions to the judicial process.[2] Although in such a situation a judge may need to make immediate comments to keep order in the court, a judge should not preside over the resulting criminal contempt proceedings if the judge fails to maintain the integrity of the court, engages in a shouting match with a party or witness, or later seeks revenge for what was said or done.

That said, judges are generally presumed to be impartial, even in cases of contempt where the action or comments occurred before them, as long as proper procedures are followed. In an early, seminal case on judicial bias in contempt cases, *Cooke v. United States* (1925), Chief Justice William Howard Taft wrote the following for a unanimous U.S. Supreme Court: "To preserve order in the court room for the proper conduct of business, the court must act instantly to suppress disturbance or violence or physical obstruction or disrespect to the court when occurring in open court."[3] However, Chief Justice Taft also noted that there are limits to this power, especially when the judge is the target of the contemnor's scorn:

> The power of contempt which a judge must have and exercise in protecting the due and orderly administration of justice and in maintaining the authority and dignity of the court is most important and indispensable. But its exercise is a delicate one and care is needed to avoid arbitrary or oppressive conclusions. This rule of caution is more mandatory where the contempt charged has in it the element of personal criticism or attack upon the judge. The judge must banish the slightest personal impulse to reprisal, but he should not bend backward and injure the authority of the court by too great leniency. The substitution of another judge would avoid either tendency but it is not always possible. Of course where acts of contempt are palpably aggravated by a personal attack upon the judge in order to drive the judge out of the case for ulterior reasons, the scheme should not be permitted to succeed. But attempts of this kind are rare. All of such cases, however, present difficult questions for the judge. All we can say upon the whole matter is that where conditions do not make it impracticable, or where the delay may not injure public or private right, a judge called upon to act in a case of contempt by personal attack upon him, may, without flinching from his duty, properly ask that one of his fellow judges take his place.[4]

In other words, if the judge is being personally attacked, the safest course of action may be to find a substitute judge to handle the contempt proceedings, as long as unnecessary delay would not result. Otherwise, a judge in this situation may create an appealable issue for the contemnor.

Usually, though, this does not raise a constitutional problem. For instance, in *Ungar v. Sarafite* (1964), the U.S. Supreme Court upheld Judge Joseph Sarafite's finding of contempt and accompanying ten day jail sentence and fine where a hostile prosecution witness, Sidney Ungar, repeatedly refused to answer the questions asked by the prosecutor and demanded a recess before offering additional testimony. The Court found the judge's actions to be constitutional, even though the witness stated clearly disruptive, recalcitrant, and disagreeable comments toward the judge, including telling the judge that he would not answer because he was being "badgered" and "coerced" by the judge and that the judge was "suppressing the evidence."[5]

Sometimes, however, judges become too emotionally involved in cases where their authority is challenged, making it impossible for those judges to impartially preside over the subsequent contempt proceedings. One of the most obvious examples of this occurred in *Mayberry v. Pennsylvania* (1971). Richard Mayberry, Herbert Langnes, and Dominic Codispoti were inmates who tried to break out of prison. Once they were captured, the three were charged in 1966 for engaging in a prison breach and holding hostages in a penal institution. All three men pleaded not guilty. Each defendant decided to represent himself at trial, although trial Judge Albert A. Fiok appointed counsel as advisors.[6]

Mayberry began to be disruptive from the first day of the trial, and would ultimately be found guilty by the judge of eleven counts of criminal contempt. On that first day, Mayberry went to the side bar to make suggestions to Judge Fiok how he would like to see the trial run and to ask for rulings on trial procedures. Mayberry stated to the judge the following: "It seems like the court has the intentions of railroading us." Mayberry then moved to have the trial judge disqualified. Judge Fiok denied that motion. Mayberry then made additional motions, including asking that the sheriff's deputies in the courtroom be dressed as civilians. Judge Fiok denied all of these motions. This exchange between Mayberry and Fiok then occurred:

> Mayberry: "I would like to have a fair trial of this case and like to be granted a fair trial under the Sixth Amendment."
> The Court: "You will get a fair trial."
> Mayberry: "It doesn't appear that I am going to get one the way you are overruling all our motions and that, and being like a hatchet man for the State."
> The Court: "This side bar is over."
> Mayberry: "Wait a minute, Your Honor."
> The Court: "It is over."
> Mayberry: "You dirty son of a bitch."[7]

As if calling a sitting judge a "hatchet man" and a "dirty son of a bitch" was not enough, on the eighth day of the trial Mayberry engaged in additional conduct that angered Judge Fiok. Mayberry's codefendant, Codispoti, was cross-examining a prison guard. When the prosecution objected to Cosispoti's questions, Judge Fiok sustained some of them. After one such sustained objection, a second incident occurred:

> Codispoti: "Are you trying to protect the prison authorities, Your Honor? Is that your reason?"

The Court: "You are out of order, Mr. Codispoti. I don't want any outbursts like that again. This is a court of justice. You don't know how to ask questions.
Mayberry: "Possibly Your Honor doesn't know how to rule on them."
The Court: "You keep quiet."
Mayberry: "You ought to be Gilbert and Sullivan the way you sustain the district attorney every time he objects to the questions."
The Court: "Are you through? When your time comes you can ask questions and not make speeches."[8]

A third interaction between Mayberry and Judge Fiok began when the defense was doing direct examination of a fellow inmate about a prison riot where Mayberry had been implicated. The defense asked many questions, a sizable number of which resulted in prosecution objections which were sustained by the court. Mayberry then engaged in what the U.S. Supreme Court would later characterize as an "outburst" in open court:

Mayberry: "Now, I'm going to produce my defense in this case and not be railroaded into any life sentence by any dirty, tyrannical old dog like yourself."
The Court: "You may proceed with your questioning, Mr. Mayberry."[9]

A fourth interaction between Mayberry and Judge Fiok that led to a contempt charge began during the direct examination of another defense witness:

Mayberry: "I ask you, Mr. Nardi, is that area, the handball court, is it open to any prisoner who wants to play handball, who cares to go to that area to play handball?"
Nardi: "Yes."
Mayberry: "Did you understand the prior question when I asked you if it was freely open and accessible area?"
The Court: "He answered your question. Let's go on."
Mayberry: "I am asking him now if he understands —"
The Court: "He answered it. Now, let's go on."
Mayberry: "I ask Your Honor to keep your mouth shut while I'm questioning my own witness. Will you do that for me?"
The Court: "I wish you would do the same. Proceed with your questioning."[10]

In what would become the fifth contempt charge against Mayberry, he and his co-defendants were protesting Judge Fiok's denial of access to certain legal documents that the defendants thought they should be able to view:

Mayberry: "You're a judge first. What are you working for? The prison authorities, you bum?"
Livingston: "I have a motion pending before Your Honor."
The Court: "I would suggest —"
Mayberry: "Go to hell. I don't give a good God damn what you suggest, you stumbling dog."

Another one of the defendants (it is not clear from the trial transcripts which one) told Judge Fiok that if he did not receive access to the requested legal documents that night, he would "blow your head off." The other co-defendant told Judge Fiok that he would not sit still and be "kowtowed and be railroaded into a life imprisonment." Then Mayberry and the judge engaged in more verbal combat:

> Mayberry: "You started all this bullshit in the beginning."
> The Court: "You keep quiet."
> Mayberry: "Wait a minute."
> The Court: "You keep quiet."
> Mr. Mayberry: "I am my own counsel."
> The Court: "You keep quiet."
> Mr. Mayberry: "Are you going to gag me?"
> The Court: "Take these prisoners out of here. We will take a ten minute recess, members of the jury."

In what became the sixth contempt charge against Mayberry, he and one of his co-defendants wanted a recess to speak with a witness. Judge Fiok denied the defense's motion. The following then occurred:

> Mayberry: "Just one moment, Your Honor."
> The Court: "This is not your witness, Mr. Mayberry. Keep quiet."
> Mayberry: "Oh, yes, he is my witness, too. He is my witness, also. Now, we are at the penitentiary and in seclusion. We can't talk to any of our witnesses prior to putting them on the stand like the District Attorney obviously has the opportunity, and as he obviously made use of the opportunity to talk to his witnesses. Now —"
> The Court: "Now, I have ruled, Mr. Mayberry."
> Mayberry: "I don't care what you ruled. That is unimportant. The fact is —"
> The Court: "You will remain quiet, sir, and finish the examination of this witness."
> Mayberry: "No, I won't be quiet while you try to deny me the right to a fair trial. The only way I will be quiet is if you have me gagged. Now, if you want to do that, that is up to you; but in the meantime I am going to say what I have to say. Now, we have the right to speak to our witnesses prior to putting them on the stand. This is an accepted fact of law. It is nothing new or unusual. Now, you are going to try to force us to have our witness testify to facts that he has only a hazy recollection of that happened back in 1965. Now, I believe we have the right to confer with our witness prior to putting him on the stand."
> The Court: "Are you finished?"
> Mr. Mayberry: "I am finished."
> The Court: "Proceed with your examination."[11]

A seventh incident took place when Mayberry was engaging in a direct examination of one of his co-defendants:

Mayberry: "No. Don't state a conclusion because Gilbert is going to object and Sullivan will sustain. Give me facts. What leads you to say that?"

...

Mayberry: "My witness isn't being in an inquisition, you know. This isn't the Spanish Inquisition."

After some exchanges with Judge Fiok, the following took place:

Mayberry: "Now, just what do you call proper? I have asked questions, numerous questions and everyone you said is improper. I have asked questions that my adviser has given me, and I have repeated these questions verbatim as they came out of my adviser's mouth, and you said they are improper. Now just what do you consider proper?"

The Court: "I am not here to educate you, Mr. Mayberry."

Mayberry: "No. I know you are not. But you're not here to railroad me into no life bit, either."

Codispoti: "To protect the record —"

The Court: "Do you have any other questions to ask this witness?"

Mayberry: "You need to have some kind of psychiatric treatment, I think. You're some kind of a nut. I know you're trying to do a good job for that Warden Maroney back there, but let's keep it looking decent anyway, you know. Don't make it so obvious, Your Honor."[12]

Next, one of Mayberry's co-defendant's was temporarily removed from the courtroom, and when the co-defendant returned, Mayberry asked to sever the trials:

Mayberry: "I have to ask for a severance."

The Court: "I have heard that before. It is denied again. Let's go on."

Mayberry: "This is the craziest trial I have ever seen."

The Court: "You may call your next witness, Mr. Mayberry."

The next witnesses that Mayberry asked to call were from the penitentiary. The defense had not submitted these persons' names on their witness list, and no subpoenas had been issued for these witnesses (Judge Fiok had previously ruled that witnesses would be restricted to those who had been subpoenaed). Mayberry then stated the following:

Mayberry: "Before I get to that I wish to have a ruling, and I don't care if it is contempt or whatever you want to call it, but I want a ruling for the record that I am being denied these witnesses that I asked for months before this trial ever began."[13]

Thus, Mayberry was almost goading the judge into ruling him in contempt. He did not stop there, however. A ninth exchange between Mayberry and Judge Fiok took place when the defendants asked about the availability of tools to the prisoners in their cells:

The Court: "I have ruled on that, Mr. Mayberry. Now proceed with your questioning, and don't argue."
Mayberry: "You're arguing. I'm not arguing, not arguing with fools."[14]

A tenth incident that led to a contempt charge took place near the end of the trial, when Mayberry was ejected from the courtroom several times. According to Judge Fiok, this contempt charge was issued because "On December 7, 1966, [Mayberry] created a despicable scene in refusing to continue calling [his] witnesses and in creating such consternation and uproar as to cause a termination of the trial."[15]

The eleventh and final incident occurred after the close of evidence, when Judge Fiok was about to give the jury its charge. At that point, Mayberry stated the following:

> Before Your Honor begins the charge to the jury defendant Mayberry wishes to place his objection on the record to the charge and to the whole proceedings from now on, and he wishes to make it known to the Court now that he has no intention of remaining silent while the Court charges the jury, and that he is going to continually object to the charge of the Court to the jury throughout the entire charge, and he is not going to remain silent. He is going to disrupt the proceedings verbally throughout the entire charge of the Court, and also he is going to be objecting to being forced to terminate his defense before he was finished.

At that point, Judge Fiok had Mayberry removed from the courtroom. Mayberry was returned shortly thereafter, gagged. Even while gagged, however, Mayberry continued his disruptive behavior. Judge Fiok then had Mayberry removed to an adjacent room where the court proceedings were audible to him over a loudspeaker. According to Judge Fiok, he charged Mayberry with contempt for this incident because he "constantly, boisterously, and insolently interrupted the Court during its attempts to charge the jury, thereby creating an atmosphere of utter confusion and chaos."[16]

There is no question that Mayberry acted rudely and that he disrupted the trial at numerous points. His behavior and statements were inappropriate. His constant outbursts and name calling must have been very trying for Judge Fiok. Chief Justice Warren Burger, in his concurring opinion in *Mayberry v. Pennsylvania*, reflected on "the exemplary patience of the trial judge under provocation few human beings could accept with equanimity."[17] However, the key constitutional moment in the case was yet to come.

The trial took place over twenty-one days. On the final day, Friday, December 9, 1966, the jury returned guilty verdicts against the defendants on both counts. The following Monday, December 12, 1966, all three defendants were brought back into court for sentencing. Before imposing sentence against them, Judge Fiok found them guilty of criminal contempt. Specifically, the judge found that Mayberry had committed contempt on eleven of the twenty-one days of trial. For this, Judge Fiok sentenced Mayberry to between one and two years imprisonment for each count of contempt, for a total of eleven to twenty-two years in prison (Codispoti received a sentence for contempt of seven to fourteen years, and Langnes received a sentence of six to twelve years). Judge Fiok then sentenced Mayberry to an additional fifteen to thirty years in prison for holding hostages in a penal institution and five to ten years in prison for prison breach. Mayberry appealed all of his convictions and sentences, including the ones for contempt, through the Pennsylvania court system, and the Supreme Court of Pennsylvania affirmed. He then appealed to the U.S. Supreme Court.[18]

The justices of the U.S. Supreme Court unanimously vacated the contempt convictions against Mayberry. Writing for the majority, Justice William Douglas began by rightly remarking on the seriousness of Mayberry's actions and comments: "Petitioner's conduct at the trial comes as a shock to those raised in the Western tradition that considers a courtroom a hallowed place of quiet dignity as far removed as possible from the emotions of the street."[19] Douglas went on to more specifically state that

> These brazen efforts to denounce, insult, and slander the court and to paralyze the trial are at war with the concept of justice under law. Laymen, foolishly trying to defend themselves, may understandably create awkward and embarrassing scenes. Yet that is not the character of the record revealed here. We have here downright insults of a trial judge, and tactics taken from street brawls and transported to the courtroom.[20]

There may be times where defendants proceeding *pro se* make mistakes or are confused as to what to do. I have seen that multiple times when presiding over trials with unrepresented defendants. Such persons, who are not trained in the finer points of civil or criminal procedure, often need some clarification from the court as to what they should do. Mayberry clearly was not one of those defendants, however. He knew what he was doing, and he wanted to be as disruptive as possible.

Because of his litany of disruptions, the U.S. Supreme Court agreed with Judge Fiok that, under these circumstances, "criminal contempt is one appropriate remedy."[21] Still, Justice Douglas asserted that as these outbursts took place, an "arsenal" was available to the trial judge to keep order in the courtroom, including instantly "holding [Mayberry] in contempt, or excluding him from the courtroom, or otherwise insulating his vulgarity from the courtroom."[22] In other words, tools short of criminal contempt were available to Judge Fiok to deal with Mayberry's behavior too. And these tools were available immediately for the judge to quell what was occurring. A contempt finding, accompanied by a fine and perhaps removal to a jail cell until the next day, may be an appropriate way to reestablish proper courtroom decorum under these circumstances. In the heat of the moment, something has to be done to protect the integrity of the court. But going a step farther and declaring a defendant to be guilty of criminal contempt after the trial has concluded raises due process questions about the impartiality of that particular judge in such a case.

On this point, Justice Douglas noted that "we do not say that the more vicious the attack on the judge the less qualified he is to act" because a "judge cannot be driven out of a case" by a party who wants to use a disruption as a pretext for a backdoor judicial substitution.[23] Douglas then stated that if a judge "does not act the instant the contempt is committed, but waits until the end of the trial, on balance, it is generally wise where the marks of the unseemly conduct have left personal stings to ask a fellow judge to take his place."[24] The immediacy of the disruption had already passed by the time Judge Fiok found Mayberry to be in contempt — the trial was over. There was no need for the same judge, who had been insulted numerous times over twenty-one days, to hear the contempt case.

When the U.S. Supreme Court reviewed Judge Fiok's course of action, they, through the pen of Justice Douglas, maintained that "the concern of due process is with the fair administration of justice."[25] That fairness was threatened here because Judge Fiok was "vilified" by Mayberry with "highly personal aspersions, even 'fighting words,'" and in such a situation one "necessarily becomes embroiled in a running, bitter controversy. No one so cruelly slandered is likely to maintain that calm detachment necessary for fair adjudication."[26] Much like a crime victim should not serve as a juror in his or her assailant's case, a judge should not preside over the criminal contempt case for the person who vilified him or her. For this reason, Justice Douglas concluded on behalf of the Court that "by reason of the Due Process Clause of the Fourteenth Amendment a defendant in criminal contempt proceedings should be given a public trial before a judge other than the one reviled by the contemnor."[27] As for Mayberry, Douglas declared that in the "present case that requirement can be satisfied only if the judgment of contempt is vacated so that on remand another judge, not bearing the sting of these slanderous remarks and having the impersonal authority of the law, sits in judgment on the conduct of petitioner as shown by the record."[28]

There is no question that impartiality was lacking in the contempt proceedings against Mayberry. The first clue that Judge Fiok probably lacked impartiality was in his summary pronouncement that Mayberry, Codispoti, and Langnes were guilty of criminal contempt. No attempt was made to let them explain their actions. This lacked due process, and it was due to bias that had been built up over a long, frustrating trial. This is not to say that Judge Fiok was a bad judge. Quite the contrary. As Chief Justice Burger noted in his concurrence, Judge Fiok had "exemplary patience" during the trial, and the Supreme Court decision overturning his contempt ruling "does not reflect on his performance; it relates rather to a question of procedure."[29] That is the reason why another judge needed to be appointed to hear that contempt case — so that a good judge would not need to be put in the impossible position of trying to be impartial under those circumstances.

Although it was not mentioned in the majority opinion, Justice John Marshall Harlan's concurrence remarked on another telling fact: the length of Mayberry's sentence. According to Harlan, "these contempt convictions must be regarded as infected by the fact that the unprecedented long sentence of twenty-two years which they carried was imposed by a judge who himself had been the victim of petitioner's shockingly abusive conduct."[30] He went on to state that this "circumstance seems to me to deprive the contempt proceeding of the appearance of evenhanded justice which is at the core of due process."[31] Indeed, even with the understanding that Mayberry's conduct was beyond outrageous, a sentence of between eleven and twenty-two years is at the very least disproportionate to the crime. At the most, it borders on being sadistic. Consider where you were twenty-two years ago and everything you have done since. Now imagine that you had spent all of that time in prison. A sentence of that length might be appropriate for homicides, some other crimes of violence, and perhaps grand larceny. For being disruptive during one's own criminal trial, a contempt sentence of that length is far too long.

Judge Fiok had his patience tried by the defendants in *Mayberry*. But if a judge is annoyed by a party to a case, that is all the more reason for recusal. In *Public Utilities Commission v. Pollak* (1952), streetcar and bus passengers sued the District of Columbia Public Utilities Commission for allowing transit companies in the city to play music through loudspeakers. The riders filed suit because they found the music annoying. The U.S. Supreme Court held in *Pollak* that the commission had the power to allow companies to play this music, and the Court also held that the constitutional rights of passengers were not violated by the music.[32] Justice Felix Frankfurter, who rode public transportation in the city, recused himself from the case. According to Frankfurter, a judge

> [M]ust think dispassionately and submerge private feeling on every aspect of a case... reason cannot control the subconscious influence of feelings of which it is unaware. When there is ground for believing that such unconscious feelings may operate in the ultimate judgment, or may not unfairly lead others to believe they are operating, judges recuse themselves. They do not sit in judgment. They do this for a variety of reasons. The guiding consideration is that the administration of justice should reasonably appear to be disinterested as well as be so in fact.[33]

This led Frankfurter to conclude that "[t]his case for me presents such a situation. My feelings are so strongly engaged as a victim of the practice in controversy that I had better not participate in judicial judgment upon it."[34] His annoyance at the playing of this music prevented Frankfurter from being impartial in the case. Judge Fiok should have taken a page from Justice Frankfurter's playbook and let someone else decide the defendant's criminal contempt cases in *Mayberry*. The U.S. Supreme Court eventually ensured that another judge would do this in the case.

The process matters in the legal system. In criminal contempt situations like this one, a second set of eyes is important to ensuring that the presiding judge is neutral and acting in the best interests of justice, not out of vengeance. After the Supreme Court vacated the contempt rulings against them, Mayberry and his two co-conspirators were retried in separate proceedings before another trial judge. Each man was found guilty again of multiple counts of criminal contempt, but this time the sentences were much shorter: Mayberry was sentenced to a total of four years nine months in prison (as opposed to his original sentence of eleven to twenty-two years), Codispoti was sentenced to three years and three months in prison (as opposed to his original sentence of seven to fourteen years), and Langnes was sentenced to two years and eight months in prison (as opposed to his original sentence of six to twelve years). The saga does not end there though. Codispoti and Langnes appealed their decisions to the U.S. Supreme Court again, this time winning a reversal of their convictions on the ground that they were entitled to a jury trial in their criminal contempt cases. Following suit, Mayberry, who did not file a second appeal to the U.S. Supreme Court, found out about Codispoti and Langnes's success on the second time. Subsequently, Mayberry filed a habeas corpus petition in federal district court, and the court granted his petition for a jury trial. It appears that these three defendants did not settle for simply having a neutral judge hear their contempt cases. They each demanded, and each eventually won, an impartial jury as well.[35]

Ultimately, the inappropriate courtroom behavior of Mayberry and his codefendants led to the U.S. Supreme Court creating an objective standard for contempt cases which presumes judicial bias when there are personal attacks between the alleged contemnor and the judge. In these cases, a substitute judge is required to try the resulting criminal contempt case. This practice has led to a greater protection of the right to a neutral judge.[36]

Notes

1. John R. Allison, "Ideology, Prejudgment, and Process Values," *New England Law Review* 28 (1994): 657-743, 718.
2. Louis S. Raveson, "Advocacy and Contempt: Constitutional Limitations on the Judicial Contempt Power; Part One: The Conflict between Advocacy and Contempt," *Washington Law Review* 65 (1990): 477-593, 563 n.298.
3. *Cooke v. United States*, 267 U.S. 517, 534 (1925).
4. *Cooke*, 267 U.S. at 539.
5. *Ungar v. Sarafite*, 376 U.S. 575, 576-84 (1964); *Ungar v. Sarafite*, 189 N.E.2d 629 (N.Y. 1963).
6. *Mayberry v. Pennsylvania*, 400 U.S. 455, 455 (1971); *Mayberry Appeal*, 255 A.2d 131, 132 (Pa. 1969); *Codispoti v. Pennsylvania*, 418 U.S. 506, 507 (1974); Rowland L. Young, "Supreme Court Report," *American Bar Association Journal* 57 (April 1971): 367-72, 368-69.
7. *Mayberry*, 400 U.S. at 456.
8. *Mayberry*, 400 U.S. at 456-57.
9. *Mayberry*, 400 U.S. at 457.
10. *Mayberry*, 400 U.S. at 457-58.
11. *Mayberry*, 400 U.S. at 459.

12. *Mayberry*, 400 U.S. at 460.
13. *Mayberry*, 400 U.S. at 461.
14. *Mayberry*, 400 U.S. at 461.
15. *Mayberry*, 400 U.S. at 461.
16. *Mayberry*, 400 U.S. at 462.
17. *Mayberry*, 400 U.S. at 468-69 (Burger, C.J., concurring).
18. *Mayberry*, 400 U.S. at 455-56; *Mayberry Appeal*, 255 A.2d at 132; *Codispoti*, 418 U.S. at 507.
19. *Mayberry*, 400 U.S. at 456.
20. *Mayberry*, 400 U.S. at 462.
21. *Mayberry*, 400 U.S. at 463.
22. *Mayberry*, 400 U.S. at 463.
23. *Mayberry*, 400 U.S. at 463.
24. *Mayberry*, 400 U.S. at 463-64.
25. *Mayberry*, 400 U.S. at 465.
26. *Mayberry*, 400 U.S. at 465-66.
27. *Mayberry*, 400 U.S. at 466.
28. *Mayberry*, 400 U.S. at 466.
29. *Mayberry*, 400 U.S. at 468-69 (Burger, C.J., concurring).
30. *Mayberry*, 400 U.S. at 469 (Harlan, J., concurring).
31. *Mayberry*, 400 U.S. at 469 (Harlan, J., concurring).
32. *Public Utilities Commission v. Pollak*, 343 U.S. 451 (1952).
33. *Public Utilities Commission v. Pollak*, 343 U.S. at 466-67 (Frankfurter, J., special opinion).
34. *Public Utilities Commission v. Pollak* 343 U.S. at 467 (Frankfurter, J., special opinion).
35. *Codispoti*, 418 U.S. at 507-10, 518; *Mayberry v. Frame*, 383 F. Supp. 212, 213-14 (1974).
36. Kimberly Morihara, "An Evaluation of the Summary Contempt Power of the Court: Balancing the Attorney's Role as an Advocate and the Court's Need for Order," *Hawaii Law Review* 19 (1997): 145-75, 156.

~ 8 ~

Non-Lawyer Judges: *North v. Russell* (1976)

Our concern in prior cases with judicial functions...has also been directed at the need for independent, neutral, and detached judgment, not at legal training.
– *North v. Russell*, 427 U.S. 328, 337 (1976)

A judge ignorant of the law is simply incapable of performing [many court] functions. If he is aware of his incompetence, such a judge will perhaps instinctively turn to the prosecutor for advice and direction. But such a practice no more than compounds the due process violation.
– *North v. Russell*, 427 U.S. 328, 344 (1976) (Justice Stewart, Dissenting)

America has had a distrust of many things over its history, including lawyers. Many early English colonists held the English legal system in disfavor, finding the profession of law to be inefficient and ungodly. Thus, most colonists did not welcome lawyers. Most legal work early on was done by "attorneys-in-fact," with cases often heard by lay judges. For example, according to one early Pennsylvania document, "[t]hey have no lawyers. Everyone is to tell his own case, or some friend for him...'Tis a happy country." Over time, this type of distrust of lawyers became normal. Indeed, according to one historian, "[d]istrust of lawyers became an institution."[1]

Such disdain for attorneys still exists today. Perhaps that explains why many people are readily amused when they hear jokes like the following:

Q: What do you call 5,000 dead lawyers at the bottom of the ocean?
A: A good start!
Q: How can you tell when a lawyer is lying?
A: His lips are moving.
Q: What's the difference between a dead skunk in the road and a dead lawyer in the road?
A: There are skid marks in front of the skunk.
Q: Why won't sharks attack lawyers?

A: Professional courtesy.
Q: What do you have when a lawyer is buried up to his neck in sand?
A: Not enough sand.
Q: Why is going to a meeting of the Bar Association like going into a bait shop?
A: Because of the abundance of suckers, leeches, maggots, and night crawlers.
Q: What's the difference between a lawyer and a herd of buffalo?
A: The lawyer charges more.

Regardless of how much this sentiment existed and continues to persist, over time the need for lawyers grew in early America. As stated by one legal historian, "[l]awyers were, in the end, a necessary evil. When all is said and done, no colony could even try to make do without lawyers. The makeshift alternatives worked in the early days; but when society became more complex — and more commercial — the lawyers became essential."[2]

As the need for lawyers increased in colonial America, so did the need for legal education. There was very little formal education that existed during the time. Most attorneys were either self-taught or trained as apprentices. The focus during this time was on practical training. The first specialized law school in the United States did not open until 1784. The longest continuously open university-affiliated law school, Harvard Law School, opened its doors in 1817. Through the 1860s, law schools tended to teach their students via a lecture method of instruction. All of that changed in 1870, when Christopher Columbus Langdell became the Dean of the Harvard Law School. Dean Langdell instituted what later became the standard three year curriculum for law schools, with a case-based approach. This involved (and still does involve) the use of the Socratic method of interrogating students who have been assigned to read appellate cases.[3]

Although the Langdell case method became the dominant form of legal instruction, it did not happen overnight. For instance, proprietary law schools (those not affiliated with universities), which tended to emphasize training in practical legal skills, were still prevalent well into the twentieth century. In the early 1920s, apprenticeships still provided the basic legal training for many persons entering the legal profession, and no states required a university-based law school degree as a condition for bar admission. Instead, ability to pass the bar exam was the primary criterion for bar admission (Interestingly enough, today successful completion of the bar examination is not required for one to become eligible to practice law in one state, Wisconsin, if a student is admitted under the "diploma privilege" by graduating from the University of Wisconsin Law School or the Marquette University Law School.).[4]

Even though the educational requirements for lawyers have become more standardized, the non-lawyer judges are continuing to write a long and storied history, especially in trial courts of limited jurisdiction. In America, this history dates back to seventeenth century New England, where lay judges were quite common, in part because of the general colonial distrust of lawyers, the hostility toward the law, the lack of printed books and law schools, and the great faith placed at the time in the abilities of juries. These lay judges tended to be "landed gentry," but they had no formal legal training. Non-lawyer judges in colonial America and the early United States existed both at the bottom and the top of the judicial system. Although one can easily see how non-lawyer judges existed at the lowest levels, it may surprise some to know that lay judges also had the final say in legal cases. For instance, New Jersey's 1776 constitution made the state's governor and council the court of appeals, and New York employed a system from 1777 into the nineteenth century whereby state senators were part of an error correcting court. In another example, the Vermont republic's supreme court did not have its first lawyer judge until 1787. Shortly after the American Revolution, just as the law was becoming more complex, the increasingly growing ranks of attorneys in the United States successfully lobbied legislatures in states like Massachusetts and Virginia to require judges in some of the higher courts to be lawyers. This effort then spread across the country, in spite of the Jacksonian sentiment in the early to mid-nineteenth century that advocated more democratic institutions, which in the legal system generally meant placing more power in juries and laypersons and less power in trained lawyers. This helps to explain why it was common practice long after the Revolutionary period for limited jurisdiction courts in rural areas to have non-lawyer judges. Maintenance of such courts was also due to these rural areas' small size, small bar, and transportation problems. Those factors also help to explain why many rural areas staff their limited jurisdiction courts with non-lawyer judges today.[5]

As this system continued, with urban courts and general jurisdiction courts usually requiring that judges be lawyers and rural limited jurisdiction courts often not creating such a mandate, the latter judges generally took on the title of "justice of the peace." By the 1930s, most municipal courts in larger cities began requiring that judges be trained lawyers, but justices of the peace in rural areas still often were not required to be lawyers. As is the case with these judges today, the office developed so that justices of the peace were usually elected, and their duties tended to be part-time. National reform efforts were underway in the twentieth century, however, leading to a decrease in the ranks of non-lawyer judges. By the 1940s, some states required all judges to be lawyers, and by the 1960s the American Bar Association, the American Judicature Society, and many academics were calling for all judges to be trained as lawyers. Still, even at the close of the twentieth century, at least twenty-nine of fifty states allowed some non-lawyer judges to adjudicate cases.[6]

This is a long way of saying that both historically and today, there has been no solitary method of obtaining the education necessary to become a lawyer, much less a judge. Instead, there have been varying paths to becoming an attorney, and there have been many non-lawyer judges in American history. That said, the overwhelming majority of lawyers today, and many judges today, were formally educated at standard three-year programs at accredited university-affiliated law schools, followed by passage of a state bar examination. And even though historically there were lay lawyers and lay judges, given the complexity of the modern legal system, can persons without this formal training preside over a court of law today? Can such judges be fair and impartial to the degree required by due process? This question was asked in *North v. Russell* (1976).

North began when Lonnie North was arrested in Lynch, Kentucky on July 10, 1974 and charged with driving while intoxicated (DWI), first offense. Under Kentucky law at the time, a first offense DWI carried with it a fine from between $100 and $500. Jail time was only a penalty for a second or greater DWI (e.g.: a second offense DWI carried a fine of $100-$500 and a jail sentence of up to six months). North's trial was promptly scheduled for July 18, 1974 at 7:00 p.m. in the Lynch City Police Court. C.B. Russell was the presiding judge. At the time, the qualifications for a police judge in a Kentucky city of Lynch's size (between 1,000 and 3,000 people) included being a voter, a resident of the city for at least one year, and bonded once taking office. Being a lawyer was not a requirement in this size of a city. Russell was not a lawyer; instead, he was a coal miner with only a high school education. He had just been appointed to the bench shortly before he heard North's case. Russell had received no training concerning the rules of evidence and later stated that he was not familiar with Kentucky statutes related to jury trials, the state's rules of criminal procedure, or Fourteenth Amendment rights of defendants. Alternatively, in police courts of cities with more than 20,000 residents, Kentucky law required judges to be lawyers, and judges in those courts almost certainly would have been familiar with such legal requirements.[7]

Upon arriving at his trial, North asked Judge Russell for a jury trial. Even though North had a right to a jury trial in his case under Kentucky law, Judge Russell denied his request. North pleaded not guilty and had a bench trial before Judge Russell. In addition to not allowing him a jury trial, Judge Russell failed to tell North that he had a right to a court-appointed attorney. Judge Russell also only allowed the arresting officer to testify, refusing to even let North tell his side of the story (although Judge Russell did apparently ask some questions of North). That same night, the judge found North guilty of a first offense DWI and sentenced him to thirty days in jail, a fine of $150, and a revocation of his driver's license. The jail sentence was not authorized under Kentucky law. Judge Russell did not inform North that he had a right to appeal his conviction.[8]

Under Kentucky law at the time, North had a right to appeal his police court conviction to a circuit court, where judges were required to be at least thirty-five years of age, citizens of Kentucky, a two-year resident of their judicial district, and a practicing attorney of at least eight years. If he had appealed his case, North had a right to a trial *de novo* (new trial) before the circuit court judge. However, North did not file an appeal, probably in part because he did not know he had the right to do so. North filed a writ of habeas corpus in the Harlan County Circuit Court, challenging his detention as a violation of the Due Process Clause and Equal Protection Clause of the Fourteenth Amendment on the grounds that he should not have been tried and sentenced by a non-lawyer judge.

North, who now had attorney Eugene Goss to represent him, argued that a non-lawyer judge like Russell lacked legal competence and that it was not fair to North to be tried by a non-lawyer judge when similarly situated defendants in police courts in larger cities would be tried before judges who were attorneys. Circuit Court Judge Edward G. Hill denied North relief after a hearing, and that decision was affirmed by the Kentucky Court of Appeals, even though that appellate court characterized what happened in North's trial as an "absurdity." Eventually, North appealed his case to the U.S. Supreme Court.[9]

At the Supreme Court, North lost his appeal by a vote of 6-2. Chief Justice Warren Burger wrote the opinion of the Court. The Chief Justice began his analysis by noting that there is an important difference between trial courts of general jurisdiction, such as Kentucky's circuit courts, and trial courts of limited jurisdiction, such as Kentucky's police courts: "there is a wide gap between the functions of a judge of a court of general jurisdiction, dealing with complex litigation, and the functions of a local police court judge trying a typical 'drunk' driver case or other traffic violations."[10] Indeed, the types of citations and cases that frequently appear in trial courts of limited jurisdiction are usually much simpler in nature than the complicated procedures that one might face in homicide cases or some types of civil litigation.

That said, Chief Justice Burger recognized that in cases where a defendant is sentenced to confinement in jail or prison, *Argersinger v. Hamlin* (1972) and *Gideon v. Wainwright* (1963) mandated that the defendant has the assistance of counsel for his or her defense.[11] North argued that his right to due process was threatened under these cases because without a lawyer judge to understand the arguments being made by defense counsel, a defendant's right to an attorney is meaningless. Burger, however, quickly dismissed this argument because "a defendant in Kentucky facing a criminal sentence is afforded an opportunity to be tried *de novo* in a court presided over by a lawyer-judge."[12] Burger went on to note that many defendants facing traffic violations or other misdemeanors may not have attorneys when they are in limited jurisdiction courts. He then stated that

> We assume that police court judges recognize their obligation...to inform defendants of their right to a lawyer if a sentence of confinement is to be imposed. The appellee judge testified that informing defendants of a right to counsel was "the standard procedure." We also assume that police court judges in Kentucky recognize their obligation to inform all convicted defendants, including those who waived counsel or for whom imprisonment was not imposed, of their unconditional right to a trial *de novo* and of the necessity that an "appeal" be filed within 30 days in order to implement that right.[13]

Burger may have been right that notifying defendants of their right to counsel was "the standard procedure," and it may have been the case that most police court judges recognized their obligation to inform defendants of their right to an appeal, but there is no evidence that Judge Russell did this for North. An uninformed and unrepresented defendant, like North, is left with little recourse in this situation, a reality that the Chief Justice failed to recognize.

Burger next differentiated North's case from *Tumey v. Ohio* (1927) and *Ward v. Village of Monroeville* (1972) (see chapter six for more on these cases). North argued that cases stood for the proposition that non-lawyer judges could not preside over trials. Burger, on the other hand, rightfully saw that those cases involved judges who were potentially biased because of the financial incentives in place to find defendants guilty. For Burger, in *Tumey* and *Ward* "the challenge was directed not at the training or education of the judge but at his possible bias due to interest in the outcome of the case, [or because] he was both mayor and judge and received a portion of his compensation directly from the fines."[14] No such potential for judicial bias existed in *North*.

Chief Justice Burger closed this section of his opinion by discussing that there is nothing about legal training that necessarily makes a legal arbiter impartial: "Our concern in prior cases with judicial functions being performed by non-judicial officers has also been directed at the need for independent, neutral, and detached judgment, not at legal training."[15] Burger then went on to state that the Court previously approved of the constitutionality of "lay magistrates and other judicial officers empowered to issue warrants," even though in such situations those officers "must deal with evaluation of such legal concepts as probable cause and the sufficiency of warrant affidavits."[16] Thus, Burger found plenty of evidence that persons without formal legal training and bar admission could make legal decisions impartially, and thus there was no due process violation.

Justice Potter Stewart dissented in *North*, and he also wrote on the behalf of Justice Thurgood Marshall. Stewart found that a trial before a judge who was not a lawyer violated both the right to counsel and due process. According to Stewart,

> [T]he essential presupposition of this basic constitutional right is that the judge conducting the trial will be able to understand what the defendant's lawyer is talking about. For if the judge himself is ignorant of the law, then he, too, will be incapable of determining whether the charge is good or bad. He, too, will be unfamiliar with the rules of evidence. And a lawyer for the defendant will be able to do little or nothing to prevent an unjust conviction. In a trial before such a judge, the constitutional right to the assistance of counsel thus becomes a hollow mockery.[17]

For Stewart, such a situation not only threatens the effectiveness of one's attorney but also the ability of the judge to be impartial. Stewart reasoned that the U.S. Supreme Court "has never required a showing of specific or individualized prejudice when it was the procedure itself that violated due process of law,"[18] and he would have found one in this case. Furthermore, Justice Stewart argued that it was impossible for a non-lawyer judge to be impartial because of the complexity of issues faced by a judge, including when accepting a guilty plea, determining the voluntariness of a confession, advising a defendant of his or her trial rights, and instructing a jury. When performing these duties, Stewart argued that a non-lawyer judge will either not realize that he or she fails to understand the law, or the judge will turn to the prosecutor to answer legal questions; in neither case can the defendant count on the judge acting fairly and impartially: "A judge ignorant of the law is simply incapable of performing these functions. If he is aware of his incompetence, such a judge will perhaps instinctively turn to the prosecutor for advice and direction. But such a practice no more than compounds the due process violation."[19] The latter scenario was exactly what occurred with Judge Russell, who claimed that he relied on the city attorney for such advice, clearly calling into question his impartiality. Indeed, when questioned after the trial under oath, Judge Russell admitted the following:

> Question: Prior to your appointment as City Judge...had you had any previous legal experience of any kind?
> Judge Russell: "No, sir."
> Question: "Have you had any legal training of any kind since your appointment?"
> Judge Russell: "Well, the only thing I can say, if I have any doubt, I just consult with the city lawyer..."
> ...
> Question: "And when you receive advice from the city attorney, do you follow that advice?"
> Judge Russell: "Yes, sir."[20]

Finally, Justice Stewart was not convinced by the majority's conclusion that North's rights were protected because he could appeal his police court decision and have a trial *de novo* before a lawyer judge in circuit court. Stewart cited *Ward*, in which the court stated that the defendant in the case was "entitled to a neutral and detached judge in the first instance," and he concluded that "there can be no meaningful constitutional difference between a trial that is fundamentally unfair because of the judge's possible bias, and one that is fundamentally unfair because of the judge's ignorance of the law."[21] His final line called upon Magna Carta as authority: "At Runnymede in 1215 King John pledged to his barons that he would 'not make any Justiciaries, Constables, Sheriffs, or Bailiffs, excepting of such as know the laws of the land...' Today, more than 750 years later, the Court leaves that promise unkept."[22]

The trial judge in *North v. Russell* did not do his job very well. Judge Russell's ignorance of basic legal rights and his reliance on the prosecutor for legal information meant that he was less than neutral in violation of the Due Process Clause, and North should have been able to have a new trial in front of a judge who could truly be neutral. But that does not mean that all non-lawyer judges are like that judge. Even Russell, a newly appointed judge, might have done a better job with more training. In this sense, Chief Justice Burger and Justice Stewart were each partially correct: North was denied due process in this case, but not every defendant who appears before a non-lawyer judge will be denied due process by virtue of the fact that the judge does not have a law degree.

There is nothing talismanic about attending law school or practicing law. One can be a learned student of the law without having a framed diploma from an accredited school of law. In Wisconsin, where municipal judges are not always required to be attorneys, there are many fine non-lawyer judges who serve with distinction. On the flip side, there is evidence that lawyer judges tend to favor the interests of the legal profession over that of the public, meaning that simply being a lawyer judge does not wipe one clean of any and all biases. Furthermore, one can attend law school, graduate, and be admitted to the state bar, and still not be knowledgeable or be ethical enough to be fair and impartial. Indeed, there are numerous cases of lawyer judges who, regardless of the ethics courses they had to take in law school and the continuing legal education ethics credits they had to take while lawyers and judges, were later found guilty of taking bribes or intervening in cases of family or friends. As will be discussed in the next chapter, judges in such cases can be something well short of neutral, and their actions can raise due process problems. But this lack of neutrality has nothing to do with the framed diploma, or lack thereof, in the judge's office; instead, it has everything to do with each particular judge's actions and legal training, wherever and however it took place.[23]

The key here is having a mandatory, comprehensive judicial "boot camp" for new judges, whether they are attorneys or not, to learn key elements of judging before taking the bench. In addition, all states need to have requirements for continuing judicial education, so that all judges — whether they have law degrees or not — are properly informed about the law and ongoing changes to it. These types of training requirements can ensure that even non-lawyer judges keep the promise of Magna Carta and "know the laws of the land."

Non-lawyer judges in trial courts of limited jurisdiction can be impartial, and having them preside over cases can be in line with due process, especially when their decisions are subject to review by lawyer judges at general jurisdiction trial courts and appellate courts. Just like we trust non-lawyers to serve on juries and decide guilt and innocence after bring told the applicable laws, limited jurisdiction judges can preside over certain types of cases without having the training necessary to practice law in all areas. Furthermore, isolated incidents like the *North* case aside, the most comprehensive study available on the subject suggests that non-lawyer judges are just as competent as lawyer judges in carrying out judicial duties in courts of limited jurisdiction.[24]

Notes

1. Susan Katcher, "Legal Training in the United States: A Brief History," *Wisconsin International Law Journal* 24 (2006): 335-75, 336-37 (quoting Daniel J. Boorstin, *The Americans: The Colonial Experience* (New York: Vintage Books, 1958), 197).

2. Katcher, "Legal Training," (quoting Lawrence M. Friedman, *A History of American Law* (New York: Simon & Schuster, 2005), 54-55).

3. John O. Sonsteng with Donna Ward, Colleen Bruce and Michael Petersen, "A Legal Education Renaissance: A Practical Approach for the Twenty-First Century," *William Mitchell Law Reivew* 34 (2007): 303-472, 321-25.

4. Sonsteng, "A Legal Education," 364 & n.354; Wisconsin Court System, "For Attorneys: Admission to Practice Law in Wisconsin, Diploma Privilege 2012," March 7, 2012, http://www.wicourts.gov/services/attorney/bardiploma.htm (accessed June 4, 2012).

5. Lawrence M. Friedman, *A History of American Law* (New York: Touchstone, 1973), 109-10; James Findley, "The Debate Over Nonlawyer Probate Judges: A Historical Perspective," *Alabama Law Review* 61 (2010): 1143-61, 1152-53; Frederic S. Le Clercq, "The Constitutional Policy That Judges Be Learned in the Law," *Tennessee Law Review* 47 (1980): 689-741, 701-03.

6. Cathy Lesser Mansfield, "Disorder in the People's Court: Rethinking the Role of Non-Lawyer Judges in Limited Jurisdiction Court Civil Cases," *New Mexico Law Review* 29 (1999): 119-200, 135-41.

7. *North v. Russell*, 427 U.S. 328, 329-30, 339-42 & n.1 & 3 (1976); Doris Marie Provine, *Judging Credentials: Nonlawyer Judges and the Politics of Professionalism* (Chicago: University of Chicago Press, 1986), 71.

8. *North*, 427 U.S. at 330; Provine, *Judging Credentials*, 71; David W. Neubauer and Henry F. Fradella, *America's Courts and the Criminal Justice System* (Belmont, CA: Wadsworth, 2011), 485.

9. *North*, 427 U.S. at 330-33; Provine, *Judging Credentials*, 71; *North v. Russell*, 540 S.W.2d 4, 4-5 (Ky Ct. App. 1975).

10. *North*, 427 U.S. at 334.

11. *Argersinger v. Hamlin*, 407 U.S. 25 (1972); *Gideon v. Wainwright*, 372 U.S. 335 (1963).

12. *North*, 427 U.S. at 334.

13. *North*, 427 U.S. at 335 (internal citations omitted).

14. *North*, 427 U.S. at 337.

15. *North*, 427 U.S. at 337.

16. *North*, 427 U.S. at 337.

17. *North*, 427 U.S. at 342-43 (Stewart, J., dissenting) (internal citations and quotations omitted).

18. *North*, 427 U.S. at 343 (Stewart, J., dissenting).

19. *North*, 427 U.S. at 344 (Stewart, J., dissenting) (internal citations omitted).

20. *North*, 427 U.S. at 344 n.4 (Stewart, J., dissenting).

21. *North*, 427 U.S. at 345 (Stewart, J., dissenting) (quoting *Ward v. Village of Monroeville*, 409 U.S. 57, 62 (1972)).

22. *North*, 427 U.S. at 346 (Stewart, J., dissenting) (internal citations omitted).

23. Neubauer and Fadella, *America's Courts*, 203; Benjamin H. Barton, *The Lawyer-Judge Bias in the American Legal System* (New York: Cambridge University Press, 2011).

24. Provine, *Judging Credentials*.

~9~

The Judge Who Was Bribed in Other Cases: *Bracy v. Gramley* (1997)

[T]he floor established by the Due Process Clause clearly requires a fair trial in a fair tribunal, before a judge with no actual bias against the defendant or interest in the outcome of his particular case.
– *Bracy v. Gramley*, 520 U.S. 899, 904-05 (1997)

There are plenty of instances where it is arguable if a judge is impartial or not. There is no question, however, that a judge who accepts a bribe is biased in that case. History demonstrates that occasionally an unethical judge will engage in this behavior and allow money to trump justice. In such instances, it is necessary that the judge is disqualified from hearing that case, removed from office, and prosecuted criminally.

When a judge accepts a bribe in a case, defendants in other cases may wonder if they were treated fairly. There is no question that accepting a bribe is unethical, but does it mean that the judge was also biased in other cases where no one bribed that judge? The U.S. Supreme Court was asked to answer this question in *Bracy v. Gramley* (1997).

The story of *Bracy* began on November 12, 1980. Sometime after 10:00 p.m. Frederick Lacey, R.C. Pettigrew, and Richard Holliman were driven to a viaduct in Chicago, Illinois and shot to death in and around a red Oldsmobile. Lacey was lying on the ground on the driver's side of the vehicle, Pettigrew was lying partially under the right front bumper, and Holliman was in the back seat. Shotgun and gunshot wounds were in various places on the men, including in the back of the head, the face, neck, chest, back, and legs. Roger Collins, William Bracy, and Murray Hooper were indicted for the armed robbery, aggravated kidnapping, and the murders of Lacey, Pettigrew, and Holliman. Collins and Bracy were tried together (Hooper was tried separately) before a jury in a Cook

County, Illinois Circuit Court in 1981. Judge Thomas J. Maloney presided over the trial.[1]

Morris Nellum was the main witness for the prosecution. In exchange for his testimony, Nellum agreed to a plea deal of three years in protective custody and for his family to be relocated into witness protection. Nellum testified that on November 12, 1980 he was at the apartment of his girlfriend, Regina Parker, at 2222 South State Street in Chicago. At approximately 9:30 p.m., Nellum claimed that Collins arrived at the apartment and asked Nellum to go with him to another apartment on that block, apartment 206 at 2240 South State Street. Nellum claimed that Collins had something he wanted Nellum "to take care of." Nellum went to the other apartment with Collins, where he arrived ten minutes later. Nellum claimed that he discovered Collins, Bracy, and Hooper holding in a bedroom three men that Nellum did not know. Nellum later identified the three men being held against their will as Lacey, Pettigrew, and Holliman. Pettigrew and Holliman were on the bed with their hands bound; Lacey was standing at the side of the bed. At this point, Collins asked Nellum to drive Collins's brown Cadillac to Roosevelt Road and Clark Street. Nellum claimed that he took Collins's keys and went to the parking lot downstairs to wait for the other men. Nellum then purported to observe Collins, Bracy, and Hooper take the three other men to a red Oldsmobile and place them in the backseat. Collins and Hooper got in the front seat of the Oldsmobile, and Bracy got in his own car parked nearby. After Collins, Hooper, and Bracy drove away, Nellum waited a few minutes before departing, as instructed. As Nellum approached the viaduct at Roosevelt Road and Clark Street, he claimed that he heard a series of gunshots. Nellum then saw Bracy, who was carrying a sawed-off shotgun, and Hooper running to Bracy's car. Collins then got into his Cadillac (still being driven by Nellum), and Nellum claimed that Collins remarked, "That damn Hooper. I told him to wait until — I wanted to use the shotgun because they can't trace the shotgun, but he used the gun instead." The two vehicles then drove to the parking lot at 2240 State Stret, where Nellum claims Bracy gave him $125 and told him to "just be cool." Nellum then stated that he drove with Collins to Lake Michigan, where Collins threw two handguns, a 38-caliber Charter Arms revolver and a .357 Ruger revolver, into the lake. Two firearms matching this description were located by police divers at the location described by Nellum.[2]

Nellum's description of these gruesome crimes seemed very compelling at first, but his story became less persuasive on cross-examination. He admitted to initially lying to police that he did not know where the weapons were located. He also denied under oath knowing the victim Lacey. The defense, however, introduced numerous photographs from August of 1980 showing Nellum and Lacey together. Finally, although he initially did not cooperate with police, he later decided to testify against Collins and Bracy in exchange for a deal with prosecutors not to charge him with murder and instead charge him with three counts of concealing a homicidal death with a three-year sentencing recommendation.[3]

In addition to Nellum, the prosecution had other witnesses. Daretha Redmond testified that sometime after 10:00 p.m. on the night of the murders she saw a group of about five men, two of whom were tied, walk past her living room window at 2240 South State Street. She later identified Collins, Nellum, and Hooper as resembling men in the group. However, on cross-examination Redmond could not say that she had seen Bracy or that she could be certain she saw Collins that night. Still, another eyewitness who lived in the same apartment building, Laverne Lyles, testified that on that night around 10:00 p.m. she saw Collins and Bracy walking out of the building with a man who had his hands tied. Lyles identified the tied man as the victim Pettigrew.[4]

Regarding the firearms, Christina Nowell testified that Bracy had stolen a .38-caliber Charter Arms revolver from her in May of 1980. When she later asked him about it in late November 1980, Nowell claimed that Bracy threatened to have her "wasted" and that he told her he had "murdered people with [her gun] and threw it in the Chicago River." The serial number on the recovered .38-calibur Charter Arms revolver matched the serial number on the gun that had been stolen from Nowell. A firearms expert testified that tests were conducted on the .38-caliber Charter Arms revolver and the .357 Ruger revolver that police recovered with the help of Nellum. The expert claimed that bullets or bullet fragments bearing the characteristics of at least one of the weapons were found in each of the three victims. However, since the guns were rusted from being in the river, the expert could not say for sure that they fired the bullets in the victims. Similarly, police found rope in apartment 206 at 2240 South Street that matched the rope found on Pettigrew's wrist, although it was a very common type of rope.[5]

Both Collins and Bracy had alibi defenses, suggesting that Nellum, Hooper, and another man named Jesse committed the crimes instead. Bracy put his sister on the witness stand, and she testified that he was at her home between 6:00 p.m. and 11:30 p.m. on the night of the murders. When his sister was cross-examined, she admitted that she had not told the authorities about this before trial. Bracy testified on his own behalf, confirming the story that he had been at his sister's home that night. He also denied stealing Nowell's gun. However, two police officers testified in rebuttal that Bracy was in the vicinity of apartment 206 on the night of the murders. Collins testified that he was with his girlfriend at the time of the murders, and he only briefly stopped by apartment 206 that evening for a brief conversation. Collins's girlfriend testified to the same, except that on cross-examination she admitted to being a heroin addict who was undergoing methadone treatment at a clinic on November 12. Collins also had other alibi witnesses who confirmed his story, but each one lacked credibility because each one had either robbery convictions, theft convictions, or both. These witnesses also struggled with some of the prosecution's questioning.[6]

Although there were some holes in the prosecution's evidence, the state secured convictions against both Collins and Bracy on all counts. At the sentencing phase of the trial, the jury found aggravating factors against Collins and

Bracy but no mitigating factors. Based on this, both men were sentenced to death for the murders, and they were also each sentenced to concurrent sixty-year prison sentences for armed robbery and aggravated kidnapping. In February 1985, the Supreme Court of Illinois upheld the convictions for Collins and Bracy and directed that their execution date be set for September 24, 1985. Their executions were stayed, first by a direct appeal to the U.S. Supreme Court. When that appeal was denied, Collins and Bracy filed for post-conviction hearings, which eventually landed them in the Supreme Court of Illinois again. That court affirmed their denial of post-conviction relief, and their execution date was reset to March 23, 1993. It looked like the end of the line for both men.[7]

However, simultaneous to these defendants' post-conviction appeals, their saga took an interesting turn. Their trial judge, Thomas J. Maloney, was indicted by a federal grand jury on charges of bribery, racketeering, income tax evasion, extortion under color of official right, and obstruction of justice. Maloney's indictment was part of Operation Greylord, a comprehensive federal investigation of judicial corruption in Chicago. Maloney served as a circuit court judge from his appointment in 1977 until his retirement in 1990. Before his time on the bench, Maloney was a criminal defense attorney whom law enforcement later learned had close ties to organized crime in Illinois. Evidence surfaced that while still a practicing lawyer, Maloney paid off judges in criminal cases in exchange for acquittals, including in a trial for a mob hit man. A mob enforcer testified that Maloney helped him evade a series of criminal charges dating back to the late 1960s. Thus, at the very least, Maloney had a history of criminal behavior unbecoming of an officer of the court.[8]

There was more, though. After his indictment, a jury convicted Maloney of accepting bribes, including in murder cases, while serving as a judge. The jury found that Maloney accepted an undetermined portion of a $100,000 payment in 1981 to acquit three New York gang members, including Lenny Chow, of murdering a rival in Chicago's Chinatown. The jury found that he accepted between $4,000 and $5,000 in 1982 to convict a defendant of voluntary manslaughter instead of the greater charge of felony murder. The jury found that in 1986 Maloney accepted $10,000 to acquit two leaders of the El Rukn gang of a double murder. Maloney was also convicted of fixing a non-homicide case, and he was indicted, but not convicted, of fixing a fifth case. Although he was not indicted for them, prosecutors also alleged that Maloney fixed other cases. They claimed that he fixed a murder case in 1980 for between $2,000 and $2,500. In addition, prosecutors claimed that Maloney accepted $5,000 in 1982 to guarantee no prison time for a defendant accused of five counts of deceptive practices. Particularly relevant for Bracy and Collins was that their murder trial was sandwiched between two other murder trials where Judge Maloney took bribes. Defense attorney William Swano testified that he bribed Maloney in the murder case of his client, Wilfred Rosario; Judge Maloney excluded Rosario's confession and acquitted him after a bench trial in May of 1981. The Bracy and Collins trial then took place in July 1981. In August of 1981, Maloney acquitted Lenny Chow in his murder trial.[9]

The appearance of bias in the Bracy/Collins murder trial looked even stronger based on some of the other actions taken by Judge Maloney during the summer of 1981. Bracy's attorney was Robert McDonnell, who was appointed by Judge Maloney to represent Bracy in June 1981. Although there were initially allegations by Bracy that McDonnell was a former law partner of Maloney, this was not the case. Perhaps more disturbing, though, was that Maloney and McDonnell knew each other and both associated with Chicago organized crime families. McDonnell had been convicted of conspiracy to distribute counterfeit money in 1966 (for which he was sentenced to two years in prison), he was convicted of tax evasion in 1968 (for which he served four years in prison), and he was disbarred in 1972. Although he was reinstated to the bar in 1980, in 1989 McDonnell was convicted of conspiracy to defraud the government and solicitation to influence the operation of an employee benefits plan. For this last charge, he was sentenced to six years in prison, and he withdrew himself from the Illinois Bar. When representing Bracy in 1981, McDonnell announced that he was ready to defend a murder charge just a few weeks after being appointed by Judge Maloney. McDonnell failed to ask for more time to prepare for the penalty phase of the trial. Judge Maloney also made numerous discretionary rulings in the Bracy/Collins trial, including excusing for cause the only African American jury panel member, ruling against a defense motion to exclude evidence, ruling against a defense motion for a separate penalty hearing, rejecting the defense's jury instructions, declining to grant a defense continuance, and admitting evidence against Bracy of an unadjudicated Arizona homicide.[10]

There were further allegations that this was only the tip of the iceberg and that Maloney accepted bribes in many more cases. In the bribery cases that were known to law enforcement, Maloney received the bribes by using an intermediary between himself and the lawyer in each case. Maloney first used a bailiff, Lucius Robinson, as his intermediary, until Robinson came under suspicion in Operation Greylord. From then on, Maloney used a former law partner, Robert McGee, as his intermediary. William Swano was frequently the lawyer who arranged for his clients to bribe Judge Maloney; McGee also bribed the judge, as did another attorney, Robert J. Cooley.[11]

This system started to crumble when a grand jury convened to investigate Robinson in May 1988. Robinson was eventually granted immunity, and he testified against Maloney. In June 1991, Maloney was indicted by a federal grand jury. At his trial, which began in March 1993, Maloney claimed that Robinson and Swano engaged in a scam whereby they never passed the bribes to the judge. However, prosecutors produced evidence that Maloney had extensively used money orders to hide his excessive spending. In April 1993, the jury convicted Maloney of multiple counts of bribery and subsequently sentenced him to serve fifteen years and nine months in a federal penitentiary. Maloney's conviction was upheld on appeal. As noted by Chief Justice William Rehnquist, Judge

Maloney "has the dubious distinction of being the only Illinois judge ever convicted of fixing a murder case."[12]

By this time, Bracy had exhausted his direct appeals and his state post-conviction remedies. Based on Maloney's convictions, Bracy petitioned a federal district court for habeas corpus relief. Bracy's argument was that Judge Maloney was accepting bribes in other cases, including other murder cases, directly before and after his criminal trial. Thus, Bracy alleged that Judge Maloney was biased against him and intentionally made discretionary rulings in favor of the prosecution in an attempt to secure a conviction against him. Bracy argued that Judge Maloney was doing this so as to not draw attention to the acquittals he secured in cases where he accepted bribes. In other words, Judge Maloney did not want to have too many acquittals, so he needed to ensure that there were convictions in some cases before him. Bracy's argument was bolstered by the testimony of William Swano (one of the attorneys who bribed Judge Maloney). According to Swano, Maloney retaliated against one of Swano's clients in a rare case where he failed to offer the judge a bribe; in bribe negotiations in a later case, McGee (Maloney's intermediate) admitted that this was the case. Swano thus subsequently testified that he learned that "to practice law in front of Judge Maloney…we had to pay."[13]

Based on this information, Bracy requested (1) the sealed transcript of Maloney's criminal trial; (2) access to the prosecution's materials in Maloney's case; (3) the opportunity to depose those persons associated with Maloney; and (4) a chance to search Maloney's rulings for a pattern of pro-prosecution bias. However, the federal district judge denied Bracy's request for additional discovery into Judge Maloney, and the court dismissed his habeas petition. That decision was affirmed by the Seventh Circuit Court of Appeals in 1996. This led Bracy to appeal his cases to the U.S. Supreme Court, which agreed to hear his case in the spring of 1997.[14]

Writing for a unanimous Court, Chief Justice Rehnquist found that Bracy's right to an impartial judge may have been violated under the Fourteenth Amendment's Due Process Clause and that he was entitled to discover additional information about Maloney to see if bias actually existed. The Chief Justice began by noting, though, that most issues like this do not raise constitutional concerns: "Of course, most questions concerning a judge's qualifications to hear a case are not constitutional ones, because the Due Process Clause of the Fourteenth Amendment establishes a constitutional floor, not a uniform standard. Instead, these questions are, in most cases, answered by common law, statute, or the professional standards of the bench and bar."[15] After making that statement, Rehnquist was clear that the Due Process Clause does have a role to play when a judge is partial to an outcome in a case: "the floor established by the Due Process Clause clearly requires a fair trial in a fair tribunal, before a judge with no actual bias against the defendant or interest in the outcome of his particular case."[16] No doubt, the bare minimum standard of constitutionally mandated due process requires this type of neutrality in the courtroom. Without it, any trial is a sham.

Chief Justice Rehnquist next noted the extreme nature of this case: "The facts of this case are, happily, not the stuff of typical judicial-disqualification disputes."[17] He then made it clear that this is not the same issue that is normally raised in cases involving judicial bribery, as a judge "who accepts bribes from a criminal defendant to fix that defendant's case is 'biased' in the most basic sense of that word, but his bias is directed against the State, not the defendant."[18] Bracy's claim, on the other hand, was that "Maloney's taking of bribes from some criminal defendants not only rendered him biased against the *State* in those cases, but also induced a sort of compensatory bias against *defendants* who did not bribe Maloney," so that the judge could avoid "being seen as uniformly and suspiciously 'soft' on criminal defendants."[19] Although this proposition is difficult to prove, Rehnquist clarified that "if it could be proved, such compensatory, camouflaging bias on Maloney's part in [Bracy's] own case would violate the Due Process Clause of the Fourteenth Amendment."[20]

Rehnquist then recounted the facts surrounding Judge Maloney's bribery convictions in murder cases, as well as the circumstances surrounding the Bracy/Collins murder trial. After then restating Bracy's corruption theory, the Chief Justice noted that this "is, of course, only a theory at this point; it is not supported by any solid evidence of [Bracy's] trial lawyer's participation in any such plan," but Rehnquist conceded that "[i]t is true, however, that McGee was corrupt and that petitioner's trial coincided with bribe negotiations in the *Chow* case and closely followed the *Rosario* murder case, which was also fixed."[21] In other words, the Court was unable to discern if Bracy's attorney, Robert McDonnell, a man who had demonstrated a lack of ethics, was working in conjunction with Judge Maloney to secure a conviction, but the evidence against one of Maloney's other former law partners, Robert McGee, lent itself to more investigation before concluding that Bracy had received a fair trial. Therefore, Rehnquist and the eight other justices concluded that Bracy showed good cause for the discovery that he sought because if he is able to obtain all of the facts in the case, Bracy may be able to demonstrate that Maloney was, in fact, biased in his trial. Rehnquist clarified that this conclusion was warranted because of the unusual circumstances involving Judge Maloney:

> Ordinarily, we presume that public officials have properly discharged their official duties. Were it possible to indulge this presumption here, we might well agree with the Court of Appeals that [Bracy's] submission and his compensatory-bias theory are too speculative to warrant discovery. But, unfortunately, the presumption has been soundly rebutted: Maloney was shown to be thoroughly steeped in corruption through his public trial and conviction. We emphasize, though, that [Bracy] supports his discovery request by pointing not only to Maloney's conviction for bribe-taking in other cases, but also to additional evidence, discussed above, that lends support to his claim that Maloney was actually biased *in [Bracy's] own case.*[22]

Thus, Bracy and Collins were granted relief from the U.S. Supreme Court. Their habeas claim was heard by United States District Judge William T. Hart of the Northern District of Illinois in 1999. Once the additional discovery was completed, Judge Hart put on the record all of the unethical practices of Judge Maloney and the questionable actions of Bracy's attorney, Robert McDonnell. However, Judge Hart found that there was no understanding between Maloney and McDonnell to help convict Bracy as a way to deflect suspicion from cases fixed by Maloney. Nor did Judge Hart find evidence that Maloney had a pattern of being biased against defendants in cases where his was not bribed. Thus, Judge Hart found no judicial bias that affected the jury's decision to convict Bracy. Judge Hart did find evidence of bias in Maloney's sentencing though. Judge Hart found fault in Maloney's failure to sever the Collins and Bracy sentencing hearings, even though Maloney allowed evidence of a prior Arizona homicide to be introduced against Bracy. Judge Hart also pointed to Maloney's sentencing at his own bribery trial, where Maloney pointed to the death sentences against Bracy, Collins, and Hooper as evidence that he was a careful, thorough, and tough judge. Jude Hart concluded that this showed evidence of compensatory bias at sentencing, and he vacated Collins's and Bracy's death sentences while simultaneously upholding their underlying convictions. A split Seventh Circuit Court of Appeals, hearing the case *en banc*, upheld Judge Hart's decision in 2002. The U.S. Supreme Court declined to review the case again. After more than two decades, Bracy's appeals had finally run their course.[23]

William Bracy died in April 2005 in the Provena St. Joseph Medical Intensive Unit in Joilet, Illinois. He was transferred to that facility from the Illinois Statesville Correctional Center when it was learned that he had lung cancer and pneumonia. He was sixty-three years of age. As for the judge who initially sentenced him, Thomas Maloney died of kidney failure in a nursing home in October 2008. He was eighty-three years old.[24]

Although neither of the principals of this case is still alive, the ruling from *Bracy v. Gramley* remains an important benchmark in measuring judicial bias. There is no evidence that Maloney was bribed in the murder trial of Bracy and Collins, but his track record as an attorney and judge, as well as his convictions for bias in cases before and after this trial, lend themselves to the conclusion that he was engaging in compensatory bias. At the very least, the vacating of Collins's and Bracy's death sentences were warranted, as there was demonstrated bias in the need for Maloney to put death penalty convictions on his record. Both Judge Hart and the Seventh Circuit could have gone a step farther, however. While there was still plenty of good evidence against Collins and Bracy, a new trial in front of a judge who was not convicted of taking bribes in other cases was the only way to ensure that the judge was free from bias. Given the testimony of Swano, there was solid evidence that Maloney was biased against non-bribing defendants at both the conviction and sentencing phases of criminal trials.

Indeed, this case conjures up visions of the judge in *Tumey v. Ohio*, a man who was tempted by having a direct financial interest in the case. Judge Maloney's bribery scheme was based on him not getting caught. There is evidence that he carried on these practices years after the Bracy/Collins trial. Maloney needed to avoid suspicion of his scheme, and convicting defendants in non-bribery cases was one way to accomplish this. Furthermore, the outcomes in any cases are suspect if they are decided by a judge who is willing to put justice up for sale to the highest bidder. Maloney was a corrupt judge, and his behavior shocks the conscience. Before his death, Bracy should have at least had the right to a trial before a judge who did not have these types of biases. Bracy probably was guilty, but he at least had a right to have the state prove this fact on a level playing field.

Although a new trial would have been sensible in Bracy's case, due concerns of judicial economy prevent doing so for everyone similarly situated. There are, thankfully, few judges who take bribes, but Judge Maloney alone presided over 6,000 cases during his judicial career. As pointed out by Court of Appeals Judge Richard Posner, this is a high number of cases, and combined with the seventeen other Illinois judges who had been convicted of accepting bribes when the Seventh Circuit Court of Appeals originally heard Bracy's appeal, this could lead to invalidating a high number of cases. In a situation like this, can we expect it reasonable to reopen tens of thousands of cases, or do concerns of judicial economy prevent such action? As one commentator suggested, defendants convicted by a judge who was bribed in other cases should automatically be given an evidentiary hearing and the right to ask the judge under oath whether that judge's bribes affected their case. This should particularly be the case for all decisions made solely by such a judge, including sentencing decisions and bench trial verdicts.[25]

What occurred with Judge Maloney was a travesty against justice. Obviously, no judge should participate in that type of conduct even once, much less multiple times like Maloney did. *Bracy* stands for the proposition that a judge's misconduct in one case can threaten that judge's impartiality in other cases. Not only should cases be revisited where such a judge took bribes, but to ensure there was no compensatory bias, other cases presided over by such a judge should be revisited as well. The right to a neutral judge and due process require nothing less.

Notes

1. *People v. Collins*, 478 N.E.2d 267, 272 (Ill. 1985); Timothy R. Terry, "Lawyers, Guns, and Money: What Price Justice?," *Journal of Law and Criminology* 88 (1998): 1087.
2. *Collins*, 478 N.E.2d at 272-73; Terry, "Lawyers, Guns, and Money."
3. *Collins*, 478 N.E.2d at 273.

4. *Collins*, 478 N.E.2d at 273.
5. *Collins*, 478 N.E.2d at 273-74.
6. *Collins*, 478 N.E.2d at 274-76.
7. *Collins*, 478 N.E.2d at 272, 286; *People v. Collins*, 606 N.E.2d 1137 (Ill. 1992).
8. *Bracy v. Gramley*, 520 U.S. 899, 901-02 (1997); *Bracy v. Gramley*, 81 F.3d 684, 696 (7th Cir. 1996) (Rovner, J., dissenting); *United States v. Maloney*, 71 F.3d 645, 650 (7th Cir. 1995); Terry, "Lawyers, Guns, and Money."
9. *Bracy*, 81 F.3d at 696 (Rovner, J., dissenting); *Maloney*, 71 F.3d at 650-51; *Bracy* 520 U.S. at 907 n.9.
10. *Bracy*, 520 U.S. at 907-08; Terry, "Lawyers, Guns, and Money;" *Bracy v. Schomig*, 286 F.3d 406, 413-14 (7th Cir. 2002).
11. *Bracy*, 81 F.3d at 696 (Rovner, J., dissenting); *Maloney*, 71 F.3d at 650-51; *Bracy* 520 U.S. at 902, 906-07.
12. *Maloney*, 71 F.3d at 651-52; *Bracy*, 81 F.3d at 696; Terry, "Lawyers, Guns, and Money;" *Bracy*, 520 U.S. at 901.
13. *Bracy*, 520 U.S. at 906 n.5.
14. *Bracy*, 520 U.S. at 902; Terry.
15. *Bracy*, 520 U.S. at 904 (internal citations omitted).
16. *Bracy*, 520 U.S. at 904-05 (internal citation and quotation omitted).
17. *Bracy*, 520 U.S. at 905.
18. *Bracy*, 520 U.S. at 905.
19. *Bracy*, 520 U.S. at 905 (italics in original).
20. *Bracy*, 520 U.S. at 905.
21. *Bracy*, 520 U.S. at 908.
22. *Bracy*, 520 U.S. at 909 (internal quotations and citations omitted) (emphasis in original).
23. *United States ex rel. Collins v. Welborn*, 79 F. Supp. 2d 898 (N.D. Ill. 1999); *Bracy*, 286 F.3d 406; *Collins v. Walls*, 537 U.S. 894 (2002); *Bracy v. Schomig*, 537 U.S. 894 (2002).
24. Melissa Sanders-Rivera, "Must Read/This is what PRISON is…," Illinois Inmates Support, April 28, 2005, http://dir.groups.yahoo.com/group/illinoisinmatesupport/message/1818 (accessed June 10, 2012); Trevor Jensen, "Thomas J. Maloney, 1925-2008: Judge Was Convicted of Rigging Cases," *Chicago Tribune*, October 22, 2008, http://truthinjustice.org/judge-maloney.htm (accessed June 10, 2012).
25. *Bracy*, 81 F.3d at 689; Thomas M. DiBiagio, "Judicial Corruption, The Right to a Fair Trial, and the Application of Plain Error Review: Requiring Clear and Convincing Evidence of Actual Prejudice or Should We Settle For Justice in the Dark?," *American Journal of Criminal Law* 25 (1998): 595-629, 601; Ian Ayres, "The Twin Faces of Judicial Corruption: Extortion and Bribery," *Denver University Law Review* 74 (1997): 1231-50, 1250.

~ 10 ~

A Judge Deciding a Case Involving a Major Campaign Supporter: *Caperton v. A.T. Massey Coal Co.* (2009)

[T]here is a serious risk of actual bias...when a person with a personal stake in a particular case had a significant and disproportionate influence in placing the judge on the case by raising funds or directing the judge's election campaign when the case was pending or imminent.
– *Caperton v. A.T. Massey Coal Co.*, 129 S. Ct. 2252, 2263-64 (2009)

The facts of *Caperton v. A.T. Massey Coal Co.* (2009) are so compelling that it has been noted by multiple commentators that the case's facts are worthy of a John Grisham legal thriller.[1] The case has its roots in a dispute over a coal mine in Virginia called the Harman Mine. In the early to mid-1990s, the mine was owned by the Inspiration Coal Corporation, which had subsidiaries that transacted business in West Virginia. Under a 1992 coal supply agreement, the Wellmore Coal Corporation was to purchase from the subsidiaries of Inspiration approximately 750,000 tons of coal per year for a period of ten years. In 1997, the A.T. Massey Coal Company acquired Wellmore. At the direction of Massey Coal, Wellmore wanted to scale back the amount of coal purchased from the Harman Mine. This led to what Hugh M. Caperton, owner of Inspiration and the Harmon Mine, later characterized as Massey Coal engaging in allegedly fraudulent misrepresentation and in Massey Coal dragging its feet regarding the closing of the contract between Wellmore and Caperton's companies. Caperton's companies then found themselves under additional financial stress, and Hugh Caperton ultimately filed for bankruptcy.

In 1998, Caperton and his companies filed suit against Massey Coal, claiming that Massey's actions were illegal and directly caused Caperton's financial problems. In August 2002, a jury returned a verdict for Caperton, finding that Massey Coal engaged in tortious interference, fraudulent misrepresentation, and fraudulent concealment. In the jury's verdict, just over $50 million in compensatory and punitive damages were awarded to Caperton.[2]

Massey Coal, less than satisfied with the trial court's verdict and damage awards, filed post-trial motions challenging both. The trial judge denied these motions in June 2004 and denied Massey's motion for a judgment as a matter of law in March 2005. After Massey's motion was denied in June 2004, Massey prepared an appeal of the decision to the Supreme Court of Appeals of West Virginia. West Virginia has no intermediate appellate court, so all appeals of state trial court decisions must be heard by the state's supreme court.[3]

In the meantime, the state held its 2004 judicial elections at the same time as the November 2004 national presidential election. Justice Warren McGraw of the state supreme court was up for reelection, running as a Democrat. A former state legislator and lieutenant governor, the sixty-five-year-old McGraw was first elected to the state supreme court in 1998.[4] McGraw's challenger was forty-seven-year-old defense attorney and West Virginia Republican Party treasurer Brent Benjamin.[5] The partisan judicial election became very nasty, with numerous attack advertisements, including ones that characterized Justice McGraw as releasing a child molester and as being a deterrent to potential business investment in the state; the campaign was so nasty that it attracted the attention of *The New York Times*.[6]

Enter Don Blankenship, Massey Coal's chairman, chief executive officer, and president. U.S. Supreme Court Justice Anthony Kennedy characterized Blankenship's involvement in the 2004 election as follows: "Knowing the Supreme Court of Appeals of West Virginia would consider the appeal in the case, Blankenship decided to support an attorney who sought to replace Justice McGraw… The attorney who sought to replace him was Brent Benjamin."[7] Setting aside for the moment Blankenship's motives, he interjected himself, and his money, into the election. Indeed, Blankenship did the following:

- He contributed $1,000 (the statutory maximum) to Benjamin's campaign committee;
- He donated nearly $2.5 million to "And For the Sake of the Kids," a 527 group that opposed McGraw's reelection and supported Benjamin; and
- He spent a little more than $500,000 on independent expenditures (direct mailings, letters soliciting donations, and television and newspaper advertisements) in support of Benjamin's candidacy.[8]

Recall those attack advertisements mentioned briefly ago. The most visceral ones were by "And For the Sake of the Kids." One ad claimed of a probationer who had his case heard by the West Virginia Supreme Court that "he sexually molested multiple West Virginia children," and that "liberal Judge Warren McGraw cast the deciding vote to set this reprehensible criminal free."[9] Another ad by "And For the Sake of the Kids," titled "Tired," seemed to blame all of West Virginia's problems on McGraw: "Tired of lost jobs? Skyrocketing car insurance bills? Doctors leaving the state? Tired of rich, greedy lawyers? Ifrational judges? Self-serving, lifetime politicians? Tired of our kids being victimized but criminals going free? Then you're tired of Judge Warren McGraw. Radical McGraw: too many lies, too expensive, too dangerous. West Virginia deserves better."[10]

These advertisements were typical of ones run by "And For the Sake of the Kids" against McGraw throughout September and October 2004.[11] Benjamin won the election against McGraw by a margin of 53 percent to 47 percent (382,036 votes to 334,301 votes).[12]

Now we return to the lawsuit between Caperton and A.T. Massey Coal. In October 2005, Caperton made a motion to disqualify Justice Benjamin from hearing the appeal under the Due Process Clause of the Fourteenth Amendment and the West Virginia Code of Judicial Conduct. Caperton neither objected to the way in which Benjamin conducted his campaign, nor how Blankenship spent approximately $3 million on Benjamin's campaign in direct contributions, 527 funding, and independent expenditures. Caperton did not argue that Benjamin was unfit to serve as a state supreme court justice in all cases. Instead, Caperton believed that state and federal law prevented Benjamin from hearing *this* case because of the conflict of interest caused by Blankenship's involvement in trying to influence an election that Benjamin ultimately won. Benjamin disagreed, denying Caperton's motion in April 2006. According to Benjamin, there existed "no objective information" to show that he had "a bias for or against any litigant," that he had "prejudged the matters which comprise this litigation," or that he would "be anything but fair and impartial."[13]

In November 2007, the West Virginia Supreme Court of Appeals, by a vote of 3-2, reversed the $50 million verdict against Massey. The court held that *res judicata* barred West Virginia courts from adjudicating the contract, as it had already been adjudicated in the Virginia courts and that a forum-selection clause in the 1992 contract required adjudication in Virginia. Benjamin concurred with the majority, thus casting the deciding vote in favor of Massey Coal and Don Blankenship.[14]

Caperton filed to have the case reheard by the West Virginia Supreme Court of Appeals. This time, each side moved for disqualification of justices: Massey Coal moved to disqualify one justice, and Caperton moved to disqualify two. Massey Coal requested that Justice Larry Starcher disqualify himself. Justice Starcher had publicly called Blankenship disparaging names, including "stupid," "evil," and a "clown" who was "trying to buy influence like buying candy for children." Starcher agreed that he could not act impartially and recused himself from the case.[15]

Caperton asked that Chief Justice Elliot Maynard disqualify himself from participating in the rehearing, due to photos from 2006 that showed Maynard on vacation in Monte Carlo with Blankenship. This vacationing occurred *after* Massey had filed its appeal with the West Virginia Supreme Court of Appeals but *before* the case was decided. A spokesperson for Massey stated that the two men were not "vacationing together" and that it was "coincidence" that they were in the same place at the same time. However, time stamps on the photographs revealed that the two men were pictured vacationing together on three consecutive days, and some photographs showed them drinking together. Due to these photographs, Chief Justice Maynard recused himself from the rehearing.[16]

The third disqualification motion was filed by Caperton. Like he did for the first hearing, Caperton moved to disqualify Justice Benjamin for the rehearing. And just as was the case before the first hearing, Justice Benjamin found himself fit to participate in the rehearing. With the chief justice having recused himself, Benjamin became acting chief justice for the rehearing. In this role, acting Chief Justice Benjamin appointed two other West Virginia judges to temporarily serve on the West Virginia Supreme Court of Appeals in place of the recused justices Starcher and Maynard. Before the case was reheard, Caperton filed one more disqualification motion against acting Chief Justice Benjamin. Benjamin again refused to recuse himself. The rehearing went ahead as scheduled. With Benjamin again in the majority, Massey won the rehearing by a vote of 3-2 in April 2008.[17] In dissent, Justice Joseph Albright forthrightly stated that "the majority has radically strayed from the fundamental principles of fairness and justice," and Justice Albright claimed that "there are now genuine due process implications arising under federal law" with respect to acting Chief Justice Benjamin's conflict of interest in the case.[18]

Upon losing the rehearing, Caperton appealed to the U.S. Supreme Court, which issued a 5-4 ruling in favor of Caperton in June 2009. The Court found that Justice Benjamin's failure to recuse himself after receiving such significant campaign assistance from Blankenship amounted to a violation of Caperton's due process rights.[19]

Justice Anthony Kennedy wrote for the five-member majority of the Court in *Caperton*. Kennedy began by stating that due process requires a fair trial in a fair tribunal, but cautioned that most matters of judicial disqualification do not raise constitutional due process questions and instead are issues left to state judicial ethics codes. Kennedy then gave an overview of two types of cases where the U.S. Supreme Court has required judicial disqualification because of due process concerns: (1) local tribunals where a judge has a financial interest in the case, and (2) cases where judges have a conflict of interest due to participation in earlier proceedings.[20]

As to the first type of case, concerning financial gain by a judge, Kennedy began with the most notable case on the subject, *Tumey v. Ohio* (1927). Recall from chapter six that *Tumey* involved a judge who received a portion of each fine when he found a defendant guilty; the judge in *Tumey* received no additional compensation when he found defendants not guilty. In *Tumey*, the U.S. Supreme Court found that this arrangement violated due process, as it provided a temptation to the average person sitting as a judge to forget the burden of proof required to find one guilty. Kennedy seized upon the following sentence in *Tumey*: "Every procedure which would offer a possible temptation to the average man as a judge to forget the burden of proof required to convict the defendant, or which might lead him not to hold the balance nice, clear and true between the State and the accused, denies the latter due process of law."[21] According to Kennedy, the *Tumey* decision was evidence that the Supreme Court "was thus concerned with more than the traditional common-law prohibition on direct pecuniary interest. It was also concerned with a more general concept of interests that tempt adjudicators to disregard neutrality."[22] In other words, although there is no question after *Tumey* that a judge cannot constitutionally receive compensation that turns on the outcome of a decision, Kennedy also claimed that under *Tumey* there are other interests judges may have in a case that lead to due process violations.

Kennedy then explored the second type of due process case that requires recusal: where a judge has been involved in the case during an earlier proceeding. The key case that Kennedy emphasized here was *In re Murchison* (1955). *Murchison* began when a judge, in accordance with state procedures, examined witnesses to determine if criminal charges should be brought in a case, in what was colloquially referred to as a "one-man grand jury." The judge called the first witness, and after the witness testified the judge found him to be untruthful and charged him with perjury; when the second witness refused to answer questions because he did not have an attorney present, the judge charged him with contempt. The judge then tried and convicted both men of the offenses charged. The U.S. Supreme Court overturned these convictions in *Murchison*, finding a conflict of interest that required the judge's disqualification under the Due Process Clause. The *Murchison* Court found that such disqualifying criteria "cannot be defined with precision," and that "[c]ircumstances and relationships must be considered," before concluding that "[a]s a practical matter it is difficult if not impossible for a judge to free himself from the influence of what took place in his grand-jury secret session."[23] Kennedy concluded from *Murchison* his opinion that the "judge's prior relationship with the defendant, as well as the information acquired from the prior proceeding, was of critical import" in the case.[24] Recall that this was also at issue in *Tumey*, as the trial judge ordered the raid on the defendant's house, thus taking on both executive and judicial functions similar to the situation in *Murchison*.

Based on these prior cases, Kennedy established the test to be used to evaluate the constitutionality of what took place in *Caperton*: "The inquiry is an objective one. The Court asks not whether the judge is actually, subjectively biased, but whether the average judge in his position is 'likely' to be neutral, or whether there is an unconstitutional 'potential for bias.'"[25] In other words, the Court would not try to ask what Justice Benjamin may or may not have been thinking when deciding on his recusal motion and when deciding the ultimate outcome of the case in the West Virginia Supreme Court of Appeals. Instead, the Court would ask if we should expect the average person in Benjamin's situation to be impartial.

In laying down this standard, Kennedy was following in the footsteps of *Tumey*. Indeed, in *Tumey* the Court did *not* find that the judge in the case was, in fact, subjectively biased. Instead, the Court found that the *temptation* violated due process: "There are doubtless [judges] who would not allow such a consideration as $12 costs in each case to affect their judgment in it; but the requirement of due process of law in judicial procedure is not satisfied by the argument that men of the highest honor and the greatest self-sacrifice could carry it on without danger of injustice."[26] Kennedy emphasized this point later in the opinion when he stated that the "difficulties of inquiring into actual bias, and the fact that the inquiry is often a private one, simply underscore the need for objective rules... the Due Process Clause has been implemented by objective standards that do not require proof of actual bias."[27]

Kennedy then announced the holding in *Caperton*:

> We conclude that there is a serious risk of actual bias — based on objective and reasonable perceptions — when a person with a personal stake in a particular case had a significant and disproportionate influence in placing the judge on the case by raising funds or directing the judge's election campaign when the case was pending or imminent. The inquiry centers on the contribution's relative size in comparison to the total amount of money contributed to the campaign, the total amount spent in the election, and the apparent effect such contribution had on the outcome of the election.[28]

Now, that holding appears quite reasonable, but the devil lies in the details, as Kennedy's statement is rather vague. His preface to the holding made this clear: "Not every campaign contribution by a litigant or attorney creates a probability of bias that requires a judge's recusal, but this is an exceptional case."[29] This begs the question, what makes this an exceptional case? Kennedy noted that Blankenship's actions had a "significant and disproportionate influence in placing Justice Benjamin on the case," including the $3 million he spent to help elect Benjamin, which was more than the spending of all of Benjamin's other supporters, three times as much as Benjamin's own campaign committee spent, and $1 million more than the campaign committees of both Brent Benjamin and Warren McGraw.[30]

One can easily see that this set of facts is "exceptional," but it does little to inform one where that line is that separates the exceptional case from the ordinary one. What about a $1 million contribution? A $100,000 contribution? A $500 contribution? That said, Kennedy's approach is in line with *Tumey*'s standard, which emphasized how economic factors can affect one's impartiality, and with *Murchison*'s standard, which eschewed precision and instead noted the need to consider "circumstances and relationships" when ruling on issues of due process and impartiality.

Even with all of his campaign expenditures and donations, there is nothing that *proves* Blankenship's efforts put Benjamin over the top with an electoral victory. However, the Court's inquiry did not rest on the cause and effect of the outside party's influence. Instead, Kennedy argued that "Blankenship's campaign contributions — in comparison to the total amount contributed to the campaign, as well as the total amount spent in the election — had a significant and disproportionate influence on the electoral outcome," so as to violate due process.[31] This argument is a bit more tenuous than the one asking if actual bias exists or not, and it is probably not one that Kennedy needed to answer. After all, whether or not anyone was swayed by Blankenship to vote for Benjamin or against McGraw (which is an incredibly difficult question of social science), the fact remains that the direct contributions and independent expenditures in this case were so substantial that Benjamin would almost certainly have taken notice of Blankenship's actions and understood them to be financial assistance to his campaign. This was enough to raise an objective due process concern of bias. That alone, under the standard began in *Tumey* and *Murchison* and later refined by Kennedy in *Caperton*, should have been enough.

Kennedy rounded out this portion of the Court's decision by noting the importance of the timing of Blankenship's campaign spending. According to Kennedy, the "temporal relationship between the campaign contributions, the justice's election, and the pendency of the case is also critical...Blankenship's extraordinary contributions were made at a time when he had a vested stake in the outcome" of a case that Benjamin would be deciding.[32] According to Kennedy, this scenario, where "a man chooses the judge in his own case," raises fears of bias the lead to a due process violation.[33]

This point by Kennedy is both important to understanding the case, yet should be only a minor consideration in the Court's inquiry. On the one hand, the timing of the contributions can be interpreted as evidence that Blankenship was trying to place a favorable justice on the West Virginia Supreme Court of Appeals shortly before the tribunal heard his case, which certainly raises due process concerns of impartiality. On the other hand, the fact that these contributions were made just before the case was going to be decided by the West Virginia Supreme Court of Appeals should not be determinate as to whether or not there was there was, in the Court's words, "a serious risk of actual bias." After all, if Blankenship had spent $3 million directly or indirectly to help elect Benjamin ten years before his case was heard by that court, the risk that Benjamin would be biased toward helping someone who had provided him with so much past financial assistance was still present. Kennedy was right to note the timing of the contributions, but that factor should also be weighted relatively lightly when compared to the size of the financial benefit at issue, which is the biggest concern with respect to potential conflicts of interest.

Chief Justice John Roberts wrote on behalf of the four dissenters (a group that also included Justices Antonin Scalia, Clarence Thomas, and Samuel Alito) in *Caperton*.[34] Chief Justice Roberts thought that the majority's decision would have the opposite of the intended effect: "I, of course, share the majority's sincere concerns about the need to maintain a fair, independent, and impartial judiciary — and one that appears to be such. But I fear that the Court's decision will undermine rather than promote these values."[35] At first blush this appears to be counterintuitive: how can a decision that requires a judge to recuse himself when a party in a pending case spends millions of dollars to help him gain a seat on the court that will hear the case lead to less judicial impartiality? Roberts claimed that the majority's "[v]aguer notions of bias or the appearance of bias," which "cannot be defined in any limited way" will "inevitably lead to an increase in allegations that judges are biased, however groundless those charges may be. The end result will do far more to erode public confidence in judicial impartiality than an isolated failure to recuse in a particular case."[36] In other words, Roberts thought that this decision would do two things: (1) due to its lack of precision, this holding will lead to many more unjustified charges of judicial bias; and (2) the resulting flood of these claims will destroy the public's confidence in the judiciary. Each of these claims will be examined in detail.

Chief Justice Roberts began his opinion by explaining that the Court had previously only found a judge's failure to recuse himself or herself to be a Due Process Clause violation in two, limited types of circumstances: "when the judge has a financial interest in the outcome of the case, and when the judge is trying a defendant for certain criminal contempts."[37] Of course, the Chief Justice is correct that those cases involved those issues, but the Court's rulings in those cases went well beyond those narrow descriptions. *Tumey* did not just involve a judge who received additional payment in cases where he found defendants guilty. In addition, *Tumey* involved a judge who was the city's mayor. Recall from chapter six that in *Tumey* Chief Justice Taft feared not just that the judge would think about his additional take-home pay in cases, but also that he might be inappropriately thinking about his municipality's finances instead of the facts of each case.[38] Thus, the larger lesson from *Tumey* was that conflicts of interest which threaten judicial impartiality — whether they are due to the temptation of direct financial gain, the pressures of serving in another public office, or a relationship with a major electoral contributor — are also a threat to due process. Likewise, *Murchison* was about more than limiting judicial participation in certain criminal contempt cases, as it also focused on the dangers of judges presiding over cases where they have prior involvement.

Now, Chief Justice Roberts was correct to cite *Tumey* for the proposition that the Due Process Clause does not necessarily decide all questions of recusal and judicial bias. After all, Chief Justice Taft stated in *Tumey* that "[a]ll questions of judicial qualification may not involve constitutional validity…matters of kinship, personal bias, state policy, remoteness of interest, would seem generally to be matters merely of legislative discretion."[39] However, putting aside that the Court has recognized many more due process rights since the *Tumey* decision in 1927, there is nothing in *Tumey* to suggest that a case involving $3 million worth of direct and indirect financial interest fails to raise due process questions. Yet, Roberts claimed that potential conflicts like this, even when presenting a probability of bias, do not necessarily require a constitutional remedy. Indeed, Roberts believed these problems of bias are not an issue for the Court because "[m]any state statutes require recusal based on a probability or appearance of bias."[40] True, but that ducks the due process question without answering it. Indeed, Roberts claimed throughout his opinion that the Court has never held this issue to be a Due Process Clause violation, so it should not do so now. However, the Court has held due process violations in similar conflict of interest cases. The nation is well-served by a Due Process Clause that prevents judges from earning extra money when they find defendants guilty; the nation is also well-served when due process deters litigants from spending large amounts of money to elect the judge they want to hear their cases. It is not constitutional overreach in either case to invoke the Due Process Clause.

Additionally, one should not be surprised that the more direct question of judicial conflicts of interest with litigants who are also major campaign contributors is only now making its way to the U.S. Supreme Court. It is only relatively recently that judicial elections have been such major events with increased partisanship and campaign spending.[41] This is due, in part, to Court decisions on First Amendment rights that allow judicial candidates to speak on controversial issues (recall the *Republican Party v. White* case from the introductory chapter) and that allow larger amounts of money to be spent on elections via independent expenditures and 527 organizations.[42] The amount of money involved in all elections, including judicial elections, has only become greater after *Caperton* with the Court's decision in *Citizens United v. FEC* (2010), which held that the First Amendment bars government limits on independent political spending by corporations and labor unions.[43] Finally, there is no guarantee that state judicial ethics codes and statutes will require recusal in these types of cases. Obviously, West Virginia did not have a clear rule or law to require recusal in this case. Chief Justice Roberts' notion that this conflict of interest can be handled by the states rings quite hollow if some states fail to do so.

Next, Chief Justice Roberts noted that the majority was too vague and that their standard makes it impossible to know when a case requires judicial recusal and when it does not: "the standard the majority articulates — 'probability of bias' — fails to provide clear, workable guidance for future cases."[44] Roberts then went on to list forty questions, each of which probed into the majority's relatively vague standard, asking how do we know when the amount of money contributed is "too much" money, how long does the probability of bias last, what if the judicial candidate disclaims the support of the litigant, how do we determine the impact that the financial contributions had on the outcome of the election, etc.[45] Granted, the majority's standard was not the clearest one articulated in a Supreme Court case. That said, the Due Process Clause has long been interpreted by the Court as vague, flexible, and adapting to different sets of circumstances. Indeed, as the Court once noted, "[d]ue process cannot be measured in minutes and hours or dollars and cents."[46] Instead, as the world changes, new issues arise under the Due Process Clause, which is designed, in part, to ensure an impartial judge. When the Court enters a new area like what was at stake in *Caperton*, more questions may be raised initially than answers given, but future cases will ultimately always give flesh to the bare bones that are formed in seminal cases like *Caperton*. As long as the Court takes one case at a time, cases decided today will always raise new questions that lead to future litigation tomorrow. Furthermore, *Caperton*'s core principle — that when a party with a personal stake in a particular case has a significant and disproportionate influence in placing the judge on the case, a serious risk of actual bias is created that violates due process — is a relatively simple concept to grasp. While there is some question how this precedent will apply in future cases, there is no doubt that as a general rule it makes sense.

Still, Chief Justice Roberts feared that *Caperton* would open the floodgates to claims of judicial conflicts of interest, asserting that it would "inevitably lead to an increase in allegations that judges are biased."[47] However, the U.S. Supreme Court has not decided a case since *Caperton* in which it was asked to decide if a judge was required to recuse himself or herself under the Due Process Clause. Given the forty questions posed by Roberts, one would expect countless cases to come before the Court for clarification. Yet, this has not happened, which can probably best be explained by the majority's belief that *Caperton* was based on "extreme facts." Even if a flurry of these claims are raised, the solution to a biased judge is simple: a new judge is assigned to handle the case! Recall that in the West Virginia Supreme Court of Appeals, two conflict of interest substitutions were made before the rehearing of *Caperton*. The substitution of Justice Benjamin with another judge who did not have financial ties to a litigant in the case would have solved the bias problem without too great of a drag on judicial economy.

Finally, Chief Justice Roberts disagreed with the majority that this was an extreme set of facts. Roberts correctly pointed out with respect to the $3 million Blankenship spent, that "[o]ther than a $1,000 direct contribution from Blankenship, *Justice Benjamin and his campaign had no control over how this money was spent.*"[48] Although this is true, it is the equivalent of sticking one's head in the sand. There may be a case where a litigant spends large sums of money to run advertisements in favor of a judicial candidate, the litigant really does not want the judicial candidate to win, and the real goal of the litigant is to establish a false "conflict of interest" that requires the judge to be recused from the case. Given the oddity of spending millions of dollars to help elect someone you despise, when you might be able to redirect that money to help someone you would like to see elected, such a scenario is far-fetched. And even if it might happen, common sense indicates that this was not what happened in *Caperton*. Blankenship spent quite a bit of money to help elect someone to a judicial post who would be deciding a case where he was a litigant, and this candidate was someone Blankenship wanted to see elected because he thought it increased the change that he would win his appeal. Justice Benjamin, whether his victory was due to Blankenship or not, was aware of Blankenship's spending, and this was not something we would objectively expect a judge to forget. Since this factor would likely weigh on his mind regardless of the arguments and evidence presented in *Caperton*, recusal was the safest course, and it is the constitutionally required course if judicial impartiality is to be preserved. Indeed, in *Tumey*, the judge who was earning extra money for finding defendants guilty did not put in place the law that gave him that benefit; he only benefitted from it. In *Caperton*, another West Virginia Supreme Court of Appeals justice "just happened" to be vacationing with Blankenship, but this level of involvement with a litigant prevented that justice from being impartial. The same was true for Justice Benjamin.

Ultimately, *Caperton* stands for the proposition that neither justice, nor a justice, should be bought by the highest bidder who is litigating a case. Although Don Blankenship was free to spend as much money as he wanted on his legal team and in defense of his position in the case, and even though he had a First Amendment right to spend millions of his own dollars to help defeat the election of a sitting state supreme court justice, he did not have a right to help engineer the election of a judge so that the judge could subsequently decide his legal case. The majority was correct to set down the rule in this case that such scenarios require recusal under the Due Process Clause to ensure that public confidence in the impartiality of judges is protected. Although more clarification will be needed before the exact contours of *Caperton* will be known, it is a good start at making sure that a just process is protected.

The Chief Justice's dissent, while passionate and raising good points, fell short of the mark. Roberts's proposed legal system would leave the Due Process Clause silent on such questions, instead abandoning these issues for resolution in state judicial ethics codes. While that might protect litigants in some, and perhaps many, cases, it would also mean that some cases in states with weak codes and laws would slip through the cracks. If the Constitution demands an impartial decisionmaker, then the recusal of judges in cases like this is demanded by the Constitution as well. Although the precise issue of judicial impartiality's relation to judicial elections is a fairly new one for the Court, thus creating the possibility that a flood of cases will result, three years after *Caperton* was decided, that flood has not yet come. In fact, there is little evidence that *Caperton* has led to any rise in the tide of cases on judicial impartiality.

As for the parties in the case, including Hugh Caperton and the A.T. Massey Coal Company, their case was remanded back to the West Virginia Supreme Court of Appeals. Justice Brent Benjamin, by virtue of the U.S. Supreme Court's decision, did not participate in the case. In the fall of 2009, the West Virginia Supreme Court of Appeals concluded that the trial court should have granted A.T. Massey Coal's motion to dismiss the case, based on the forum selection clause in the contract between the litigants that required adjudication of disputes in Virginia.[49] Thus, Blankenship ultimately prevailed on the legal claim against Caperton. There was no question about the justices being impartial this time around. The case was given a fair hearing in the West Virginia Supreme Court of Appeals in front of justices who had no legal or financial ties to Blankenship. Due process prevailed. Because of his electoral spending spree and the resulting U.S. Supreme Court case, Don Blankenship ensured (although not intentionally) that litigants in future cases could not do what he tried to do — spend millions of dollars to get a favorable judge on his own case.

Notes

1. *See, e.g.*, Richard Gillespie, "Buying a Judicial Seat for Appeal: *Caperton v. A.T. Massey Coal Company, Inc.*, is Right out of a John Grisham Novel," *Journal of the National Association of Administrative Law Judiciary* 30 (2010): 309-352; Joan Biskupic, "Supreme Court Case with the Feel of a Best Seller," *USA Today*, February 16, 2009, http://www.usatoday.com/news/washington/2009-02-16-grisham-court_N.htm (accessed January 29, 2012); Scott Finn, "Caperton v. Massey: What a Long, Strange Case It's Been," West Virginia Public Broadcasting, June 9, 2009, http://www.wvpubcast.org/newsarticle.aspx?id=9955 (accessed January 29, 2012).

2. *Caperton v. A.T. Massey Coal*, 2007 W. Va. LEXIS 119, 6-20.

3. *Caperton v. A.T. Massey Coal*, 129 S. Ct. 2252, 2257 (2009); David W. Neubauer and Henry F. Fradella, *America's Courts and the Criminal Justice System, 10th Edition* (Belmont, CA: Wadsworth, 2011), 446.

4. "Justice Warren McGraw," McGraw 4 Justice, 2004, http://www.nurelm.com/examples/warren_mcgraw/ (accessed January 29, 2012).

5. Finn, "Caperton v. Massey: What a Long, Strange Case It's Been;" West Virginia Humanities Council, "Brent Benjamin," *The West Virginia Encyclopedia*, November 22, 2010, http://www.wvencyclopedia.org/articles/2319 (accessed January 29, 2012).

6. *See* Adam Liptak, "Judicial Races in Several States Become Partisan Battlegrounds," *The New York Times*, October 24, 2004, http://www.nytimes.com/2004/10/24/politics/campaign/24judicial.html (accessed January 29, 2012).

7. *Caperton*, 129 S. Ct. at 2257.

8. *Caperton*, 129 S. Ct. at 2257.

9. Liptak, "Judicial Races in Several States Become Partisan Battlegrounds."

10. And for the Sake of the Kids, "Tired," June 24, 2009, http://www.youtube.com/watch?v=xL9Lj6WlILg (accessed January 29, 2012).

11. *See, e.g.*, And for the Sake of the Kids, "Believe," June 15, 2009, http://www.youtube.com/watch?feature=endscreen&v=qyb8xLTJ6SM&NR=1 (accessed January 29, 2012); And for the Sake of the Kids, "Wrong Again," June 24, 2009, http://www.youtube.com/watch?v=kzCSMqVMZjI&feature=related (accessed January 29, 2012); And for the Sake of the Kids, "Brothers," June 15, 2009, http://www.youtube.com/watch?v=Xl2wZXJvWk4&feature=related (accessed January 29, 2012).

12. *Caperton*, 129 S. Ct. at 2257.

13. *Caperton*, 129 S. Ct. at 2257-58.

14. *Caperton*, 2007 W. Va. LEXIS 119.

15. *Caperton*, 129 S. Ct. at 2258; ———, "U.S. Supreme Court Is Asked to Fix Troubled West Virginia Justice System," *The New York Times*, October 11, 2008, http://www.nytimes.com/2008/10/12/washington/12scotus.html (accessed January 29, 2012).

16. *Caperton*, 129 S. Ct. at 2258; Adam Liptak, "Motion Ties W. Virginia Justice to Coal Executive," *The New York Times*, January 15, 2008, http://www.nytimes.com/2008/01/15/us/15court.html (accessed January 29, 2012).

17. *Caperton*, 129 S. Ct. at 2258.
18. *Caperton v. A.T. Massey Coal*, 223 W. Va. 624, 685 n.16, 686 (2008).
19. *Caperton*, 129 S. Ct. at 2256-57 (2009).
20. *Caperton*, 129 S. Ct. at 2259-62.
21. *Caperton*, 129 S. Ct. at 2260 (quoting *Tumey v. Ohio*, 273 U.S. 510, 532 (1927)).
22. *Caperton*, 129 S. Ct. at 2260.
23. *Caperton*, 129 S. Ct. at 2261 (internal quotations omitted).
24. *Caperton*, 129 S. Ct. at 2262.
25. *Caperton*, 129 S. Ct. at 2262.
26. *Tumey*, 273 U.S. at 532.
27. *Caperton*, 129 S. Ct. at 2263.
28. *Caperton*, 129 S. Ct. at 2263-64.
29. *Caperton*, 129 S. Ct. at 2263.
30. *Caperton*, 129 S. Ct. at 2264.
31. *Caperton*, 129 S. Ct. at 2264.
32. *Caperton*, 129 S. Ct. at 2264-65.
33. *Caperton*, 129 S. Ct. at 2265.
34. Justice Scalia also wrote a brief dissent: *Caperton*, 129 S. Ct. at 2274-75 (Scalia, J., dissenting).
35. *Caperton*, 129 S. Ct. at 2267 (Roberts, C.J., dissenting).
36. *Caperton*, 129 S. Ct. at 2267 (Roberts, C.J., dissenting).
37. *Caperton*, 129 S. Ct. at 2267 (Roberts, C.J., dissenting).
38. *Tumey*, 273 U.S. at 533.
39. *Tumey*, 273 U.S. at 523.
40. *Caperton*, 129 S. Ct. at 2268 (Roberts, C.J., dissenting) (italics omitted).
41. *See* David E. Pozen, "The Irony of Judicial Elections," *Columbia Law Review*, 108 (2008): 265-330.
42. *See Republican Party of Minnesota v. White*, 536 U.S. 765 (2002) and *Federal Election Commission v. Wisconsin Right to Life, Inc.*, 551 U.S. 449 (2007).
43. *Citizens United v. FEC*, 130 S. Ct. 876 (2010).
44. *Caperton*, 129 S. Ct. at 2269 (Roberts, C.J., dissenting).
45. See *Caperton*, 2269-72 (Roberts, C.J., dissenting).
46. *Taylor v. Hayes*, 418 U.S. 488, 500 (1974).
47. *Caperton*, 129 S. Ct. at 2267 (Roberts, C.J., dissenting).
48. *Caperton*, 129 S. Ct. at 2273 (Roberts, C.J., dissenting) (emphasis in original).
49. *Caperton v. A.T. Massey Coal Co.*, 225 W. Va. 128 (2009).

Part Three:

Due Process and the Right to an Impartial Decisionmaker in Quasi-Judicial, Non-Court Settings

~ 11 ~

Parole Revocation: *Morrissey v. Brewer* (1972)

[D]ue process requires that after the arrest, the determination that reasonable ground exists for revocation of parole should be made by someone not directly involved in the case...there should be an uninvolved person to make this preliminary evaluation of the basis for believing the conditions of parole have been violated.
– *Morrissey v. Brewer*, 408 U.S. 471, 485-86 (1972)

[T]he minimum requirements of due process...include...
a neutral and detached hearing body such as a traditional parole board.
– *Morrissey v. Brewer*, 408 U.S. 471, 488-89 (1972)

Up to this point, we have examined cases which have taken place in a courtroom. The question of impartiality has applied to a judge, a jury, or both. Yet, there are other contexts in which public institutions exercise quasi-judicial powers and must make legal decisions which implicate due process and the need for impartiality and neutrality. As the next few chapters will demonstrate, the rights at stake here can be just as great as those that are to be decided at a criminal trial. In some contexts, one's property or one's ultimate freedom hangs in the balance, thus necessitating that the decisionmaker follows the highest constitutional standards. Parole revocation is one area where a person's liberty is at stake.

Parole is the early, conditional release from prison before a full sentence has been served. It is done for inmates who have demonstrated good behavior while incarcerated. In states that maintain discretionary parole, an inmate's case is typically reviewed by a parole board which is trusted with the power to determine if the inmate is worthy of release. The increased freedom is granted on the stipulation that the parolee regularly reports to a parole officer for a specified period of time. A parolee must also live under certain conditions that are more restrictive than those imposed on the average citizen. For instance, these restrictions may include abstaining from alcohol and not having associations or correspondence with certain people. Parolees may also need to receive permission from their parole officers before taking part in certain activities, including changing employment, changing addresses, obtaining or driving automobiles, or traveling outside of the county or state. Failure to follow these rules, failure to report to a parole officer, or commission of a new crime can result in the revocation of parole and the return of the parolee to prison. The practice of parole is nothing new in the United States, as some states, most notably New York and Massachusetts, began using indeterminate sentencing and instituting parole boards in the 1880s. During the twentieth century, parole became an established part of the American criminal justice system as a way to help convicted criminals reintegrate into society. It also serves to help lower prison costs by creating an incentive for inmates to behave well and to be released from prison earlier than scheduled.[1]

Just as there is often discretion in the jury's decision to convict a defendant, the judge's decision to sentence that defendant, and the parole board's decision to release a prisoner, there is frequently discretion in the decision to revoke a parolee's parole and send that person back to prison. And when there is discretion, a decisionmaker might make that decision with bias. In such instances, what constitutional standards apply? This question was answered by the U.S. Supreme Court in *Morrissey v. Brewer* (1972).

The story of *Morrissey* began when John J. Morrissey pleaded guilty to false drawing or uttering of checks in January of 1967 in the Linn County District Court in Iowa. The judge sentenced Morrissey to a prison term of not more than seven years. Morrissey was transported to the Iowa State Penitentiary, where he stayed as a guest of the Hawkeye State until he was paroled on June 20, 1968. He then enjoyed his relative freedom until his parole officer ordered him arrested on a parole violation seven months later on January 24, 1969. His parole officer submitted a report on January 28, 1969, detailing numerous parole violations, including buying an automobile under an assumed name and operating it without permission, falsely reporting to police his address and insurance company after a minor accident, obtaining credit under an assumed name, and failing to report his place of residence to his parole officer. In the report, Morrissey's parole officer asserted that he interviewed Morrissey, and that the parolee could not explain why he failed to contact his parole officer. The report also stated that Morrissey admitted in the interview to buying a car, obtaining credit under an assumed name, and being involved in an auto accident. His parole officer recommended that Morrissey's parole be revoked because of Morrissey's "continual violating of his parole rules." After reviewing Morrissey's parole officer report, the Iowa Board of Parole agreed and revoked his parole on January 31, 1969. Morrissey was then sent back to the Iowa State Penitentiary. Following state practice, Morrissey was not given a hearing before his parole was revoked, but he was afforded a hearing before the Board of Parole on February 12, 1969. The Board found him to be in violation of his parole.[2]

Not satisfied with this result, Morrissey filed a petition with the Lee County, Iowa District Court, alleging that he should have been granted a hearing to determine if he had, in fact, violated his parole *before* he was sent back to prison. Without such a hearing, Morrissey claimed that he was denied due process. The district court denied his petition on June 26, 1969. He then filed a petition for a state writ of habeas corpus, which was denied. His appeal to the Supreme Court of Iowa was denied on September 12, 1969. Morrissey's next step was to file for a federal writ of habeas corpus, where he again argued that his right to due process was violated because he was not afforded a hearing before his parole was revoked. A federal judge in the Southern District Court of Iowa denied that petition on April 15, 1970.[3]

G. Donald Booher's story is quite similar to that of Morrissey's. Booher pleaded guilty to forgery in April of 1966 in the O'Brien County District Court in Iowa. Booher was sentenced to serve a maximum term of ten years in prison. After serving a portion of this term in the Iowa State Penitentiary, Booher was paroled on November 14, 1968. Less than one year later, in August of 1969, Booher was arrested for violating his parole. According to a report submitted on September 8, 1969, the conditions that his parole officer claimed Booher violated were leaving the county without consent, obtaining an Iowa driver's license under an assumed name, unlawfully operating a motor vehicle, and not being gainfully employed. Booher's parole officer wrote that he had interviewed Booher, who admitted to leaving the county without permission, operating the automobile, and obtaining a license under an assumed name. The parole officer recommended parole revocation. The Iowa Board of Parole reviewed the report of Booher's parole officer, and based on this the board revoked Booher's parole on September 13, 1969. Just like Morrissey, Booher then returned to the Iowa State Penitentiary. He was given a hearing on October 14, 1969, where the Board of Parole confirmed its earlier revocation decision.[4]

Booher also then turned to the courts for relief. He filed for a writ of habeas corpus in Lee County, Iowa, claiming that his due process rights were violated because his parole was taken without a prior hearing. On November 26, 1969, the court denied his petition. Booher also filed numerous other unsuccessful motions in the Lee County District Court. He did not file a habeas appeal to the Iowa Supreme Court because by then Morrissey's case had been denied by the same court. In addition, Booher was advised by the County Attorney of O'Brien County, Iowa that the state supreme court had already ruled that a parolee was not entitled to a hearing on parole revocation. Booher, like Morrissey, then filed a federal habeas petition, which was denied by the United States District Court for the Southern District of Iowa on June 16, 1970.[5]

When both Morrissey and Booher appealed to the Eighth Circuit Court of Appeals, that court consolidated the cases. By a split vote of 4-3, that court held that due process did not require a hearing for either parolee. The majority of the court of appeals characterized parole as a privilege and not a right, and citing a previous ruling of the Iowa Supreme Court, the court of appeals stated that "parole is a matter of grace on the part of the sovereign" and that "a defendant acquires no vested rights when granted a parole." Unhappy with this ruling, Morrissey and Booher appealed to the U.S. Supreme Court. They came armed with some rather telling information. In the 540 most recent Iowa revocations, only one was reversed by the Board of Parole at the parolees' post-revocation hearings. Unlike every other court that had previously heard their claims, the Supreme Court found that both men's rights had been violated in *Morrissey v. Brewer.*[6]

Writing for the Court, Chief Justice Warren Burger first noted the rights associated with being on parole from prison: "Implicit in the system's concern with parole violations is the notion that the parolee is entitled to retain his liberty as long as he substantially abides by the conditions of his parole."[7] Burger explained that there are two questions to be resolved anytime a parole revocation decision is to be made. First, a factual question must be answered to determine if a parolee in fact did violate any conditions of his or her parole, including committing a new crime. If it has been determined that a parolee *did* violate one of these conditions, then the second question is to determine if the parolee should be sent back to prison or if other remedial steps should be taken. Burger characterized the first question as relatively simple and the second as potentially much more complex, because the second question "involves the application of expertise in the parole authority in making a prediction as to the ability of the individual to live in society without committing antisocial acts," and it is a determination that is "predictive and discretionary."[8]

The Chief Justice then proceeded to define how many rights were at stake, and they were not all of the rights that are afforded to the average American citizen who is accused of a crime: "the revocation of parole is not part of a criminal prosecution and thus the full panoply of rights due a defendant in such a proceeding does not apply to parole revocations."[9] Since parole occurs after a defendant has had a criminal trial, there are certain assumptions built into the process, including the assumption that the prisoner is guilty of the crime charged. Thus, the liberty calculus is altered by this determination of factual guilt. According to Burger, parole revocation "deprives an individual, not of the absolute liberty to which every citizen is entitled, but only of the conditional liberty properly dependent on observance of special parole restrictions."[10]

The first issue at stake in *Morrissey* was whether parole revocation causes one a grievous loss of rights protected by the Fourteenth Amendment or not. If there is a liberty or property interest that is implicated in parole revocation, then due process applies, and the issue remains *how much* process is due, as not all procedural deprivation of rights require the same procedures. As explained by the Chief Justice, "due process is flexible and calls for such procedural protections as the particular situation demands."[11] Burger then went on to describe the liberty at stake for one who is on parole:

> The liberty of a parolee enables him to do a wide range of things open to persons who have never been convicted of any crime. The parolee has been released from prison based on an evaluation that he shows reasonable promise of being able to return to society and function as a responsible, self-reliant person. Sub-

ject to the conditions of his parole, he can be gainfully employed and is free to be with family and friends and to form the other enduring attachments of normal life. Though the State properly subjects him to many restrictions not applicable to other citizens, his condition is very different from that of confinement in a prison. He may have been on parole for a number of years and may be living a relatively normal life at the time he is faced with revocation. The parolee has relied on at least an implicit promise that parole will be revoked only if he fails to live up to the parole conditions. In many cases, the parolee faces lengthy incarceration if his parole is revoked.[12]

Thus, a great deal of liberty is at stake for a parolee facing revocation, and the penalty imposed can be very great. Although the average parolee, either now or in 1972, lives under many more restrictions than the average person, the average parolee still enjoys many freedoms that the average prison inmate does not. This led Burger to declare that "the liberty of a parolee, although indeterminate, includes many of the core values of unqualified liberty and its termination inflicts a 'grievous loss' on the parolee and often on others," which is "within the protection of the Fourteenth Amendment," calling for "some orderly process, however informal."[13]

Given that these liberty interests are at stake, the Court needed to confirm what process is due to a parolee facing revocation. Since a parolee has already been convicted of a crime and subsequently granted conditional release, the process required to return that parolee back to prison is necessarily less than the process due to a criminal defendant who has not been convicted. Still, the Court found that some procedural guarantees are necessary for the parolee before facing revocation, and these are not outweighed by administrative problems in providing a timely hearing to such parolees. Burger then took his argument into an interesting direction. He claimed that it is not just the parolee who has a stake in his or her conditional liberty. In addition, Burger claimed that "[s]ociety has a stake in whatever may be the chance of restoring [a parolee] to normal and useful life within the law."[14] Thus, society has an interest in making sure that parole is not revoked for erroneous reasons and in making sure that parolees are treated with basic fairness. This is a unique argument by Burger, and it is one that he did not fully explore. What is clear, however, is that "there is no interest on the part of the State in revoking parole without any procedural guarantees at all," thus requiring at least an informal hearing to verify facts before a parole board exercises its discretion.[15]

So what process was constitutionally due to Morrissey and Booher? As parolees, they were guaranteed a preliminary hearing by an independent officer, followed by a more formal hearing by a parole board or something similar to it. Chief Justice Burger's first point of emphasis was in a neutral, independent decisionmaker in the preliminary determination of whether or not a parolee has violated his or her parole:

[D]ue process requires that after the arrest, the determination that reasonable ground exists for revocation of parole should be made by someone not directly

> involved in the case. It would be unfair to assume that the supervising parole officer does not conduct an interview with the parolee to confront him with the reasons for revocation before he recommends an arrest. It would also be unfair to assume that the parole officer bears hostility against the parolee that destroys his neutrality; realistically the failure of the parolee is in a sense a failure for his supervising officer. However, we need make no assumptions one way or the other to conclude that there should be an uninvolved person to make this preliminary evaluation of the basis for believing the conditions of parole have been violated. The officer directly involved in making recommendations cannot always have complete objectivity in evaluating them.[16]

Given the seriousness of the liberty interest at stake, the decisionmaker on the issue of parole revocation must be neutral. But as Burger correctly pointed out, a parole officer may be less than impartial in this context. The parole officer is often the one who investigates what a parolee is doing and then the one who recommends revocation for parole violations, much akin to the role of the law enforcement and prosecution in criminal cases. Although there are many law enforcement personnel and prosecutors who do their jobs quite well and who can be objective, there is no question that we still want a neutral third party to review the case and give the accused a fair hearing before another set of eyes. The same holds true in the parole revocation context, where a parolee should have his or her case reviewed by someone other than the investigating party.

Chief Justice Burger also recalled *Goldberg v. Kelly* (1970), a case where a welfare caseworker was found to have violated the Constitution for taking away a recipient's welfare benefits without a hearing first. In *Goldberg*, the Court did not find bias in that caseworker, yet it still required that an independent decisionmaker had to review the decision in a pre-termination hearing.[17] The same logic held true in *Morrissey*: without determining that a parole officer is biased, his or her decision must be reviewed by an independent, impartial decisionmaker. However, Burger went on to clarify that, just like *Goldberg*, for parole revocation, this "independent officer need not be a judicial officer," because "[t]he granting and revocation of parole are matters traditionally handled by administrative officers."[18] With this in mind, Burger and the Court required that in the parole revocation context, the determination of whether or not parole should be revoked shall be "made by someone such as a parole officer other than the one who has made the report of parole violations or has recommended revocation."[19] Even though the *Goldberg* Court did not require that a welfare benefits termination hearing be "before the traditional 'neutral and detached' officer," Burger thought it necessary that "the minimum requirements of due process" for a parole revocation include "a 'neutral and detached' hearing body such as a traditional parole board."[20] Thus, Burger and the Court found that the greater liberty interest in a parolee's freedom required a greater level of neutrality in the person or persons conducting the revocation hearing.

Burger drew a line between the requirements for the preliminary hearing officer and the revocation board. As noted above, the preliminary hearing officer needs to only be independent from the parole officer handling the parolee's case. The body making the formal revocation determination, however, needs to be more fully neutral and detached. Although impartiality is implicated in both hearings, the latter hearing requires more and assumes that the role of the decisionmaker is more akin to that of a court.

Putting in place the right to impartial decisionmakers at both the preliminary and formal hearing stages for parole revocation, Burger turned to other due process mandates at these hearings, including the rights to notice, to present evidence, and to a limited form of confrontation and cross-examination. He then specified that the hearing officers need to make decisions that are based on what occurs at the hearings: "The hearing officer shall have the duty of making a summary, or digest, of what occurs at the hearing in terms of the responses of the parolee and the substance of the documents or evidence given in support of parole revocation and of the parolee's position."[21] Furthermore, this must be "a written statement by the factfinders as to the evidence relied on and reasons for revoking parole."[22] Although Burger did not frame it this way, this requirement ultimately protects the right to a neutral decisionmaker because a written statement detailing what evidence was compelling and why the parole revocation decision was made helps to ensure that decisionmakers are making rulings based on the evidence in front of them, and not based on some bias for a parole officer or against a parolee. Finally, Burger and the Court required that a formal hearing before the parole board, if desired by the parolee, must take place before the final decision on parole revocation. Based on these standards, the Court remanded Morrissey and Booher's cases to let the district court determine if these procedures were properly followed.[23]

Justice William Brennan wrote a concurring opinion, which was joined by Justice Thurgood Marshall. Brennan agreed with the majority that under the Due Process Clause parole cannot be revoked unless there is (1) a preliminary hearing at arrest to determine if there is probable cause that parole conditions were violated and (2) a final hearing to determine if those conditions were, in fact, violated. Brennan also agreed with the majority's procedural requirements at these hearings, including the due process requirement that "in each case the decisionmaker must be impartial, there must be some record of the proceedings, and the decisionmaker's conclusions must be set forth in written form indicating both the evidence and the reasons relied upon."[24] Brennan only wrote separately to confirm these points and to state that he believed the Due Process Clause also requires the assistance of counsel at these hearings.[25]

Justice William Douglas wrote a partial dissent in *Morrissey*. Also appealing to *Goldberg v. Kelly*, Douglas found a property interest in the right to parole, due to the degree of liberty which is associated with such a status. Drawing upon *Goldberg*, Douglas proclaimed that "[v]iolations of conditions of parole may be technical, they may be done unknowingly, they may be fleeting and of no consequence," so the "parolee should, in the concept of fairness implicit in due process, have a chance to explain" because the "charges may or may not be true."[26]

For Douglas, the Fourteenth Amendment's procedural due process requirements include that a parole revocation hearing "should not be before the parole officer, as he is the one who is making the charge and there is inherent danger in combining the functions of judge and advocate."[27] In doing so, Douglas made the point more forthrightly than Burger did that the parole officer's function is similar to that of a prosecutor and the parole board's function is more like that of a judge: "the parole officer — whatever may be his duties under various state statutes — in Iowa appears to be an agent having some of the functions of a prosecutor and of the police: the parole officer is therefore not qualified as a hearing officer."[28] Thus, for a parolee to be afforded due process, the person conducting the review should be impartial, and the parole officer cannot fulfill that task, given his or her investigatory roles. In addition, Douglas disagreed with the preliminary hearing approach of the majority, instead wishing that parolees be entitled to their freedom until the parole board makes the final determination as to revocation. Due to these considerations, Douglas would have gone farther than the other justices and reversed the judgments outright.[29]

The Court was right in *Morrissey* to require a system of both preliminary and later full hearings, in front of neutral arbiters, for parolees facing revocation. Understanding that parole revocation proceedings trigger due process protections is no giant leap, as they do involve a liberty interest, albeit less than what is at stake in criminal proceedings. Still, the role of the probation officer is analogous to the prosecutor, making it necessary for another official to review that person's determination before sending a parolee back to prison. Although Justice Douglas offered a more comprehensive approach to reviewing parolee revocation before that person returns to prison, such review may prove to be unrealistic. Furthermore, since the parolee already has less than the full panoply of rights and is under significant supervision, holding a preliminary hearing promptly, with full review after incarceration, is in line with the Fourteenth Amendment's requirement of due process. There is a balance here, as a parolee has less of a personal interest in avoiding temporary detainment, and, therefore, less procedural protection is needed in response to such detainment. The preliminary hearing bridges the gap between temporary detention and the more formal hearing by the parole board later.[30]

For the present purposes, the most important aspect of either the preliminary hearing or the more formal hearing is the need for the decisionmaker to be "neutral and detached." The parole officer who arrests the parolee does not fit this bill. In addition, to be neutral the decisionmakers at these revocation hearings must produce written statements that explain the reasons for revocation and the evidence relied upon to make this decision. This further requirement protects the neutrality requirement, both in appearance and reality, because it helps to prevent the decisionmaker from being a rubber stamp for the original parole officer. Instead, a factual basis must support a decision to revoke one's parole.[31]

Morrissey and Booher were not provided an opportunity to have their revocation decisions reviewed by a neutral decisionmaker prior to being sent back to prison. They needed a preliminary hearing before such a decisionmaker in order for their due process rights to be protected. Indeed, as the data in Iowa showed, without a preliminary review, there was a slim to none chance that any parolee would have a revocation decision overturned, implying a possible lack of impartiality if the first review is at that late stage in the process.

Although there is little known about what ever happened to either Morrissey or Booher, their case had a far reaching impact. In addition to requiring a whole host of due process procedures for parolees facing revocation (including the right to a neutral decisionmaker), *Morrissey* served as a precedent that helped to expand these requirements into other areas. For instance, the U.S. Supreme Court used *Morrissey* as precedent when it declared in *Gagnon v. Scarpelli* (1973) that due process requires probationers to be afforded the same preliminary and final revocation hearings as are required for parolees. As part of this process, the *Gagnon* court also required that the final probation revocation hearing must be before "a neutral and detached hearing body."[32] Furthermore, the Court relied on *Morrissey* in *Wolff v. McDonnell* (1974) to impose due process procedural requirements for prison inmates facing disciplinary procedures. One of the requirements addressed by the Court in *Wolff* was the need for an impartial decisionmaker; the majority in that case ultimately declined to find that a prison adjustment committee was not impartial according to Due Process Clause requirements.[33]

Notes

1. Bryan A. Garner, ed., *Black's Law Dictionary* (St. Paul, MN: West, 2009), 1127; Adam L. Pollock, "Using Parole to Constitutionally Reconcile the Criminal Punishment Goals of Desert and Incapacitation," *University of Pennsylvania Journal of Constitutional Law* 8 (2006): 115-141, 132-33; *Morrissey v. Brewer*, 408 U.S. 471, 477-79 (1972).
2. *Morrissey v. Brewer*, 443 F.2d 942, 943 & n.1 (8th Cir. 1971); *Morrissey*, 408 U.S. at 472-73, 476.
3. *Morrissey*, 443 F.2d at 944-45 &n.3; *Morrissey*, 408 U.S. at 474.
4. *Morrissey*, 443 F.2d at 944 & n.2; *Morrissey*, 408 U.S. at 473-74, 476.
5. *Morrissey*, 443 F.2d at 944-45 &n.3; *Morrissey*, 408 U.S. at 474.
6. *Morrissey*, 443 F.2d at 945-46; *Morrissey*, 408 U.S. at 474-75.
7. *Morrissey*, 408 U.S. at 479.
8. *Morrissey*, 408 U.S. at 479-80.
9. *Morrissey*, 408 U.S. at 480.
10. *Morrissey*, 408 U.S. at 480.
11. *Morrissey*, 408 U.S. at 481.
12. *Morrissey*, 408 U.S. at 482.
13. *Morrissey*, 408 U.S. at 482.
14. *Morrissey*, 408 U.S. at 484.
15. *Morrissey*, 408 U.S. at 484.

16. *Morrissey*, 408 U.S. at 485-86.
17. *Goldberg v. Kelly*, 397 U.S. 254 (1970).
18. *Morrissey*, 408 U.S. at 486.
19. *Morrissey*, 408 U.S. at 486.
20. *Morrissey*, 408 U.S. at 486, 488-89.
21. *Morrissey*, 408 U.S. at 487.
22. *Morrissey*, 408 U.S. at 489.
23. *Morrissey*, 408 U.S. at 490.
24. *Morrissey*, 408 U.S. at 491 (Brennan, J., concurring).
25. *Morrissey*, 408 U.S. at 491 (Brennan, J., concurring).
26. *Morrissey*, 408 U.S. at 495 (Douglas, J., dissenting in part).
27. *Morrissey*, 408 U.S. at 498 (Douglas, J., dissenting in part) (internal citations omitted).
28. *Morrissey*, 408 U.S. at 499-500 (Douglas, J., dissenting in part).
29. *Morrissey*, 408 U.S. at 500 (Douglas, J., dissenting in part).
30. Randy Lee, "Twenty-Five Years after *Goldberg v. Kelly*: Traveling from the Right Spot on the Wrong Road to the Wrong Place," *Capital University Law Review* 23 (1994): 863-1002, 953.
31. Mihal Nahari, "Due Process and Probation Revocation: The Written Statement Requirement," *Fordham Law Review* 56 (1988): 759-82, 770-71.
32. *Gagnon v. Scarpelli*, 411 U.S. 778, 786 (1973) (quoting *Morrissey*, 408 U.S. at 489).
33. *Wolff v. McDonnell*, 418 U.S. 539 (1974).

~ 12 ~

Medical License Review: *Withrow v. Larkin* (1975)

> [A] fair trial in a fair tribunal is a basic requirement of due process. This applies to administrative agencies which adjudicate as well as to courts. Not only is a biased decisionmaker constitutionally unacceptable but our system of law has always endeavored to prevent even the probability of unfairness.
> – *Withrow v. Larkin*, 421 U.S. 35, 46–47 (1975)

As noted in the introduction, the practice of licensing medical doctors dates back centuries. The practice originated in Europe in the Middle Ages, as a way to structure medieval society and as part of the standardization and code creation that was occurring generally in Europe during that period. The first evidence of real licensure, involving a required academic curriculum, field experience, an examination, and standards of practice, emerged in the 1230s under Hohenstaufen emperor Frederick II. Over time, other kingdoms in Europe began to follow suit, often with requirements to complete university coursework and examinations, before a university chancellor conferred the medical license upon the graduate. Early on, the chancellors presided over religious universities and were representatives of the Catholic Church, meaning that new doctors were given the privilege to practice in any Christian country; practicing without a license could subject one to excommunication in addition to other legal prosecution. The facts of *Dr. Bonham's Case* (1610) indicate that the Royal College of Physicians in London was empowered by the English Parliament to regulate the local practice of medicine at least as early as the sixteenth century. Except for graduates of Oxford and Cambridge, the president and three members of the college examined and approved those who were allowed to practice medicine anywhere in England.[1]

During the early colonial period in America, much like there were few licensed lawyers, there was no licensure of medical doctors. There was a shortage of doctors, so those with medical skills were welcomed, and an apprentice system developed over time. By the mid-eighteenth century, however, the idea of licensing of physicians was taking root. For instance, in 1753, a New York newspaper remarked that regulation of the medical profession was necessary to prevent "the dismal havock [*sic*] made by quacks and pretenders." Spurred on by this public sentiment, the New York Provincial Assembly passed the first colonial licensure law in 1760. In 1772, New Jersey enacted a medical licensure law, and colonial America was soon on its way to having a more-fully regulated medical profession. Medical societies in the new United States began advocating more heavily for European-style licensing, with educational and experiential requirements, even in the midst of the American Revolutionary War. By 1781, Massachusetts and New Hampshire instituted licensure requirements for medical practice. All other states soon followed suit, although with westward expansion the educational requirements on the frontier were often inadequate. After the Civil War, however, states began creating state boards of examiners, with Texas taking the lead in 1873. By 1895, nearly all states had such boards, and more sound regulation of the profession was taking place.[2]

Of course, there are very important reasons for medical licensure. The most self-evident of these is the serious consequence that could occur if a medical professional makes an error due to incompetence or ignorance. In such cases where there is a wrong diagnosis or an improper treatment, a patient could die. Unlike the legal profession, where an error by an attorney or a judge could be reviewed by an appellate court, a fatal error by a medical physician has immediate, irreversible effects. Concerns such as these are what spurred on the development of medical licensure, both in the United States and abroad.[3]

On the other hand, there are very serious consequences if a qualified physician is not able to practice medicine. That physician's livelihood is threatened, as that person is prevented from working in his or her chosen field after investing considerable time and expense to become an expert in medicine. Furthermore, if such a person cannot practice, a community of patients is denied care by a medical professional. If there is a shortage of physicians in a geographical area, such a decision could result in people not receiving needed treatment. Thus, decisions made by state medical examining boards can have a great impact, whether they are denying or permitting one's license. Given what is at stake, there are legal ramifications to a decision either way. This means that those persons making these decisions need to be impartial, and since these decisions are made by state licensing boards, a lack of impartiality raises problems under the Fourteenth Amendment's Due Process Clause. Indeed, this was one of the problems raised in *Dr. Bonham's Case*, where he was tried within the college's own court for practicing law without a license, and the college proceeded to imprison him and keep part of the fine upon conviction, until that decision was overruled by Sir Edward Coke. The issue of the impartiality of a medical examining board's suspension of a doctor's license was raised in a more modern context in *Withrow v. Larkin* (1975).

As noted above, by the late nineteenth century, all states had established some sort of medical examining board to license physicians. Wisconsin was no exception. The Wisconsin Medical Examining Board, a body made up of practicing Wisconsin physicians, was authorized to "investigate, hear and act upon practices by persons licensed to practice medicine and surgery...that are inimical to public health." In addition, the state, like all other states, forbade anyone from practicing medicine without a license from the medical examining board, and it prohibited various other acts of professional misconduct. If a licensed physician engaged in such misconduct, the medical examining board was authorized by state statute to invoke various sanctions, including warnings, reprimands, license suspensions, and the initiation of license revocations and criminal actions.[4]

Duane Larkin was a Michigan resident who was licensed to practice medicine in that state. In August of 1971, Larkin obtained a Wisconsin medical license under a reciprocity agreement between the two states. Larkin's medical practice in Wisconsin consisted of him performing abortions out of a Milwaukee office. However, on June 20, 1973, the medical examining board sent Larkin a notice that it would hold an investigative hearing about him on July 12, 1973 to decide if he had engaged in certain proscribed acts. According to the notice, the hearing was to determine if Larkin had "engaged in practices that are inimical to the public health...in conduct unbecoming a person licensed to practice medicine, and...in conduct detrimental to the best interests of the public." The real motivation of the medical examining board investigation appears to have been the elimination of abortion providers like Dr. Larkin. He was informed that his hearing would be closed to the public and that he would not be permitted to cross-examine witnesses. He would, however, be able to attend with his attorney. The notice stated that possible sanctions included almost every sanction that the board could impose: a warming, a reprimand, license revocation, and initiation of criminal action.[5]

Not willing to wait around to see what might transpire at the hearing, on July 6, 1973, Larkin filed for a temporary restraining order (TRO) and a permanent injunction against the medical examining board's investigation and hearing. The U.S. District Court for the Eastern District of Wisconsin denied the motion for a TRO. On July 12, 1973, Larkin filed an amended complaint, claiming that his constitutional rights were being violated by the relevant Wisconsin statutes and the actions of the medical examining board. The district court denied Larkin's motion for a TRO.[6]

The medical examining board went forward with its investigative hearing on July 12-13, 1973. The board heard witness testimony, and Larkin's attorney was present during the proceedings. On September 18, 1973, the medical examining board sent Larkin a notice that a contested hearing would be held on October 4, 1973, to determine if he had engaged in acts prohibited by the state's medical code, including if Larkin had practiced medicine in the state under a false name, if he engaged in unfair competition, or if he otherwise engaged in actions that were detrimental to the profession or the public. More specifically, the board was holding the hearing to determine if Larkin "has practiced medicine in this state since September 1, 1971, under the name of Glen Johnson," if Larkin "permitted Young Wahn Ahn, M.D., an unlicensed physician, to perform abortions at his abortion clinic during the year 1972," and if Larkin "split fees with other persons during the years 1971, 1972, and 1973," in violation of state law. In response to this contested hearing, Larkin moved the federal district court for another restraining order. On October 1, 1973, the U.S. District Judge Myron L. Gordon granted Larkin's motion. Judge Gordon found that Larkin had raised a substantial due process question. Since due process requires "an independent decisionmaker," Judge Gordon had concerns because "it appears that the examining board is authorized not only to investigate physicians and present charges, but to rule on those charges and impose punishment, at least to the extent of reprimanding or temporarily suspending," thus leading the judge to question if the contested hearing "may occur without the intervention of an independent neutral and detached decisionmaker." Based on this, Judge Gordon granted Larkin's motion to convene a three-judge court to review his constitutional claims.[7]

The medical examining board obeyed the court order and did not hold a contested hearing on October 4, 1973. However, the board held a final investigative session on that date (Larkin sought a TRO to prevent this session, but it was denied by the court). At the conclusion of the "investigative session," the board reached the following decision: "it is hereby determined that there is probable cause to believe that licensee has violated the criminal [statutes], and that there is probable cause for an action to revoke the license of the licensee for engaging in unprofessional conduct." Furthermore, the board filed a verified complaint with the Milwaukee County District Attorney to initiate the revocation of Larkin's Wisconsin medical license and begin criminal proceedings against him.[8]

However, at the same time that these legal proceedings were moved against Larkin by the state, his constitutional claim was progressing through the federal courts. On November 19, 1973, a three-judge federal district court found that the state statute which authorized the medical examining board to act as both an investigative body and an adjudicatory body violated due process.[9] In an opinion issued on December 21, 1973, the three-judge district court stated the following:

> [F]or the board temporarily to suspend Dr. Larkin's license at its own contested hearing on charges evolving from its own investigation would constitute a denial to him of his rights to procedural due process. Insofar as [Wisconsin law] authorizes a procedure wherein a physician stands to lose his liberty or property, absent the intervention of an independent, neutral and detached decision maker, we concluded that it was unconstitutional and unenforceable.[10]

After the three-judge district court entered its decision, the medical examining board appealed its case to the United States Supreme Court. After hearing oral arguments on December 19, 1974, the Court issued its decision on April 16, 1975.[11]

Justice Byron White wrote the opinion for a unanimous Court. He began his analysis of the constitutional issue in *Withrow* by reciting an oft-quoted line from *In re Murchison* (1955): "a fair trial in a fair tribunal is a basic requirement of due process."[12] White went on to state that this "applies to administrative agencies which adjudicate as well as to courts" and that "[n]ot only is a biased decisionmaker constitutionally unacceptable but our system of law has always endeavored to prevent even the probability of unfairness."[13] Justice White then went on to clarify that in pursuit of the end of an impartial decisionmaker, "various situations have been identified in which experience teaches that the probability of actual bias on the part of the judge or decisionmaker is too high to be constitutionally tolerable," including those "in which the adjudicator has a pecuniary interest in the outcome and in which he has been the target of personal abuse or criticism from the party before him."[14]

With that as a jurisprudential backdrop, Justice White went on to clarify what he saw as the difficulties faced by Larkin:

> The contention that the combination of investigative and adjudicative functions necessarily creates an unconstitutional risk of bias in administrative adjudication has a much more difficult burden of persuasion to carry. It must overcome a presumption of honesty and integrity in those serving as adjudicators; and it must convince that, under a realistic appraisal of psychological tendencies and human weakness, conferring investigative and adjudicative powers on the same individuals poses such a risk of actual bias or prejudgment that the practice must be forbidden if the guarantee of due process is to be adequately implemented.[15]

Thus, White pronounced a high burden for Larkin to prove that the same members of the medical examining board could not serve as both investigators and adjudicators in Larkin's case. In support of this proposition, White made use of multiple cases. The first of these was *FTC v. Cement Institute* (1948), where the U.S. Supreme Court upheld the Federal Trade Commission's investigation and subsequent hearing concerning unfair competition by a trade association. White then cited *NLRB v. Donnelly Garment Co.* (1947), where the Court allowed a hearing examiner, who had recommended findings of fact, to preside at further hearings that were required when reviewing courts held that the evidence had been erroneously excluded. Finally, White cited *Richardson v. Perales* (1971), where the Court upheld the constitutionality of a system in which a Social Security examiner had responsibility for developing the facts and then making a decision as to disability claims.[16]

These cases notwithstanding, Justice White failed to elaborate a more recent case which was discussed in the last chapter: *Morrissey v. Brewer* (1972). There the Court ruled that a parole officer could not serve as both the investigating officer and the adjudicator in parole revocation hearings. Instead of making use of this case, White relegated it to a brief mention in part of a footnote, where he characterized it as posing "a very different question," because it held that "when review of an initial decision is mandated, the decisionmaker must be other than the one who made the decision under review."[17] According to Justice White, "[a]llowing a decisionmaker to review and evaluate his own prior decisions raises problems that are not present here," because under Wisconsin law, "the Board is at no point called upon to review its own prior decisions."[18] Although the latter portion of this statement is certainly correct, the rest of White's analysis was a very narrow view of *Morrissey*. In both cases, the entity that investigates should not also serve as the adjudicative body. Whether or not there was an official prior decision is not as important as ensuring that the same entity does not serve these two different functions. Anything less than this threatens the impartiality of the decisionmaker because it significantly increases the likelihood that the decisionmaker will be biased based on the process of investigation or by collecting facts ahead of the hearing that may not be admissible at the hearing.

Once Justice White stated his position above, however, he immediately backed off of it. According to White, "[t]hat is not to say that there is nothing to the argument that those who have investigated should not then adjudicate. The issue is substantial, it is not new."[19] White's answer to this discrepancy was not resolution. Instead, he found that there was no constitutional conclusion that could be attained, as the extent that "distinctive administrative functions should be performed by the same persons," has been debated by many legislatures and that "[n]o single answer has been reached."[20] Justice White then deferred to legislatures, particularly Congress, in judging when the same persons within administrative agencies should be able to exercise both investigatory and adjudicatory functions. In his view, "the growth, variety, and complexity of the administrative processes have made any one solution highly unlikely."[21] For White, the Court's jurisprudence pointed in a different direction than what the district court found: "our cases, although they reflect the substance of the problem, offer no support for the bald proposition...that agency members who participate in an investigation are disqualified from adjudicating. The incredible variety of administrative mechanisms in this country will not yield to any single organizing principle."[22] Presumably, White was referring back to the cases he previously cited because he did not cite any cases in this paragraph of his opinion to support this presumption.

Justice White next differentiated the medical examining board's involvement in Larkin's cases from the one-man grand jury that the Court found unconstitutional in *In re Murchison* (1955). As explained in chapter ten above, the Court found fault with this practice because the same judge who charged witnesses with perjury and contempt then presided over their respective trials. In ruling that this practice violated Murchison's right to an impartial judge under the Due Process Clause, the Court noted that "[a]s a practical matter it is difficult if not impossible for a judge to free himself from the influence of what took place in his grand-jury secret session."[23] However, White proceeded to narrowly interpret *Murchison* and distinguish the medical examining board's actions from the one-man grand jury in *Murchison*. According to White, "*Murchison* has not been understood to stand for the broad rule that the members of an administrative agency may not investigate the facts, institute proceedings, and then make the necessary adjudications."[24] White found this to be true, even though the *Murchison* Court found it unacceptable for the same judge to engage in adjudication in addition to witnessing the relevant activities and serving as an investigator of them. Nevertheless, under White's narrow interpretation of *Murchison*, the medical examining board did not violate Larkin's rights:

> When the Board instituted its investigative procedures, it stated only that it would investigate whether proscribed conduct had occurred. Later in noticing the adversary hearing, it asserted only that it would determine if violations had been committed which would warrant suspension of [Larkin's] license. Without doubt, the Board then anticipated that the proceeding would eventuate in an adjudication of the issue; but there was no more evidence of bias or the risk of bias or prejudgment than inhered in the very fact that the Board had investigated and would now adjudicate.[25]

Since White relegated *Murchison* to such an insignificant case, and since he ignored the *Murchison* Court's problem with combining investigative and adjudicative function in the same person(s), it was easy for him and the rest of the Court in *Withrow* to approve of the medical examining board's actions.

Justice White went on to note that "we should be alert to the possibilities of bias that may lurk in the way particular procedures actually work in practice."[26] Even so, White subsequently declared that the board's processes did not in themselves contain an unacceptable risk of bias because Larkin and his attorney were able to attend the investigative proceeding. According to White,

> No specific foundation has been presented for suspecting that the Board had been prejudiced by its investigation or would be disabled from hearing and deciding on the basis of the evidence to be presented at the contested hearing. The mere exposure to evidence presented in nonadversary investigative procedures is insufficient in itself to impugn the fairness of the Board members at a later adversary hearing. Without a showing to the contrary, state administrators "are assumed to be men of conscience and intellectual discipline, capable of judging a particular controversy fairly on the basis of its own circumstances."[27]

Of course, nothing in prior cases stated that bias was eliminated simply from being allowed to be present with one's lawyer at the proceedings. A biased decisionmaker can certainly be biased when the subject of the proceedings is there, even with counsel, as numerous cases in the previous chapters make clear. Since the investigative proceedings were closed to the public and limited Larkin's procedural rights in other ways, his presence alone did not prevent the medical examining board from being biased against him.

After dealing away the constitutional concern with the same medical examining board members being both investigators and adjudicators, Justice White then turned specifically to the issue of the board, when it was prohibited from going forward with its contested hearing, making formal findings of fact and conclusions of law that there was probable cause to determine that Larkin had violated state law. White easily found no problem with this practice either. According to White, judges often issue arrest warrants and preside over preliminary hearings before then presiding over criminal trials for the same defendants. This practice has never been thought to violate the Constitution. Furthermore, according to White, "[i]t is also very typical for the members of administrative agencies to receive the results of investigations, to approve the filing of charges or formal complaints instituting enforcement proceedings, and then to participate in the ensuing hearings," and "it is not contrary to due process to allow judges and administrators who have had their initial decisions reversed on appeal to confront and decide the same questions a second time around."[28] White then summed up this point as follows: "just as there is no logical inconsistency between a finding of probable cause and an acquittal in a criminal proceeding, there is no incompatibility between the agency filing a complaint based on probable cause and a subsequent decision, when all the evidence is in, that there has been no violation of the statute."[29]

While there is no question that judges are involved in various stages of the same case, when they do so they are carrying out an adjudicatory function at all of the points in those cases. When judges make rulings on arrest warrants and preliminary hearings, they are doing so as judges, not as police investigators. In other words, they are only acting at the "contested" stage, not the "investigatory" stage. The medical examining board, on the other hand, was carrying out an investigatory function and then used those findings, in absence of its planned contested hearing, to recommend criminal proceedings against Larkin and the revocation of his medical license. In this sense, the analogy to a judge would not be to findings at a preliminary hearing and a subsequent trial; instead, what the board did was more akin to police investigation of a case, followed by making formal findings of fact at a preliminary hearing. Doing this combines the functions of two different branches of government and means that the decisionmaker is already biased against the individual in question before the contested hearing begins.

Even if one accepts Justice White's analogy that what the medical examining board was doing in its investigatory hearing and later hearing was the same as a judge deciding a preliminary hearing and then presiding over a criminal trial of the same defendant, the training for such board members is not commensurate with that of judges or even some more formalized federal administrative agency members. With more formal training, judges and administrators are able to distinguish burdens of proof when making factual and legal determinations. This will especially be true with judges, including non-lawyer judges who are required to take part in continuing judicial education seminars or conferences. This cannot be guaranteed with licensing and disciplinary boards, where there may be no ongoing professional development to better understand these legal differences. Although members of a medical examining review board may be experts in the field of medicine, there is no guarantee that they will also be experts in the relevant law. This can greatly increase the danger of prejudgment and bias in these board members when compared to judges.[30]

Justice White closed his opinion with a word of caution, though, for the way that administrative agencies carry out these functions: "That the combination of investigative and adjudicative functions does not, without more, constitute a due process violation, does not, of course, preclude a court from determining from the special facts and circumstances present in the case before it that the risk of unfairness is intolerably high."[31] At least Justice White and the Court allowed for review of administrative, licensing, and disciplinary board decisions when there is a serious risk of unfairness in the process. Unfortunately, such risk existed in *Withrow*, but the Court could not see it.

Recall Justice White's statement from early on in his *Withrow* opinion: "a fair trial in a fair tribunal is a basic requirement of due process. This applies to administrative agencies which adjudicate as well as to courts. Not only is a biased decisionmaker constitutionally unacceptable, but our system of law has always endeavored to prevent even the probability of unfairness."[32] While that is a profound statement, Justice White's words ring hollow when one reflects upon the decision that followed. Dr. Larkin did not receive a fair and impartial hearing under the circumstances because the medical examining board carried out functions which made it biased as to the outcome before Larkin had an opportunity to present his side of the case. The board members had, quite probably, prejudged the outcome of the second hearing, based on their first, investigatory hearing. More process was due to Dr. Larkin.

Not only was the Court's decision in *Withrow* against the principles that the Court announced only three years previously in *Morrissey*, it also failed to heed the commands of *Tumey v. Ohio* (see chapter six). There, the Court did not find it possible for a mayor-judge to be impartial due to the financial interests at stake. The Court, for similar reasons, found unconstitutional the actions of a mayor-judge in *Ward v. City of Monroeville* because, as mayor, he had the municipality's financial obligations on his mind. When particularly faced with defendants who were outsiders (not their own constituents), the powerful influence of money might cause them to be less than impartial. However, similar influences existed over the medical examining board members in *Withrow* because they faced an outsider — Michigan physician Larkin — and they had a great deal of discretion. Furthermore, the members of the medical examining board may have made the decision that they did because of their beliefs on abortion, thus viewing Dr. Larkin as an "outsider [who] was flouting a local profession's culture and strongly held personal values," which led board members to see themselves as "defending their state from an incursion that they viewed as harmful and immoral." If true, this is the epitome of bias by a decisionmaker that prejudged the outcome and used existing regulatory law as a pretext to punish a doctor for performing procedures that they opposed for religious, political, or ideological reasons.[33]

The ultimate resolution of the case took place in January of 1976, when Dr. Larkin surrendered his Wisconsin medical license. He did this in response to the medical examining board's decision to hold another hearing on his license after the U.S. Supreme Court allowed it to take part in both the investigatory and adjudicatory phases of Larkin's case. Unfortunately, in the end, the members of the medical examining board got exactly what they wanted, without needing to act impartially.[34]

Notes

1. Henry E. Sigerist, "The History of Medical Licensure," *Journal of the American Medical Association* 104 (1935), 1057-60, 1057-59; Mary Sarah Bilder, "The Corporate Origins of Judicial Review," *Yale Law Journal* 116 (2006): 502-566, 531; Samuel Edmund Thorne, *Essays in English Legal History* (London: Hambledon Press, 1985), 269.
2. Sigerist, "History of Medical Licensure," 1060; John Duffy, *From Humors to Medical Science: A History of American Medicine* (Urbana: University of Illinois Press, 1993), 40.
3. Sigerist, "History of Medical Licensure," 1057.
4. *Withrow v. Larkin*, 421 U.S. 35, 37 &n.1 (1975).
5. *Withrow v. Larkin*, 421 U.S. at 38-39 & n.2; Gillian E. Metzger, "Abortion, Equality, and Administrative Regulation," *Emory Law Journal* 56 (2007): 865-906, 869-70.
6. *Withrow*, 421 U.S. at 39.
7. *Withrow*, 421 U.S. at 40-41 & n.4; *Larkin v. Withrow*, 368 F. Supp. 793, 795 (E.D. Wis. 1973).
8. *Withrow*, 421 U.S. at 421 U.S. at 41-42 & n.5.
9. *Withrow*, 421 U.S. at 42.
10. *Larkin v. Withrow*, 368 F. Supp. 793 at 797.
11. *Withrow*, 421 U.S. at 42-43.
12. *Withrow*, 421 U.S. at 46 (quoting *In re Murchison*, 349 U.S. 133, 136 (1955)) (internal quotations omitted).
13. *Withrow*, 421 U.S. at 47.
14. *Withrow*, 421 U.S. at 47.
15. *Withrow*, 421 U.S. at 47.
16. *Withrow*, 421 U.S. at 47-50; *FTC v. Cement Institute*, 333 U.S. 683 (1948); *NLRB v. Donnelly Garment Co.*, 330 U.S. 219 (1947); *Richardson v. Perales*, 402 U.S. 389 (1971).
17. *Withrow*, 421 U.S. at 58 n. 25.
18. *Withrow*, 421 U.S. at 58 n. 25.
19. *Withrow*, 421 U.S. at 51.
20. *Withrow*, 421 U.S. at 51.
21. *Withrow*, 421 U.S. at 51.
22. *Withrow*, 421 U.S. at 52.
23. *Murchison*, 349 U.S. at 138.
24. *Withrow*, 421 U.S. at 53.

25. *Withrow*, 421 U.S. at 54.

26. *Withrow*, 421 U.S. at 54.

27. *Withrow*, 421 U.S. at 55 (quoting *United States v. Morgan*, 313 U.S. 409, 421 (1941)).

28. *Withrow*, 421 U.S. at 56-57.

29. *Withrow*, 421 U.S. at 57.

30. Michael R. Lanzarone, "Professional Discipline: Unfairness and Inefficiency in the Administrative Process," *Fordham Law Review* 51 (1983): 818-37, 825.

31. *Withrow*, 421 U.S. at 58.

32. *Withrow*, 421 U.S. at 46-47 (internal citations and quotations omitted).

33. Nancy A. Welsh, "What Is '(Im)Partial Enough' in a World of Embedded Neutrals?," *Arizona Law Review* 52 (2010): 395-471, 456-57.

34. "Dr. Larkin Gives up State License," *The Milwaukee Sentinel*, January 7, 1976, I18.

~ 13 ~

Mental Health Commitments for Juveniles: *Parham v. J.R.* (1979)

[T]he risk of error inherent in the parental decision to have a child institutionalized for mental health care is sufficiently great that some kind of inquiry should be made by a 'neutral factfinder' to determine whether the statutory requirements for admission are satisfied.
– *Parham v. J.R.*, 442 U.S. 584, 606 (1979)

In the absence of a voluntary, knowing, and intelligent waiver, adults facing commitment to mental institutions are entitled to full and fair adversary hearings in which the necessity for their commitment is established to the satisfaction of a neutral tribunal...These principles also govern the commitment of children.
– *Parham v. J.R.*, 442 U.S. 584, 627 (1979) (Justice Brennan, Dissenting)

American colonies began making laws in the eighteenth century to care for those who were deemed by colonial governments to be "feebleminded" or "insane." By 1742, Rhode Island passed a statute allowing local town councils to take responsibility for caring for the mentally ill. The first public hospital in the United States for the mentally ill was established in Williamsburg, Virginia in the mid-eighteenth century. The royal Virginian governor called for the building of a hospital in 1766, and a bill authorizing the project passed the colonial legislature in 1769. According to the legislature, such a hospital was necessary "to make provision for the support and maintenance of ideots [*sic*], lunatics, and other persons of unsound minds." However, early on, neither this facility, nor others like it, received many patients. The Williamsburg facility only received its first patient four years later in 1773, and it remained relatively unfilled for many years. This fit the custom at the time, as most mentally ill persons were given care at home or in almshouses. This may have been for the best, as professional mental health treatment did not really exist at the time. Even the forward-thinking Williamsburg facility was run by a layperson, not a medical doctor, during this period.[1]

This began to change in the mid-nineteenth century, when health care advocate Dorothea Dix began a campaign of advocating for government intervention in the care of the mentally ill. Her efforts led to the building of over thirty state hospitals for the care of such persons. By 1875, thirty two states had sixty facilities for the care of the mentally ill. By 1955, there were 265 of these public institutions. In the 1940s through the 1960s, Congress became more involved in the delivery of mental health services by providing funding for the building of medical health facilities and services. However, many experts allege that mental health services were never fully funded and that they continue to be underfunded to this day.[2]

Regardless of how many facilities exist and at what expense, there is no question that patients, either for their own personal protection or to protect the public, will sometimes need to be committed to these facilities. This type of involuntary civil commitment dates back to the sixteenth century in Europe and later migrated to the United States. *In re Oakes* (1845), an early case decided by the Massachusetts Supreme Court, upheld the involuntary commitment of a man who exhibited unusual behavior. According to the Massachusetts Supreme Court, involuntary commitment may be ordered in cases where a person is dangerous to others or where such commitment would be beneficial to the person's own welfare. However, the court also upheld Oakes's commitment without a trial or other judicial action. This case served as a guidepost for other civil commitments across the county for another century, before due process rights were more forcefully asserted and protected in these types of proceedings.[3]

The modern application of due process rights to proceedings involving involuntary mental health commitments began with *O'Connor v. Donaldson* (1975). There, the U.S. Supreme Court found constitutional fault with the involuntary commitment of a non-dangerous person who was capable of surviving safely by himself or with the help of family members and friends.[4] Similarly, in *Addington v. Texas* (1979), the Court required that to be involuntarily committed to a mental health facility, the government must provide a standard of proof greater than the preponderance of evidence standard, which is the minimum standard of proof in civil court proceedings. For the Court, due process required a higher standard for these civil commitment cases because of the significant deprivation of liberty involved.[5]

During the same period in which the U.S. Supreme Court was laying down due process requirements for involuntary mental health commitments, the Court was also applying due process rights to criminal cases involving juveniles. The seminal case in this regard was *In re Gault* (1967), where the Court required that juveniles being accused of delinquency must be given due process protections that include timely notice of the charges, the right to the assistance of counsel, the right against compelled self-incrimination, the right to confront and cross-examine adverse witnesses.[6] With this ruling on juvenile due process rights and previous cases on the due process rights applying to civil commitment proceedings, it was only a matter of time before the U.S. Supreme Court would face a case on the due process rights of juveniles facing civil commitment, including how the right to a neutral decisionmaker applies in this context. *Parham v. J.R.* (1979) was that case.

To understand what led to the *Parham* case, one needs a bit of background on the two principle juveniles involved in the case, J.R. and J.L. J.R. was born on August 14, 1965. Due to what a federal court would later characterize as "severe parental neglect," J.R. was removed from his parents' home at three months of age and placed into the custody of the Georgia Department of Family and Children Services (DFCS). J.R. then began a journey where he lived in various foster homes. In October 1966, a state court gave the Georgia DFCS permanent custody of J.R. for the purpose of placing him for adoption. However, the state was not successful in placing J.R. for adoption, and he continued to move from one foster home to the next. While with his seventh and final set of foster parents, J.R. was receiving outpatient mental health treatment, but this did not prevent him from being disruptive and acting in ways that led him to be labeled as incorrigible at school. He was placed in outpatient treatment at a county medical health center for several months, but this did not improve his behavior. Based on this, J.R.'s foster parents requested that he be removed from their home.[7]

Once J.R.'s behavior was brought to the attention of the Georgia DFCS, the agency applied to have him admitted to Central State Hospital. DFCS gave Central State J.R.'s complete sociomedical history to that point, and an admission team at the hospital conducted three interviews of J.R. On June 25, 1970, J.R. was admitted to Central State. Hospital personnel described him as "[b]orderline mentally ill," and as having an "[u]nsocialized, aggressive reaction of childhood." J.R. was seven years old at the time. In 1973, personnel at Central State began to request DFCS to remove J.R. from the facility and place him in long term foster care or an adoptive home, because hospital personnel claimed that J.R. would "only regress if he does not get a suitable home placement and as soon as possible." However, DFCS was not able to place J.R. into adoptive care.[8]

Under a similar set of circumstances was a juvenile whose initials were J.L. He was born on October 1, 1963. He was adopted at birth, and his parents divorced when he was three years of age. J.L. then lived with his mother, who later remarried and had another child. Once he started school, J.L. became uncontrollable and was later expelled. Due to his aggressive behavior, his mother and step-father later had J.L. undergo outpatient care for two months at Central State Hospital in Georgia. In May of 1970, when J.L. was still six years of age, his mother and step-father applied to have him admitted indefinitely for inpatient care at Central State. Personnel there admitted J.L., finding that he was mentally ill, specifically that he had "[h]yperkinetic reaction of childhood."[9]

Early on in his time at Central State, J.L.'s mother and step-father participated in family therapy, whereby J.L. was allowed to go home for short periods of time. Since his behavior was erratic during these stays, his mother and step-father soon asked that their participation in the program be terminated. In the fall of 1972, Central State discharged J.L. to his mother as part of a furlough program where he lived at home and attended school at the hospital. However, his mother and step-father felt that they could not control J.L., and he was readmitted to the hospital. J.L.'s parents gave up their parental rights to him in 1974, thus placing him in the guardianship of the county government. By this time, Central State had already told DFCS that J.L. needed to be removed from that facility for his own good. DFCS tried unsuccessfully to find foster care for J.L.[10]

Georgia's process at that time for admitting children to mental health hospitalization began when a parent or guardian filled out a hospital application. The superintendent of each hospital was given the authority to temporarily admit any child for observation and diagnosis of mental illness. If the superintendent found evidence of mental illness, then the child could be admitted as long as, and for any conditions that were, allowed by law. It appears that these procedures were followed for J.R. and J.L. However, the specific procures followed by each Georgia mental health facility (place of evaluation, how many staff members review an application, how patients are reviewed for release, etc.) varied from institution to institution in the 1970s.[11]

In October of 1975, J.R. and J.L. filed a lawsuit to challenge their confinement. Each of them sued James Parham, Commissioner of Georgia's Department of Human Resources, which had responsibility for DFCS; Dr. Douglas Skelton, Director of the State Division of Mental Health; and Dr. W. T. Smith, Chief Medical Officer of Central State Hospital. J.R. and J.L. requested that the U.S. District Court for the Middle District of Georgia place them in less drastic environments that would be more suitable to their needs. More specifically, they claimed that they and minor children similarly situated had been deprived of their liberty without due process of law in violation of the Fourteenth Amendment. They claimed that their involuntary confinement in a state mental hospital was done without them being given a meaningful and complete opportunity to be heard.[12]

By the time their suit was filed in federal district court, they had each spent a significant portion of their respective lives in hospital confinement: J.R. had been confined for five years and four months of his total life of thirteen years and two months; J.L. had been confined for five years and five months of his life of twelve years and one month. The U.S. district court found fault with the confinement of these juveniles, observing that they were denied due process. Part of the court's concern was that neither J.R. nor J.L. was given notice and an opportunity to be heard before an impartial tribunal on the question of their respective confinements. According to U.S. District Judge Wilbur D. Owens, Jr., "[m]ost parents accept and faithfully perform their parental duties and given this unlimited statutory authority to admit their children to a mental hospital, would use that authority only when it is genuinely necessary to do so," but "as the evidence indicates, there are some parents who abuse that authority and who under the guise of admitting a child to a mental hospital actually abandon their child to the state." For Judge Owens, the Georgia statute which gave parents the ability to arbitrarily admit their children to a mental health facility indefinitely, coupled with potential errors that could be made by admitting psychiatrists, violated due process where there was no opportunity by the children to challenge that decision. Essentially, the judge said that a judicial "double-check" was required for such a major decision. The state appealed the decision, eventually to the U.S. Supreme Court. Unfortunately, by the time the Court heard the decision, J.L. had died in state custody.[13]

Chief Justice Warren Burger wrote the opinion of the Court in *Parham v. J.R.* The Chief Justice began his analysis by stating that when a liberty interest is at stake under the Fourteenth Amendment, the Court analyzes the question according to a balancing test from *Mathews v. Eldridge* (1976). Some explanation is in order here. *Mathews* involved a litigant, George Eldridge, who had his Social Security disability benefit payments terminated prior to an evidentiary hearing. Eldridge claimed that not giving him a hearing prior to this termination violated his Fifth Amendment Due Process rights. The *Mathews* Court held that procedural due process was *not* violated in this case. The Court came to this conclusion by determining that procedural due process is a flexible standard, and its exact requirements would vary by each case, depending on three factors:

> First, the private interest that will be affected by the official action; second, the risk of an erroneous deprivation of such interest through the procedures used, and the probable value, if any, of additional or substitute procedural safeguards; and finally, the Government's interest, including the function involved and the fiscal and administrative burdens that the additional or substitute procedural requirement would entail."[14]

This was the test that the *Parham* Court would apply as well, to determine what due process requires for juveniles who were being involuntarily confined to mental health facilities. Burger went on to then note what was at stake in *Parham*, according to the *Mathews* test:

> In applying these criteria, we must consider first the child's interest in not being committed. Normally, however, since this interest is inextricably linked with the parents' interest in and obligation for the welfare and health of the child, the private interest at stake is a combination of the child's and parents' concerns. Next, we must examine the State's interest in the procedures it has adopted for commitment and treatment of children. Finally, we must consider how well Georgia's procedures protect against arbitrariness in the decision to commit a child to a state mental hospital.[15]

Using this test, Burger, citing *Addington* and *Gault*, began by stating that "a child, in common with adults, has a substantial liberty interest in not being confined unnecessarily for medical treatment and that the state's involvement in the commitment decision constitutes state action under the Fourteenth Amendment."[16] He also made it clear that the act of commitment can become a social stigma in addition to its deprivation of freedom. At the same time, Burger claimed that the resulting harms of inpatient involuntary psychiatric care are not as great as "being labeled by the state as delinquent, criminal, or mentally ill and possibly dangerous."[17] Instead, Burger characterized the state action with respect to J.R., J.L., and similarly situated juveniles as providing the diagnosis and treatment that medical specialists conclude the respective child requires. In addition, a person who does receive needed treatment "may well face even greater social ostracism resulting from the observable symptoms of an untreated disorder."[18] Even so, Burger concluded that "we assume that a child has a protectible interest not only in being free of unnecessary bodily restraints but also in not being labeled erroneously by some persons because of an improper decision by the state hospital superintendent."[19] In other words, the child has an interest in the state making the correct decision regarding the need for treatment.

Next, Chief Justice Burger moved on to the second prong of the *Mathews* test, which asks about the risk of an erroneous deprivation of the relevant liberty interest through the procedures used and the probable value of any additional or substitute procedural safeguards. In particular, Burger emphasized the interests here of the parents in institutionalizing their children. He began this portion of his analysis with an important observation: "Our jurisprudence historically has reflected Western civilization concepts of the family as a unit with broad parental authority over minor children... parents generally 'have the right, coupled with the high duty, to recognize and prepare [their children] for additional obligations.'"[20] According to Burger, one of these parental duties includes recognizing symptoms of illness, including mental illness, and subsequently seeking and following medical advice because children generally lack the "maturity, experience, and capacity for judgment required for making life's difficult decisions."[21] Burger also made it clear that the law has historically "recognized that natural bonds of affection lead parents to act in the best interests of their children."[22] Furthermore, this parental authority is not lessened simply because the child objects: "The fact that a child may balk at hospitalization or complain about a parental refusal to provide cosmetic surgery does not diminish the parents' authority to decide what is best for the child."[23]

This notwithstanding, much like Judge Owens sadly noted, Chief Justice Burger forthrightly admitted that "experience and reality may rebut what the law accepts as a starting point; the incidence of child neglect and abuse cases attests to this" because "some parents may at times be acting against the interests of their children."[24] Due to these relatively rare situations, "a state is not without constitutional control over parental discretion in dealing with children when their physical or mental health is jeopardized."[25] Based on this, Burger and the Court reached the following with respect to the rights of children and parents in the voluntary commitment setting:

> [W]e conclude that our precedents permit the parents to retain a substantial, if not the dominant, role in the decision, absent a finding of neglect or abuse, and

> that the traditional presumption that the parents act in the best interests of their child should apply. We also conclude, however, that the child's rights and the nature of the commitment decision are such that parents cannot always have absolute and unreviewable discretion to decide whether to have a child institutionalized. They, of course, retain plenary authority to seek such care for their children, subject to a physician's independent examination and medical judgment.[26]

Thus, the court found a balance between the rights of the child and the parent in this context, with the heavy presumption that the parent's decision will be in the best interest of the child, unless factors are present to suggest otherwise.

Burger next elaborated on the third part of the *Mathews* test, which examined the state's interests. First among these interests is limiting the costly mental health facilities of the state to those who are truly mentally ill. For this reason, Georgia gave superintendents of its regional hospitals the power to determine if prospective patients were mentally ill and if they would benefit from inpatient care. Furthermore, Burger pointed out that the state has "a significant interest in not imposing unnecessary procedural obstacles that may discourage the mentally ill or their families from seeking needed psychiatric assistance."[27] Indeed, if admitting mentally ill children becomes an overly burdensome process, parents may be deterred by the state from seeking such medical care for their children when it is needed. Finally, Burger stated that the state has an interest in "allocating priority to the diagnosis and treatment of patients as soon as they are admitted to a hospital rather than to time-consuming procedural minutes before the admission."[28] In other words, patients who need care should have it as soon as possible, and psychiatrists, psychologists, and similarly trained medical professionals who are preparing for hearings are spending that much less of their limited time delivering this treatment.

Based on the synthesis of these three parts of the *Mathews* test, Chief Justice Burger concluded that "the risk of error inherent in the parental decision to have a child institutionalized for mental health care is sufficiently great that some kind of inquiry should be made by a 'neutral factfinder' to determine whether the statutory requirements for admission are satisfied."[29] Burger mandated that this inquiry by a neutral decisionmaker should include an interview with the child, as well as a probe of the child's background from all available sources, such as parents, schools, and other social agencies. For the decisionmaker to truly be independent and neutral, "[i]t is necessary that the decisionmaker have the authority to refuse to admit any child who does not satisfy the medical standards for admission."[30] Furthermore, if a child is admitted under these circumstances, not only should there be an initial review, but ongoing review of the need for inpatient care is mandatory: "it is necessary that the child's continuing need for commitment be reviewed periodically by a similarly independent procedure."[31] According to Burger, this combination of procedures properly balances the rights of the child, the decisionmaking power of the parent, and the relevant government interests.

The Chief Justice then outlined the constitutional requirements for the neutral decisionmaker in the context of juvenile mental illness commitments. According to Burger, "[i]t is not necessary that the deciding physician conduct a formal or quasi-formal hearing. A state is free to require such a hearing, but due process is not violated by use of informal, traditional medical investigative techniques."[32] For Burger, this was the case because "well-established medical procedures already exist," meaning that the Court would not "undertake to outline with specificity precisely what this investigation must involve."[33] Instead, the Chief Justice noted that the "mode and procedure of medical diagnostic procedures is not the business of judges."[34] The key here for Burger was that "the decision should represent an independent judgment of what the child requires and that all sources of information that are traditionally relied on by physicians and behavioral specialists should be consulted."[35] In this respect, Burger was following the same line of reasoning as in *North v. Russell* (1976) (discussed in chapter eight). Indeed, much like the Court in *Russell* found that formal legal training was not required for judges, the Court three years later in *Parham* did not require legal training for personnel handling mental health commitments of juveniles. This should not come as a surprise, as Burger wrote the opinions for the Court in both cases. In each case, Burger emphasized the need for a decisionmaker to be independent and neutral under the circumstances, instead of requiring that law-trained judges need to make all decisions.

Furthermore, Chief Justice Burger questioned the usefulness of a full adversarial hearing in this context and whether or not such a hearing would help further the goal of the decisionmaker's neutrality:

> Although we acknowledge the fallibility of medical and psychiatric diagnosis, we do not accept the notion that the shortcomings of specialists can always be avoided by shifting the decision from a trained specialist using the traditional tools of medical science to an untrained judge or administrative hearing officer after a judicial-type hearing. Even after a hearing, the nonspecialist decisionmaker must make a medical-psychiatric decision. Common human experience and scholarly opinions suggest that the supposed protections of an adversary proceeding to determine the appropriateness of medical decisions for the commitment and treatment of mental and emotional illness may well be more illusory than real.[36]

For this reason, Burger and the majority did not require such hearings for these types of mental health commitments. Instead, he stated that "we are satisfied that an independent medical decisionmaking process, which includes the thorough psychiatric investigation described earlier, followed by additional periodic review of a child's condition, will protect children who should not be admitted" and that "we do not believe the risks of error in that process would be significantly reduced by a more formal, judicial-type hearing."[37]

Given this standard, Burger reviewed the juvenile commitment practices that were used in Georgia. Georgia's system at the time involved a diagnostic medical inquiry by the admitting physician at each mental hospital. When parents were concerned about their children possibly having a mental illness, they would typically have the child examined by a psychologist or psychiatrist. If the abnormal behavior continued, this was often followed by outpatient treatment and then referral to a mental hospital. At that point, usual Georgia practice would be an admissions team of at least two mental health professionals examining the child, looking over medical records, and then making a diagnosis as to whether the child needed institutionalized care. For children who were admitted, the normal practice would be to periodically review their need for continued care "by at least one independent, medical review group." Burger wrote that these procedures are not arbitrary and that they comport with requirements of due process, including the need for the decisionmaker to be neutral.[38] Indeed, he and the other members of the majority were "satisfied that the voluminous record as a whole supports the conclusion that the admissions staffs of the hospitals have acted in a neutral and detached fashion in making medical judgments in the best interests of the children."[39]

After describing the due process standards for situations where a child's parents request his or her admission to a mental health facility, Chief Justice Burger elaborated on cases where children were wards of the state when they are admitted to such hospitals. Although the former situation described J.L.'s case, J.R.'s situation fit the latter category. Burger found that "the differences in the two situations do not justify requiring different procedures at the time of the child's initial admission to the hospital."[40] According to Burger, this is true because, although no adult may care for a child as deeply as one's natural parents, the state is still presumed to want to protect these children and act in their best interests. Like in the case of a child whose parents are requesting his or her admittance to a mental health facility, a child who is a ward of the state is given due process if "an independent medical judgment made from the perspective of the best interests of the child after a careful investigation" occurs.[41] For J.R., Burger concluded that due process was afforded because three physicians independently concluded that institutional care was in his best interests, and he found that there was no constitutional violation for either J.R. or J.L..[42]

Justice William Brennan wrote an opinion partly concurring and partly dissenting in the case. He was joined by Justice Thurgood Marshall and Justice John Paul Stevens. Justice Brennan agreed with the majority that commitment of a juvenile to a mental health facility by one's parents or by state guardians implicates liberty and other interests that trigger due process. However, Brennan thought that hearings should be provided to juveniles facing such commitments.

Early on in his opinion, Brennan aptly laid out the interests implicated by a juvenile being committed to such facilities:

> Commitment to a mental institution necessarily entails a massive curtailment of liberty and inevitably affects fundamental rights. Persons incarcerated in mental hospitals are not only deprived of their physical liberty, they are also deprived of friends, family, and community. Institutionalized mental patients must live

> in unnatural surroundings under the continuous and detailed control of strangers. They are subject to intrusive treatment which, especially if unwarranted, may violate their right to bodily integrity. Such treatment modalities may include forced administration of psychotropic medication, aversive conditioning, convulsive therapy, and even psychosurgery. Furthermore, as the Court recognizes, persons confined in mental institutions are stigmatized as sick and abnormal during confinement and, in some cases, even after release.[43]

Given the substantial freedom that one can lose under these circumstances, Brennan had no problem agreeing with the majority that Fourteenth Amendment interests are implicated by these commitments. Brennan then compared this to the rights accorded to adults facing involuntary commitment: "In the absence of a voluntary, knowing, and intelligent waiver, adults facing commitment to mental institutions are entitled to full and fair adversary hearings in which the necessity for their commitment is established to the satisfaction of a neutral tribunal...These principles also govern the commitment of children."[44] Since minors are also protected by the Constitution, Brennan reasoned that they deserve as much, if not more, due process protections as that afforded to adults.

For Brennan, one cannot count on the diagnosing physician to be the neutral decisionmaker that protects a child's due process rights in these cases. According to Brennan, psychiatric diagnosis and therapy decisions are full of uncertainties, and this fact is exacerbated in these cases because the child is being examined during a period of great stress, economic and social class may separate the child and the doctor, and psychiatrists tend to err on the side of medical attention. Thus, children in these situations are prone to being admitted to mental health facilities when such action is not necessary. A study of Georgia mental health services conducted four years before the U.S. Supreme Court decided *Parham* confirmed this when the study concluded that more than half of the state's institutionalized children were not in need of mental health confinement.[45]

Justice Brennan reasoned that children like J.L. who were committed by their parents have rights independent of their parents. In particular, Brennan found that the rights at stake here — freedom from "wrongful incarceration, physical intrusion, and stigmatization" — have great significance for the individual being committed.[46] Furthermore, Brennan noted that although one can generally presume that parents act in their children's best interests, that presumption cannot be sustained in the commitment context. Brennan cited multiple studies that showed that parental decisions to institutionalize their children are often the result of other problems in the family, and he surmised that even well-meaning parents often lack the expertise necessary to evaluate the wisdom of inpatient care.[47]

In order to balance out the rights of children being committed with the rights of their parents to act in the best interests of their children, Brennan advocated a post-confinement commitment hearing. Brennan did not think that due process required a pre-confinement hearing because that might deter parents from seeking needed mental health treatment for their children and it might traumatize the parent-child relationship. However, Brennan thought that due process was satisfied if an admitting psychiatrist interviews that child, and if admission is required, then a short time later a formal commitment proceeding is required. In particular, Brennan implicitly questioned the impartiality of hospital staff members serving as the decisionmakers at this stage: "At later hearings, the case for and against commitment would be based upon the observations of the hospital staff and the judgments of the staff psychiatrists, rather than upon parental observations and recommendations. The doctors urging commitment, and not the parents, would stand as the child's adversaries."[48] Although he did not spell it out, one can read Brennan's words to implicate that even psychiatrists acting in good faith may be predisposed to act on the advice of others, including parents, thus making them less than neutral when making these decisions.[49]

For children who were wards of the state and who were being admitted to mental health facilities for inpatient care, Brennan argued that due process required even more. First, he reasoned that one cannot assume that state social workers will act in the best interests of the juvenile they want to commit any more than one could assume that criminal trials are unnecessary because prosecutors are only supposed to prosecute those who are guilty. Thus, Brennan would have required pre-commitment hearings.[50]

Although Chief Justice Burger took some steps to protect the due process right for a juvenile to have an impartial decisionmaker review his or her confinement, Justice Brennan's approach ultimately serves as the better protection of this constitutional entitlement. Burger was right to emphasize the need for impartial review at the time of commitment and for follow-up review periodically after a juvenile is admitted to such a facility. When a juvenile has been committed in this fashion, either when this process is initiated by a juvenile's parents or by the state as guardian, that child has his or her freedom significantly restrained and may face social stigma. There is no question that this implicates due process, including the due process right to an impartial decisionmaker.

Where Chief Justice Burger fell short, however, was in the need for a formal judicial hearing before children are admitted in these contexts. Although these juvenile admittances are voluntary from the perspective of the parents or the state, they may very well be involuntary from the perspective of the child. Threatening to take away the freedom from these children and imposing what may be unwanted medical care on them should require review by the courts first. In a context where one's liberty may be taken away, the best way to ensure that the decisionmaker will be impartial is to have a judicial officer make the determination. As proclaimed by Justice Brennan, when confronted with a juvenile admitted under these circumstances, there are certain factors which make it significantly likely that such juveniles are admitted, even when it may not be necessary. Consider how this situation is also quite different from the medical license review that was at issue in *Withrow v. Larkin*. In that case, one's ultimate freedom was not at stake, so review could be done by a medical review board, not necessarily by a court.

Chief Justice Burger, however, was afraid of something else which might cause one to doubt the impartiality and competency of judges making these decisions — that judges are not medical experts. While this is true, judges must make decisions in a variety of contexts where they are applying a legal standard to a field of knowledge that is outside of the law. Consider, for instance, when judges must decide when to admit expert testimony or when judges must determine if an insanity defense may be put to a jury. Furthermore, medical personnel are of a different status than the non-lawyer judges that were at issue in *North v. Russell*. Non-lawyer judges, although not trained in law schools, may (and should) have continuing judicial training to help them remain impartial. Thus, they still have knowledge of constitutional and legal standards, and they are experienced with it, in ways that medical personnel may not be. Those medical experts may be excellent resources to help judges make these decisions, but medical personnel alone should not be in charge of these decisions on juvenile admittance to mental health facilities. As pointed out by Justice Brennan, there are factors that suggest such medical personnel may be less objective than judges when making these decisions.

The periodic review of juveniles who have been admitted to mental hospitals is a bit different. Much like how parole boards are made up of non-legal personnel and they decide if an inmate should be released, physicians at a medical health facility can be charged to make a discretionary discharge decision. Under the standard articulated by Brennan, a judge would have previously made the impartial decision that medical treatment (and the concomitant loss of liberty) was necessary. Thus, the decision of when that status should be changed can be delegated to medical personnel.

Ultimately, Chief Justice Burger and the majority collapsed the interests of the child into those of the parent and the state, rather than allowing for a neutral, independent judge to assess whether the child has a protectable interest in being free from bodily restraint. They also discounted the financial incentive that for-profit health care facilities may have in admitting children who may not be in need of inpatient mental health treatment. Indeed, by the early 1980s, such for-profit psychiatric hospitals made up close to one half of the market share. The economic incentive involved here has caused many such private facilities to aggressively advertise their services to potential new patients, including targeting rebellious teenagers. This incentive is only compounded by the vague and overly-broad admission criteria that are often used to admit juveniles for mental health treatment. Indeed, using the Diagnostic and Statistical Manual of Mental Disorders, Fourth Edition (DSM-IV), published by the American Psychiatric Association, is problematic because the definitions for conduct disorder, oppositional defiant disorder, personality disorder, and adjustment or transitional disorder are so vague that nearly every juvenile may qualify as having a "disorder" at some point.[51]

If such financial pressures are too much for judges in *Tumey* and *Ward*, then they should be too much for medical doctors who have no legal training in making decisions about juvenile commitments. In fact, the situation in *Parham* was more significant constitutionally, because it involved the right to an impartial decisionmaker when one's freedom is at stake; in *Tumey* and *Ward*, only fines were at stake.

Finally, as will be further explained in chapter fifteen and the concluding chapter, one should question the Court's reliance on the *Mathews* standard in this context. *Mathews* involved the denial of welfare benefits. While this can be a substantial burden on a recipient who no longer has those funds to pay for living expenses, commitment for a potentially unlimited amount of time to a mental health facility is a much more significant deprivation. Indeed, to lose one's freedom is much more substantial than to lose one's property.

The impartiality of the medical personnel is not saved by well-meaning parents who are trying to admit their children to such facilities. Although parents generally have the best interests of their children in mind, parents dealing with an unruly child may not be thinking clearly and may make mistakes regarding the need for inpatient treatment. Even under the best of conditions, most laypersons will not know when child psychiatric care is appropriate, and these problems are exacerbated by the stress that parents are under when they have a child who displays severe behavioral problems. Similar difficulties exist when a child is a ward of the state. Social service agencies are often underfunded and may seek mental health commitments for problem children when they cannot be successfully placed in foster care. Given these potential circumstances, it is no surprise that admitting physicians have a tendency to over diagnose, not wanting to explain to the parent or state worker why admission is not warranted.[52]

The surest way to protect the neutrality of a decisionmaker when one's freedom is at stake is to hold a judicial hearing. Unfortunately, neither J.L. nor J.R. was given such an opportunity before spending years in the custody of a mental health facility. By the time the U.S. Supreme Court reviewed their cases, J.L. was already deceased; since J.R.'s case involved the rights of a juvenile, the records are sealed, and his ultimate fate is unknown. What is known is that his due process right to an impartial decisionmaker was not vindicated by the U.S. Supreme Court.

Notes

1. Gerald N. Grob, *The Mad Among Us: A History of the Care of America's Mentally Ill* (New York: The Free Press, 1994), 20; Elizabeth A. Segal, *Social Welfare Policy and Social Programs: A Values Perspective* (Belmont, CA: Cengage Learning, 2010), 259; Donna R. Kemp, *Mental Health in America: A Reference Handbook* (Santa Barbara, CA: ABC-CLIO, 2007), 2.
2. Grob, *The Mad Among Us*, 2; Segal, *Social Welfare Policy*, 259.

3. Robert G. Meyer and Christopher M. Veaver, *Law and Mental Health: A Case-Based Approach* (New York: The Guilford Press, 2006), 128-29.
4. *O'Connor v. Donaldson*, 422 U.S. 563 (1975).
5. *Addington v. Texas*, 441 U.S. 418 (1979).
6. *In re Gault*, 387 U.S. 1 (1967).
7. *Parham v. J.R.* 442 U.S. 584, 590 (1979); *J.L. v. Parham*, 412 F. Supp. 112, 116 (M.D. Ga. 1976).
8. *Parham*, 442 U.S. at 590; *J.L.*, 412 F. Supp. at 116-17.
9. *Parham*, 442 U.S. at 589; *J.L.*, 412 F. Supp. at 117.
10. *Parham*, 442 U.S. at 589-90; *J.L.*, 412 F. Supp. at 117.
11. *Parham*, 442 U.S. at 590-95.
12. *Parham*, 442 U.S. at 589-90; *J.L.*, 412 F. Supp. at 117-18.
13. *Parham*, 442 U.S. at 589; *J.L.*, 412 F. Supp. at 117, 137-39.
14. *Mathews v. Eldridge*, 424 U.S. 319, 335 (1976).
15. *Parham*, 442 U.S. at 600.
16. *Parham*, 442 U.S. at 600.
17. *Parham*, 442 U.S. at 600.
18. *Parham*, 442 U.S. at 601.
19. *Parham*, 442 U.S. at 601.
20. *Parham*, 442 U.S. at 602 (quoting *Pierce v. Society of Sisters*, 268 U.S. 510, 535 (1925)) (brackets in original).
21. *Parham*, 442 U.S. at 602.
22. *Parham*, 442 U.S. at 602.
23. *Parham*, 442 U.S. at 604.
24. *Parham*, 442 U.S. at 603 (internal quotations and citation omitted).
25. *Parham*, 442 U.S. at 603.
26. *Parham*, 442 U.S. at 604.
27. *Parham*, 442 U.S. at 605.
28. *Parham*, 442 U.S. at 605.
29. *Parham*, 442 U.S. at 606.
30. *Parham*, 442 U.S. at 607.
31. *Parham*, 442 U.S. at 607.
32. *Parham*, 442 U.S. at 607.
33. *Parham*, 442 U.S. at 607.
34. *Parham*, 442 U.S. at 607-08.
35. *Parham*, 442 U.S. at 608.
36. *Parham*, 442 U.S. at 609 (internal citations omitted).
37. *Parham*, 442 U.S. at 613.
38. *Parham*, 442 U.S. at 613-16.
39. *Parham*, 442 U.S. at 616.
40. *Parham*, 442 U.S. at 617-18.
41. *Parham*, 442 U.S. at 618.
42. *Parham*, 442 U.S. at 619-21.
43. *Parham*, 442 U.S. at 627 (Brennan, J., dissenting in part and concurring in part) (internal citations and quotations omitted).
44. *Parham,* 442 U.S. at 627 (Brennan, J., dissenting in part and concurring in part).

45. *Parham*, 442 U.S. at 629 (Brennan, J., dissenting in part and concurring in part).

46. *Parham*, 442 U.S. at 632 (Brennan, J., dissenting in part and concurring in part).

47. *Parham*, 442 U.S. at 632 (Brennan, J., dissenting in part and concurring in part).

48. *Parham*, 442 U.S. at 635 (Brennan, J., dissenting in part and concurring in part).

49. *Parham*, 442 U.S. at 636-37 (Brennan, J., dissenting in part and concurring in part).

50. *Parham*, 442 U.S. at 637-38 (Brennan, J., dissenting in part and concurring in part).

51. Samuel M. Leaf, "How Voluntary is the Voluntary Commitment of Minors? Disparities in the Treatment of Children and Adults under New York's Civil Commitment Law," *Brooklyn Law Review* 62 (1996): 1687-1730, 1707, 1721-23; Dennis E. Cichon, "Developing a Mental Health Code for Minors," *Thomas M. Cooley Law Review* 13 (1996): 529-614, 534.

52. Cichon, "Mental Health Code of Minors," 553-56.

~ 14 ~

Prison Discipline: *Edwards v. Balisok* (1997)

The due process requirements for a prison disciplinary hearing are in many respects less demanding than those for criminal prosecution, but they are not so lax as to let stand the decision of a biased hearing officer who dishonestly suppresses evidence of innocence.
– *Edwards v. Balisok*, 520 U.S. 641, 647 (1997)

After defendants have been duly convicted of their crimes, they are sentenced. For those who are sentenced to jail or prison, they will serve time either in a county jail or in a state penitentiary. Once they have arrived at those facilities, inmates are subject to obvious restrictions on their freedom. If an inmate is accused of breaking jail or prison rules, he or she may be exposed to additional discipline beyond what the judge required at sentencing. The question remains, however, what to do when inmates claim that they were falsely accused of breaking jail or prison rules. What kind of process is due to such inmates when they wish to challenge this type of discipline? And what requirements are in place regarding the need for an impartial decisionmaker in these cases?

Edwards v. Balisok (1997) began with Jerry Bibb Balisok, A.K.A. Ricky A. Wetta, purchasing the Columbian Hotel in Wenatchee, Washington for $135,000 in June of 1988. In September of that year, Balisok took out a $4 million insurance policy on the hotel, which burned down less than one month later. Shortly thereafter, Balisok was indicted for conspiracy to commit arson based on the testimony of Daniel Binford, who claimed that Balisok had offered him $10,000 to burn down the hotel. Emmett Thompson II, however, ultimately set the fire according to Balisok's instructions. In order to silence this potential witness, Balisok took Thompson target shooting on September 5, 1989, and when they were walking back to their car afterwards, Balisok shot Thompson in the head and arm. Thompson managed to escape, and federal authorities gave him immunity in exchange for his testimony against Balisok.[1]

When Balisok was put on trial for attempted murder in the first degree, he argued self-defense, claiming that Thompson tried to stab him with a dagger before Balisok shot him. However, the jury did not buy this explanation. Instead, the jurors found Balisok guilty, and the judge sentenced him to twenty years in prison.[2]

Thereafter, Balisok was sent to the Washington State Penitentiary in Walla Walla. On August 16, 1993, he was charged with violating four prison regulations. It is not clear from the records what these four regulations were. Under Washington's state penitentiary disciplinary code, there are certain procedures that are required when a prisoner is accused of committing this type of infraction. First, a report must be prepared and submitted by a staff member. This report needs to then be forwarded to a hearing officer. Before a disciplinary hearing takes place, the prisoner must be given various other due process protections. A hearing for Balisok was scheduled for September 2, 1993, where Balisok was found guilty of four infractions. His sentence for these violations included ten days in isolation, twenty days in segregation, and a loss of thirty days of good-time credits he had earned toward his release. Balisok appealed this decision within the prison's appeal system, but his request was denied because he did not comply with procedural requirements, including exceeding the page limit of his written appeal.[3]

These sentences affected Balisok's Fourteenth Amendment rights. The impositions of isolation and segregation limited the amount of freedom that Balisok retained while in prison. Although his freedom was diminished once he was convicted in court, he still retained some rights. In addition, his earning of good-time credits in prison through good behavior affected his release date. By having these credits revoked, the return of Balisok's full freedom was affected by this determination.

Believing that his due process rights were violated by what happened, Balisok filed a civil suit against prison officials Gary Edwards and Tana Wood in January of 1994. Balisok made his claim under 42 U.S.C. § 1983, which is a section of the federal statutes that allows persons to sue government actors who have allegedly violated constitutional rights. This is often a suit filed by criminal suspects against police officers, or by inmates against correctional personnel, if they claim that their Fourteenth Amendment rights have been violated. Balisok pleaded that the procedures used by Washington State violated due process, specifically that the hearing officer Edwards concealed exculpatory witness statements and refused to ask certain questions of requested witnesses. According to Balisok, Edwards's actions denied him the right to present his defense. Furthermore, Balisok alleged that Edwards did not provide a statement of the facts supporting the finding of guilt against him. Balisok ultimately claimed that Edwards was biased against him. Finally, Balisok was suing Wood for rejecting his appeal for the allegedly erroneous reason of it exceeding the required page limit. For these violations, Balisok requested both compensatory and punitive damages, as well as an injunction to prevent future violations of this type.[4]

A federal district court declined to rule in his favor, reasoning that a judgment for Balisok would imply that his disciplinary hearing and resulting sanctions were constitutionally defective. Still, the federal district court did not dismiss Balisok's case either, instead waiting for final resolution from the state court system on the issue of his good-time credits. The Ninth Circuit Court of Appeals reversed this decision, holding that Balisok's § 1983 action challenging the procedures in his disciplinary hearing could go forward immediately. The U.S. Supreme Court then decided to hear the appeal.[5]

Justice Antonin Scalia wrote the opinion of the Court in *Edwards v. Balisok*. Justice Scalia denied Balisok's claim for a rather technical legal reason: Balisok's civil complaint did not go far enough. Balisok only "limited his request to damages for depriving him of good-time credits *without due process*, not for depriving him of good-time credits *undeservedly* as a substantive matter."[6] In other words, if Balisok had been able to show that he had been substantively denied his rights, then the Court would have decided his request for damages on the issue of whether he was denied due process. Instead, since Balisok only asked relief on the process used to deprive him of his good-time credits, the Court would not hear his claim. The reason the Court could not hear such a complaint was that "the nature of the challenge to the procedures could be such as necessarily to imply the invalidity of the judgment."[7] The Court was not willing to challenge the validity of the outcome via finding a defect in the procedures without Balisok having already demonstrated this substantive fact. In ruling this way, Scalia was following the precedent in a previous Supreme Court case, *Heck v. Humphrey* (1994), where the justices held that "a state prisoner's claim for damages is not cognizable under 42 U.S.C. § 1983 if 'a judgment in favor of the plaintiff would necessarily imply the invalidity of his conviction or sentence,' unless the prisoner can demonstrate that the conviction or sentence has previously been invalidated."[8]

Nevertheless, Justice Scalia did address Balisok's due process claims, including the potential bias of the hearing officer. Balisok's assertion here was that the exclusion of exculpatory evidence was due to "the deceit and bias of the hearing officer." Scalia dealt with this issue by stating the general rule for judicial impartiality in criminal cases: "A criminal defendant tried by a partial judge is entitled to have his conviction set aside, no matter how strong the evidence against him."[9] Indeed, there is no question that regardless of other factors, a criminal conviction is invalidated as violative of due process if the decisionmaker is biased. However, Scalia was quick to limit the extent of this concept in the current context: "The due process requirements for a prison disciplinary hearing are in many respects less demanding than those for criminal prosecution, but they are not so lax as to let stand the decision of a biased hearing officer who dishonestly suppresses evidence of innocence."[10] Although due process still applies, it applies less when the decisionmaker is deciding the partial freedom of a prisoner versus the full freedom of a criminal defendant.

This point notwithstanding, Scalia and the Court refused to decide if Edwards was, in fact, biased against Balisok or what the requirements of such an analysis would look like because of the fear that it would question the ultimate substantive outcome of the decision on Balisok's good-time credits. Instead, Scalia stated that the "*evidentiary requirements* of due process are satisfied if there is 'some evidence' in the record to support a prison disciplinary decision revoking good time credits."[11] Scalia then concluded that Balisok's claim for declaratory relief and money damages, "based on allegations of deceit and bias on the part of the decisionmaker that necessarily imply the invalidity of the punishment imposed, is not cognizable under § 1983."[12] However, Scalia did note that Balisok could still request prospective injunctive relief, which had not been litigated yet in the courts below.

The *Edwards* case stands for the proposition that a prisoner may not seek damages under 42 U.S.C. § 1983 for a deprivation of good time credits without due process of law if a judgment in the prisoner's favor would imply the invalidity of the punishment imposed, unless the prisoner can demonstrate that the punishment has already been invalidated. Ultimately, the court decided this case the way it did because it did not see civil claims, such as § 1983 claims, as the appropriate way to challenge the unlawfulness of one's conviction or confinement. This decision is in line with the notion that the federal courts will give proper respect to state court decisions, but it goes beyond that principle in that it gives credence not just to state court decisions but also to the decisionmaking processes of prison hearing officers. Those personnel may have little to no legal training, meaning that they may not know what impartiality in decisionmaking truly is under the Fourteenth Amendment.[13]

Perhaps the Court was right that civil § 1983 claims are not the best vehicle to challenge the validity of confinement issues for prisoners. However, the tortured logic that this produces fails to adequately protect due process rights, including the right to an impartial decisionmaker. In order to prevail on his claim, Balisok would have needed to first demonstrate that his punishment for violating prison rules has already been invalidated. Of course, Balisok is unlikely to do that if he cannot raise it as a civil matter in state court, if he has an unsuccessful habeas corpus petition, or if his appeal was denied, like in this case, because his petition *was too long*! This catch-22 leaves prisoners in Balisok's situation without any legal recourse to challenge the alleged partiality of their decisionmaker. As one legal commentator described the *Edwards* decision, "if the Court continues down this path, it will surely wash its hands completely of prisoners' due process rights."[14]

At the very least, the court's decision in *Edwards* is confusing to lawyers and lower court judges when handling these types of claims. At the very worst, it means that prisoners like Balisok who claim a violation of their due process rights, including their basic right to a neutral decisionmaker, cannot be effectively litigated.[15]

Given that Balisok's freedom within the prison was at stake in the decision on his isolation and segregation, and given that his ultimate release date was at issue in the decision on his good-time credits, he deserved to have his claims heard. Although Justice Scalia was correct in that more process is due to one facing criminal prosecution than one facing prison discipline, the liberty implications are still significant in this case, demanding that a neutral decisionmaker preside over these types of prison hearings. Having his claim heard in court was the minimum that due process required for Balisok to ensure that his hearing decisionmaker was neutral. Failure of that made Scalia's words, that due process will not "let stand the decision of a biased hearing officer who dishonestly suppresses evidence of innocence," ring hollow. Without granting him the right to move forward in his civil suit, we cannot know if Balisok did, in fact, have this right denied to him.

Notes

1. *State v. Balisok*, 866 P.2d 631, 631-32 (Wash. 1994).
2. *State v. Balisok*, 866 P.2d at 632; *State v. Balisok*, 843 P.2d 1086, 1086 (Wash. Ct. App. 1992).
3. *Edwards v. Balisok*, 520 U.S. 641, 644 (1997); Tiffany A. Werner, "*Edwards v. Balisok* — Is the Court Washing Its Hands of Prisoners' Due Process Rights?," *Seton Hall Law Review* 28 (1997): 650-81, 655 n.17 & n.20.
4. *Edwards*, 520 U.S. at 644-47; David W. Neubauer and Henry F. Fradella, *America's Courts and the Criminal Justice System* (Belmont, CA: Wadsworth, 2011), 72.
5. *Edwards*, 520 U.S. at 644.
6. *Edwards*, 520 U.S. at 645 (emphasis in original).
7. *Edwards*, 520 U.S. at 645.
8. *Edwards*, 520 U.S. at 643 (quoting *Heck v. Humphrey*, 512 U.S. 477, 487 (1994)).
9. *Edwards*, 520 U.S. at 647.
10. *Edwards*, 520 U.S. at 647.
11. *Edwards*, 520 U.S. at 648 (emphasis in original) (quoting *In re Johnson*, 109 Wash. 2d 493, 497 (1987).
12. *Edwards*, 520 U.S. at 648.
13. Rhonda Wasserman, *Procedural Due Process: A Reference Guide to the United States Constitution* (Westport, CT: Praeger, 2004), 118; Werner, "*Edwards v. Balisok*," 677-78.
14. Werner, "*Edwards v. Balisok*," 678-79, 681; Melissa L. Koehn, "The New American Caste System: The Supreme Court and Discrimination among Civil Rights Plaintiffs," *University of Michigan Journal of Law Reform* 32 (1998): 49-104, 95.
15. Werner, "*Edwards v. Balisok*," 679-80; Koehn, "New American Case System," 96.

~ 15 ~

Enemy Combatant Cases: *Hamdi v. Rumsfeld* (2004)

It is during our most challenging and uncertain moments that our Nation's commitment to due process is most severely tested; and it is in those times that we must preserve our commitment at home to the principles for which we fight abroad.
– *Hamdi v. Rumsfeld*, 542 U.S. 507, 532 (2004)

An interrogation by one's captor, however effective an intelligence-gathering tool, hardly constitutes a constitutionally adequate factfinding before a neutral decisionmaker.
– *Hamdi v. Rumsfeld*, 542 U.S. 537, 532 (2004)

At certain moments in our history, the United States has faced the crisis of major war. These are wars that consume the nation and test the abilities and ideals and fortitude of most, if not all, citizens. Although America has largely assumed the role of the "world's policeman" over the past several decades, many military incursions that this country has undertaken during and after the Cold War fail to qualify as these types of crises. Indeed, truly grave war crises have only struck America once every few generations, the most notable ones in U.S. history being the Revolutionary War, the Civil War, World War II, and the post-September 11th War on Terrorism. In each case, the country found itself under some sort of major attack, our citizens suffered great loss of life, and the threat and fear of war reverberated into every home. At least in the first three situations, the war ended with victory. In the fourth, chapters are still left to be written.

Anytime our country or any other one is in an extended war, prisoners will be captured on the battlefield. When this occurs, questions arise what to do with them. Obviously, one does not want to simply release a prisoner of war or a terrorist, only to have that individual immediately take up arms again. At the same time, a civilized society with an enlightened system of justice will work strongly to prevent the wrongly accused from being held in captivity indefinitely without trial or charge. To protect the rights of prisoners of war, international treaties have been written, turning military questions into legal ones. Often, countries agree to such terms not solely out of respect for human rights, but also out of reciprocal self-interest for the lives of their own citizens and soldiers. Nevertheless, these documents are meant to protect those who have been taken prisoner during war.

When America is tested in wars that raise these types of issues, a natural reaction can be to reflect upon our founding documents. These documents were written to give us guidance and to limit the power of government, both in peace and in war. Constitutional language alone, however, often gives us little practical guidance because it can be quite vague, a consequence of our requirement that supermajorities were needed to ratify the document and amend it. Indeed, when needing so many votes in Congress and at the state level to change the Constitution, the language of amendments is often constructed in vague ways so that its meaning depends on the eye of the beholder. Although this may give us some eloquent text, it also means that such language can leave us with more questions than answers. This can make interpreting such provisions a daunting task, especially during times of peril.

Of course, there are many questions like these that, although difficult to answer, are well resolved. In some cases, it is because the relevant constitutional language is clearer; in others, the sheer volume of cases that regularly occur in a given area of constitutional law have led to the settling of important questions over time. Indeed, for ordinary crimes, the Bill of Rights and centuries of case law have spawned well-known rules on issues such as when and how police may conduct searches of suspects, what evidence must be excluded at trial, a suspect's right against compelled self-incrimination, the right to a jury trial and a whole host of procedural protections that are carried with it, the right to counsel, the right against cruel and unusual punishment, and many more. But with those suspected of making war on the United States or plotting terrorist acts, fewer cases exist to guide us. Thus, in these emergency situations, times when we should be the most prepared, we often have the least amount of legal guidance on how to proceed with respect to due process rights of the accused. What occurred on September 11, 2001 brought these issues again to the forefront of our national consciousness.

There is no question that the events of September 11, 2001 marked one of the most significant dates in American history. On that day, nineteen members of Al Qaeda hijacked four airplanes and navigated them on suicide missions. Two planes were purposely crashed into the World Trade Center in New York City, which caused the buildings to collapse later that day. A third jet was flown into the Pentagon in Washington, D.C. On the fourth jet, likely on a collision course with a target in Washington, D.C., passengers tried to wrestle the controls from the hijackers, resulting in the plane crashing into a field in western Pennsylvania. All told, nearly 3,000 people lost their lives that day.[1]

Shortly thereafter, the U.S. government began responding to these terrorist acts. On September 16, 2001, President George W. Bush noted to the American people that he expected the retaliation to take a significant amount of time: "the American people are beginning to understand, this crusade, this war on terrorism, is going to take a while."[2] Congress, wanting to contribute to the newly forming War on Terrorism, passed "The Authorization for Use of Military Force" (AUMF) on September 18, 2001. The document stated that "the President is authorized to use all necessary and appropriate force against those nations, organizations, or persons he determines planned, authorized, committed, or aided the terrorist attacks that occurred on September 11, 2001."[3] With the AUMF in hand, President Bush launched a joint American-British military action, Operation Enduring Freedom, on October 7, 2001, against Al Qaeda and the Taliban in Afghanistan. Anyone captured in Operation Enduring Freedom, and those taken into custody in other places around the globe as suspected terrorists, were labeled "enemy combatants." Under AUMF, President Bush claimed that he possessed the power to hold these enemy combatants as long as necessary. Very soon, hundreds of persons were labeled enemy combatants, most of whom were eventually brought to the U.S. naval base at Guantanamo Bay, Cuba.[4] Many of these individuals were held without any type of charge being filed or trial being scheduled. Before long, some of these detainees, and those acting on their behalf, turned to the federal courts for relief. Yaser Esam Hamdi is one of those individuals.

Yaser Esam Hamdi was born in Louisiana in 1980 and, according to the dictates of the Fourteenth Amendment, was therefore a United States citizen. However, while still a child he moved with his family to Saudi Arabia. The details of Hamdi's life become less clear in the late 1980s and the 1990s, but it is certain that by 2001 he was living in Afghanistan. In November of that year, Hamdi was captured by the Northern Alliance, and shortly thereafter he was handed over to the U.S. military. Subsequent to government agents' interrogation of Hamdi, in January 2002 the federal government labeled him an enemy combatant and relocated him to Camp X-Ray at the U.S. naval base at Guantanamo Bay, Cuba. After later discovering that Hamdi was a U.S. citizen, the military moved him again, this time to a naval brig in South Carolina. Even though it was now evident that Hamdi was an American citizen, the federal government continued to classify him as an enemy combatant, and it claimed the power to hold him indefinitely without trial or charge.[5]

The federal government classified Hamdi as an enemy combatant due to a declaration written by Michael Mobbs, Special Advisor to the Under Secretary of Defense for Policy. The Mobbs Declaration, the only evidentiary support that the U.S. government provided to the courts for Hamdi's detention, claimed that Hamdi fought with the Taliban in Afghanistan in the summer and fall of 2001, until the Northern Alliance seized him after a battle. The Mobbs Declaration also asserted that when Northern Alliance forces captured Hamdi, he was in possession of an AK-47. Hamdi's father, Esam Fouad Hamdi, was not persuaded by the Mobbs Declaration, claiming that his son was in Afghanistan to do "relief work." According to Hamdi's father, the young man was traveling on his own for the first time, and he was unable to leave Afghanistan once Operation Enduring Freedom began in October 2001. Thus, Hamdi's father petitioned for a writ of habeas corpus on his son's behalf, claiming that his son was being held in error and in violation of the U.S. Constitution.[6]

Hamdi's father questioned the conclusions of the Mobbs Declaration because it was just what it purported to be — a declaration. What Michael Mobbs engaged in to write the document was not the formal fact finding expected in the judiciary. Mobbs, who was ultimately an employee of the executive branch, had never met Hamdi. According to his declaration, Mobbs only did a "review of relevant records and reports," and he made his declaration based on his belief that he was "also familiar with the facts and circumstances related to the capture of...Hamdi and his detention by U.S. military forces." This was all of the evidence used to classify him as an enemy combatant.[7]

Furthermore, it has been well-established that the Northern Alliance and other groups turning over suspect terrorists were less than reliable sources of information during this period. The United States was paying bounties in Afghanistan and Pakistan to those who turned in members of the Taliban and Al Qaeda. Reportedly, these bounties were up to $5,000 for each Taliban prisoner and $20,000 for each Al Qaeda fighter. Although this helped encourage locals to turn in enemies of the United States, it also emboldened bounty hunters and warlords to capture innocent civilians and rivals, coerce them into giving false confessions, and subsequently turn them over to U.S. military commanders. It is unclear whether or not any bounty was paid for Hamdi.[8]

The level of fact finding that took place for Hamdi was far afield from what is normally expected by due process. Indeed, based on the cases reviewed in previous chapters, one has to question the impartiality of one Department of Defense official to determine if Hamdi was engaged in acts of war against the U.S. and its allies. Would there be repercussions against Mobbs for declaring anything but that Hamdi was an enemy of the United States, given that the military had already classified him that way? Would there be political fallout to the Bush Administration if Mobbs found that a U.S. citizen had been illegally detained? Would it be particularly embarrassing to the military if Mobbs declared that the Northern Alliance rounded up Hamdi and falsely identified him as a terrorist so they could receive a U.S. bounty? Perhaps a more neutral factfinder, one who did not have a preconceived notion of the case outcome, would have investigated the sources within the Northern Alliance, interviewed them instead of reading their statements, and asked what their motives were when turning in Hamdi.

These considerations might help explain why the Mobbs Declaration was so thin. Federal District Court Judge Robert G. Doumar understood it as such. When Judge Doumar reviewed Hamdi's habeas petition, he characterized the Mobbs Declaration as "little more than the government's 'say-so;'" Judge Doumar stated that if he were to accept the Declaration as justification for Hamdi's detention, he "would be acting as little more than a rubber-stamp" for the executive branch.[9] Judge Doumar ordered the government to turn over numerous documents for judicial review, including Hamdi's statements, a list of his interrogators, statements by the Northern Alliance members who captured Hamdi, and the names and titles of U.S. government officials who determined Hamdi's classification as an enemy combatant.

The Bush Administration, however, disagreed with the federal district court and appealed its ruling. Hamdi's case was eventually argued in front of the U.S. Supreme Court in April 2004, with a decision issued partially in his favor only two months later in June 2004. Although the justices ultimately disagreed over what due process rights needed to be afforded to Hamdi, all but one, Justice Clarence Thomas, found constitutional violations in the Bush Administration's actions in the case.

Justice Sandra Day O'Connor wrote the plurality opinion, which was joined fully by Chief Justice William Rehnquist, Justice Anthony Kennedy, and Justice Stephen Breyer. In O'Connor's opening paragraph, she set the stage for the Court's middle-of-the road ruling: "due process demands that a citizen held in the United States as an enemy combatant be given a meaningful opportunity to contest the factual basis for that detention before a neutral decisionmaker."[10] Thus, O'Connor signaled that neither side would be completely happy with the Court's approach, as the government could not hold Hamdi indefinitely without some neutral fact-finding, yet Hamdi was not guaranteed the normal due process protections given to criminal defendants. O'Connor and the plurality took this approach because they freely admitted that the "capture and detention of lawful combatants and the capture, detention, and trial of unlawful combatants" is one of the incidents of war; furthermore, "[t]here is no bar to this Nation's holding one of its own citizens as an enemy combatant."[11] For O'Connor, war changes the rules to the game.

Even so, O'Connor believed that some due process rules still exist during the War on Terrorism. O'Connor noted if an enemy combatant wanted to challenge that designation, he or she needed to be given a real opportunity to do so, even if this was not a full-blown criminal proceeding. Noting that each side had "legitimate concerns" and "substantial interests" (the power to wage war effectively versus the protection of individual liberties), O'Connor announced the standard to be followed in these types of cases: "The ordinary mechanism that we use for balancing such serious competing interests, and for determining the procedures that are necessary to ensure that a citizen is not 'deprived of life, liberty, or property, without due process of law,' is the test that we articulated in *Mathews v. Eldridge* (1976)."[12]

Recall from chapter thirteen that *Mathews* involved a litigant, Eldridge, who had his Social Security disability benefit payments terminated prior to an evidentiary hearing. The *Mathews* Court held that procedural due process was *not* violated in this case. In laying down that ruling, the Court determined that the requirements of due process would vary by each case, depending on three factors:

> First, the private interest that will be affected by the official action; second, the risk of an erroneous deprivation of such interest through the procedures used, and the probable value, if any, of additional or substitute procedural safeguards; and finally, the Government's interest, including the function involved and the fiscal and administrative burdens that the additional or substitute procedural requirement would entail.[13]

Much like the analysis of involuntary juvenile mental health commitments in *Parham*, this was the test that the *Hamdi* Court would apply to determine what due process requires for enemy combatants challenging their detention.

Applying the first prong of the *Mathews* balancing test in *Hamdi*, "the private interest...affected by the official action," O'Connor described a basic, yet extremely important, right: "the interest in being free from physical detention by one's own government."[14] O'Connor described this as the norm, not the exception, even in the post-September 11th world: "Nor is the weight on this side of the *Mathews* scale offset by the circumstances of war or the accusation of treasonous behavior, for it is clear that commitment for *any* purpose constitutes a significant deprivation of liberty that requires due process protection."[15] She came to this conclusion because "at this stage in the *Mathews* calculus, we consider the interest of the *erroneously* detained individual."[16] If one is approaching Hamdi's claim by using a *Mathews* analysis, this is quite sensible; after all, the hallmark of a neutral decisionmaker is that he or she should not have made up his or her mind about the case at hand. If that has happened, then liberty may have been erroneously deprived, and a court should review the case from that vantage point. O'Connor concluded this portion of the analysis by stating that "[w]e reaffirm today the fundamental nature of a citizen's right to be free from involuntary confinement by his own government without due process of law, and we weigh the opposing governmental interests against the curtailment of liberty that such confinement entails."[17]

O'Connor next applied the third prong of the *Mathews* analysis, which focused on the government's interest:

> On the other side of the scale are the weighty and sensitive governmental interests in ensuring that those who have in fact fought with the enemy during a war do not return to battle against the United States...our Constitution recognizes that core strategic matters of warmaking belong in the hands of those who are best positioned and most politically accountable for making them.[18]

Clearly, O'Connor was yielding to the needs of the executive branch to wage war effectively. Not only was the plurality cognizant of the need to hold enemy combatants as part of the war making power, but also of the difficulties involved in providing due process to those labeled enemy combatants during war:

> [M]ilitary officers who are engaged in the serious work of waging battle would be unnecessarily and dangerously distracted by litigation half a world away, and discovery into military operations would both intrude on the sensitive secrets of national defense and result in a futile search for evidence buried under the rubble of war. To the extent that these burdens are triggered by heightened procedures, they are properly taken into account in our due process analysis.[19]

With the concerns for Hamdi's rights and the need for the government to be able to effectively wage war, O'Connor tried to strike a balance between the two. She began by noting that it is "during our most challenging and uncertain moments that our Nation's commitment to due process is most severely tested; and it is in those times that we must preserve our commitment at home to the principles for which we fight abroad."[20] She and the rest of the plurality thought that the standard of review that existed in the Mobbs Declaration was insufficient to protect Hamdi's due process rights, but these justices also determined that the more involved judicial review ordered by the district court judge did not adequately protect the government's serious interests. Thus, trying to balance these interests and simultaneously lessen the risk of erroneous deprivation of a detainee's liberty interests, O'Connor and the plurality held the following: "a citizen-detainee seeking to challenge his classification as an enemy combatant must receive notice of the factual basis for his classification, and a fair opportunity to rebut the Government's factual assertions before a neutral decisionmaker."[21] In other words, at a minimum, the basic due process requirements of a neutral decisionmaker and the demands of notice and hearing, rules which have been long established in non-enemy combatant cases, need to be met. The Mobbs Declaration clearly did not meet this standard.

However, O'Connor was not advocating anything akin to full criminal trial rights for enemy combatants: "the exigencies of the circumstances may demand that, aside from these core elements [of notice and hearing], enemy-combatant proceedings may be tailored to alleviate their uncommon potential to burden the Executive at a time of ongoing military conflict."[22] What did this mean? According to O'Connor, it meant that hearsay may be admissible in enemy combatant reviews and that the burden of proof could be placed on the defense: "Hearsay, for example, may need to be accepted as the most reliable available evidence from the Government in such a proceeding. Likewise, the Constitution would not be offended by a presumption in favor of the Government's evidence, so long as that presumption remained a rebuttable one and fair opportunity for rebuttal were provided."[23]

This raises some immediate red flags when examining due process considerations, including the reliability of the evidence presented (such as Northern Alliance hearsay) and the fairness of requiring someone who is held in captivity to prove his or her innocence. In addition, one wonders what other procedures might be acceptable at these proceedings, as the Court noted the use of hearsay evidence and the shifting of the burden of proof were only *examples* of what due process requires in these cases.

More directly for our purposes is how neutral the decisionmaker will be in these types of cases. O'Connor did go on to note the following: "Any factfinding imposition created by requiring a knowledgeable affiant to summarize these records to an independent tribunal is a minimal one."[24] She also made it clear that an "interrogation by one's captor, however effective an intelligence-gathering tool, hardly constitutes a constitutionally adequate factfinding before a neutral decisionmaker."[25] O'Connor even forthrightly stated that "[w]e have no reason to doubt that courts faced with these sensitive matters will pay proper heed both to the matters of national security that might arise in an individual case and to the constitutional limitations safeguarding essential liberties that remain vibrant even in times of security concerns."[26] However, O'Connor also implied that a military tribunal is a sufficient way to provide due process to those accused of being enemy combatants: "There remains the possibility that the standards we have articulated could be met by an appropriately authorized and properly constituted military tribunal."[27] Thus, military officers could be the neutral decisionmakers under O'Connor's scheme. While this is more balanced than simply allowing Michael Mobbs to serve as judge and jury, it still leaves all decisions within the militiary: military officials decide who is designated as an enemy combatant, military officials prosecute the case, and military officials sit in judgment of the person who is accused. Those "neutral" decisionmakers are still employees of the executive branch, and they ultimately answer to the president. For a civilian, the neutrality of the decisionmaker in these tribunals has to be immediately suspected. Furthermore, if the burden can be shifted to the defendant and if the government can use hearsay evidence against the defendant, the neutrality of such a decisionmaker is threatened even more.

Justice Antonin Scalia was quick to point out in a dissenting opinion (joined by Justice John Paul Stevens) that the plurality's approach had significant holes in it. Scalia argued that a system was already in place to ensure that a neutral decisionmaker will exist in cases like Hamdi's:

> Where the Government accuses a citizen of waging war against it, our constitutional tradition has been to prosecute him in federal court for treason or some other crime. Where the exigencies of war prevent that, the Constitution's Suspension Clause, Art. I, § 9, cl. 2, allows Congress to relax the usual protections temporarily. Absent suspension, however, the Executive's assertion of military exigency has not been thought sufficient to permit detention without charge.[28]

Noting that Congress did not suspend the writ of habeas corpus, Scalia found no reason to authorize the type of detention advocated by the Bush Administration, nor did he believe there existed cause to decide Hamdi's fate in front of a military commission. Instead, Scalia saw two remaining options for the government in this case: seek a federal indictment against Hamdi for treason and other crimes, or else release him. For Scalia, the tried and tested method of a criminal jury trial was the proper procedure to follow:

> The gist of the Due Process Clause, as understood at the founding and since, was to force the Government to follow those common-law procedures traditionally deemed necessary before depriving a person of life, liberty, or property. When a citizen was deprived of liberty because of alleged criminal conduct, those procedures typically required committal by a magistrate followed by indictment and trial.[29]

Thus, the neutral decisionmaker envisioned by Scalia would be an impartial jury and judge in a criminal proceeding.

In a very pointed way, Scalia also questioned the plurality's use of the *Mathews* test in Hamdi's case:

> [J]ust as though writing a new Constitution [the plurality] comes up with an unheard-of system in which the citizen rather than the Government bears the burden of proof, testimony is by hearsay rather than live witnesses, and the presiding officer may well be a "neutral" military officer rather than judge and jury. It claims authority to engage in this sort of "judicious balancing" from *Mathews v. Eldridge*, a case involving...*the withdrawal of disability benefits!* Whatever the merits of this technique when newly recognized property rights are at issue (and even there they are questionable), it has no place where the Constitution and the common law already supply an answer.[30]

Scalia took a direct shot at the plurality for all of the procedures it envisions, including the notion that military officers would be neutral in these cases. Justice David Souter, joined by Justice Ruth Bader Ginsburg, also refused to join the plurality on this point, stating the following:

> It is not that I could disagree with the plurality's determinations...that someone in Hamdi's position is entitled at a minimum to notice of the Government's claimed factual basis for holding him, and to a fair chance to rebut it before a neutral decisionmaker... On the other hand, I do not mean to imply agreement that...an opportunity to litigate before a military tribunal might obviate or truncate enquiry by a court on habeas.[31]

The *Hamdi* decision was not the end of the Court's involvement in enemy combatant cases, nor was it the last word by the federal government on who would decide if suspected enemy combatants were, in fact, enemy combatants. The Bush Administration, following the *Hamdi* plurality opinion, created Combatant Status Review Tribunals (CSRTs) in the summer of 2004 for enemy combatants who challenged their designations. The decisionmakers for these CSRTs consisted of a panel of three commissioned officers of the United States Armed Forces. Again, this did little to obviate the lack of impartiality in the decisionmaker. Furthermore, when detainees were allowed to plead their cases to these CSRTs, they did not have attorneys to represent them; instead, each detainee was assisted by a "personal representative" — a military officer who had reviewed a detainee's file. CSRT procedures did not allow detainees to see all of the evidence against them, attend all of the proceedings, or call the witnesses of their choosing.[32]

In December 2005, Congress, wanting to have its say on the determination of detainee statuses, passed the Detainee Treatment Act (DTA). Among other things, the DTA limited the ability of enemy combatant detainees to challenge their CSRT hearing determinations in federal court via a habeas corpus petition, thus limiting the ability of detainees to have their hearing decisions reviewed by a neutral judge. However, in an attempt to have more oversight over the executive branch, the DTA also required the Secretary of Defense to report to Congress on CSRT procedures, and it required the President to appoint a civilian official, subject to Senate confirmation, who would give final review to CSRT determinations.[33]

The Supreme Court jumped back into the fray on this issue in *Hamdan v. Rumsfeld* (2006), where it found that the CSRTs, as then constituted, were not authorized by Congress, nor were they something inherent in executive power. The Court also found that the exclusion of detainees from portions of their hearings violated the Uniform Code of Military Justice and the Geneva Conventions.[34] Congress and the President then tried once more to reestablish military tribunals for suspected enemy combatants with the passage of the Military Commissions Act (MCA) in 2006. The MCA, among other things, eliminated federal habeas corpus jurisdiction over detainees whose cases were reviewed under the procedures of the DTA. In *Boumediene v. Bush* (2008), the Supreme Court ruled that the procedures of the DTA were not an adequate substitute for the writ of habeas corpus, thus finding that MCA was an unconstitutional suspension of the writ of habeas corpus.[35]

Whether it was the Mobbs Declaration, the CSRTs created by the Bush Administration, or the military commissions as they existed after the DTA or the MCA, the missing component in each situation was a truly neutral decisionmaker. The executive branch, as well as many members of Congress, wanted something less than a federal court to review cases where enemy combatants challenged their status designations. They did this, in part, for the very laudable and important goal of national security. However, it appears that they also wanted these alternative decisionmakers to decide these cases because those decisionmakers would be more prone to accept the government's side of the story. That falls far short of neutrality.

That leaves us with the fate of Yaser Hamdi. When the Supreme Court decided his case in June 2004, he had been in government custody for nearly three years. Less than four months later, in October 2004, the U.S. government released Hamdi to Saudi Arabia. His freedom was only given to him under the following stipulations: (1) he refrains from traveling to Afghanistan, Israel, and some other countries; (2) he does not return to the United States until at least 2014; (3) he renounces his U.S. citizenship; and (4) he renounces any commitment to the principles of violent jihad.[36] According to the Pentagon, Hamdi was let go because "considerations of United States national security did not require his continued detention."[37] Thus, what military officials classified as a matter of national security before the Supreme Court decided the *Hamdi* case evaporated in short order when the Supreme Court reviewed the case. After the Court required even a minimal due process guarantee to a decisionmaker whose neutrality was questionable, the government released Hamdi instead of putting him before a CSRT, which essentially showed that he had never been any real threat to national security.

It came years too late, but the Supreme Court made sure that a more neutral decisionmaker would be required to indefinitely hold suspected enemy combatants like Hamdi without trial or charge. Although the Court plurality in *Hamdi* did not truly ensure that decisionmakers in similar future cases would be neutral (like Justice Scalia would have done), it did require something approaching neutrality and led the way for Hamdi to be released. A neutral decisionmaker would at least give a fair listening to Hamdi's side of the story, something unlikely with an executive branch declaration. Since he was captured, Hamdi has consistently maintained that he never fought for the Taliban or supported Al Qaeda.[38] There is no evidence that since his release in 2004 Hamdi has been involved with either group.

Notes

1. *The 9/11 Commission Report: Final Report of the National Commission on Terrorist Attacks upon the United States* (New York: Norton, 2004), 1-46; Eric T. Kasper, "The Influence of Magna Carta in Limiting Executive Power in the War on Terror," *Political Science Quarterly* 126 (2011-12): 547-78, 563.
2. Todd S. Purdum, "After the Attacks: The White House; Bush Warns of a Wrathful, Shadowy and Inventive War," *New York Times*, September 17, 2001, http://www.nytimes.com/2001/09/17/us/after-attacks-white-house-bush-warns-wrathful-shadowy-inventive-war.html (accessed September 18, 2011).
3. Authorization for Use of Military Force, S.J. Res. 23 (2001).
4. Daniel Moeckli, "The Selective 'War on Terror': Executive Detention of Foreign Nationals and the Principle of Non-Discrimination," *Brooklyn Journal of International Law* 31 (2006): 495-534; Kasper, "The Influence of the Magna Carta," 564.
5. *Hamdi v. Rumsfeld*, 542 U.S. 507, 510 (2004); Kasper, "The Influence of the Magna Carta," 568.
6. *Hamdi*, 542 U.S. at 511-13; "U.S. Nationals Detained as Unlawful Combatants," *American Journal of International Law* 96 (2002): 981-83, 981; Kasper, "The Influence of the Magna Carta," 568.
7. *Hamdi*, 542 U.S. at 513; Kasper, "The Influence of the Magna Carta," 568.
8. Pnina Lahav, "The Scholarship of Lawrence M. Friedman: The Republic of Choice, the Pledge of Allegiance, the American Taliban," *Tulsa Law Review* 40 (Summer 2005): 599-626, 604 n44; Jan McGirk, "Fighting Terror," *Boston Globe*, Nov. 17, 2002, A30.
9. *Hamdi v. Rumsfeld*, 243 F. Supp. 2d 527, 535 (E.D. Va. 2002).

10. *Hamdi*, 542 U.S. at 509.
11. *Hamdi*, 542 U.S. at 518-19.
12. *Hamdi*, 542 U.S. at 528-29 (internal citations omitted).
13. *Mathews v. Eldridge*, 424 U.S. 319, 335 (1976).
14. *Hamdi*, 542 U.S. at 530 (internal citations and quotations omitted) (emphasis in original).
15. *Hamdi*, 542 U.S. at 530 (internal citations and quotations omitted).
16. *Hamdi*, 542 U.S. at 530 (emphasis in original).
17. *Hamdi*, 542 U.S. at 531.
18. *Hamdi*, 542 U.S. at 531.
19. *Hamdi*, 542 U.S. at 531-32 (internal citations omitted).
20. *Hamdi*, 542 U.S. at 532.
21. *Hamdi*, 542 U.S. at 533.
22. *Hamdi*, 542 U.S. at 533.
23. *Hamdi*, 542 U.S. at 533-34.
24. *Hamdi*, 542 U.S. at 534.
25. *Hamdi*, 542 U.S. at 537.
26. *Hamdi*, 542 U.S. at 539.
27. *Hamdi*, 542 U.S. at 538.
28. *Hamdi*, 542 U.S. at 554 (Scalia, J., dissenting).
29. *Hamdi*, 542 U.S. at 556 (Scalia, J., dissenting).
30. *Hamdi*, 542 U.S. at 575-76 (Scalia, J., dissenting)(internal citations omitted)(ellipses and emphasis in original).
31. *Hamdi*, 542 U.S. at 553-54 (Souter, J., concurring in part, dissenting in part, and concurring in the judgment).
32. Paul Diller, "Habeas and (Non-)Delegation," *University of Chicago Law Review* 77 (2010): 585-655, 620.
33. *Hamdi*, 542 U.S. at 621-23.
34. *Hamdan v. Rumsfeld*, 548 U.S. 557 (2006).
35. *Boumediene v. Bush*, 553 U.S. 723 (2008).
36. Barbara J. Olshansky, *Democracy Detained: Secret Unconstitutional Practices in the U.S. War on Terror* (New York: Seven Stories Press, 2007), 71.
37. Jerry Markon, "Hamdi Returned to Saudi Arabia; U.S. Citizen's Detention as Enemy Combatant Sparked Fierce Debate," *Washington Post*, 12 October 2004, A2.
38. Olshansky, *Democracy Detained*, 71.

Conclusions

[T]he Missouri Plan [of selecting judges]...obviously reduces threats to judicial impartiality, even if it does not eliminate all popular pressure on judges.
– *Republican Party of Minnesota v. White*, 536 U.S. 765, 791 (2002)
(Justice O'Connor, concurring)

The U.S. Supreme Court has heard many cases, and has consequently spent a great deal of ink, to clarify what it means under the U.S. Constitution to have a decisionmaker who is neutral. Indeed, the Court had given us much to digest with regard to the impartiality of jurors, judges, and decisionmakers in other contexts where legal rights are at stake. After reading through the myriad of pages written about this topic, some greater lessons can be gleaned about it, and some suggestions can be made to help bolster these related rights to jury impartiality and due process.

From the outset, it is clear from *Irvin v. Dowd* (1961) that juror impartiality does not have to mean possessing absolutely no knowledge about a case. Instead, jurors need only be able to set aside preconceived notions about a case and consider only the evidence presented at trial. In *Sheppard v. Maxwell* (1966), jurors were not able to remain impartial in this way because they encountered a tide of prejudicial and inadmissible evidence before and during trial. There is no question that the press has a First Amendment right to publish information about criminal trials because of their noteworthiness to the general public. However, a defendant's Sixth Amendment right to an impartial jury should be balanced against this. After *Sheppard*, trial judges were on notice that they needed to strike this balance by imposing remedies such as ordering a change of venue, sequestering a jury, holding a continuance if a judicial election is looming, limiting the number of reporters in a courtroom, placing reporters farther away from parties, placing a gag order on parties and witnesses, and even declaring a mistrial. The need for judges to oversee juror impartiality was confirmed by the lessons of *Frank v. Mangum* (1915) and *Moore v. Dempsey* (1923). In a world where prosecutions might be driven by prejudice, judicial oversight to protect jurors' impartiality is essential. Whether in that context or the one surrounding *Sheppard*, active steps must sometimes be taken by the judge to protect this important right.

One of the other important lessons of juror impartiality is that this Sixth Amendment right is only as full as it is today because of two clauses in the Fourteenth Amendment. Indeed, new life was breathed into this right after it was incorporated to apply to the states in *Duncan v. Louisiana* (1968) via the Due Process Clause and because it is now inextricably linked to the Equal Protection Clause in cases involving juror selection. In *Batson v. Kentucky* (1986), the Supreme Court put in place procedures to help prevent racial discrimination in jury selection: if there is a claim of a juror being struck because of his or her race, the party claiming discrimination must make a *prima facie* showing of discrimination, and if that can be done, then the other party must articulate a neutral explanation why the jurors of that race were eliminated. The *Batson* Court also, rightfully, continued to allow the trusted practice of peremptory challenges as a way to protect a defendant's ability to strike potential jurors of questionable impartiality. Although social science research suggests that some groups, particularly African Americans, may be excluded at higher than acceptable rates for jury service, the Court has largely maintained the system articulated in *Batson*. The Court did, thankfully, take a step toward correcting this imbalance by declaring unconstitutional in *Miller-El v. Dretke* (2005) the Texas jury shuffle. This jury shuffle is one of the worst examples of a practice that invites racial discrimination in violation of a defendant's right to an impartial jury. It essentially turns justice into a game of cards, based sometimes on little more than the color of a person's skin (unlike peremptory challenges, which only are exercised *after* potential jurors are questioned).

After the Court refused to outlaw sex discrimination in juror selection in *Hoyt v. Florida* (1961), the Court finally righted this wrong in *Taylor v. Louisiana* (1975), an important milestone in juror impartiality. Among other things, the case demonstrates the need for a jury to represent a cross-section of the community, so that the public has confidence in the fairness of the justice system. This case, when contrasted with the Court's failing in *Hoyt*, also teaches us the dangers of stereotyping potential jurors.

One final lesson to be learned about juror impartiality involves death-qualification of juries. *Witherspoon v. Illinois* (1968) ruled that jurors cannot be excluded for expressing only general doubts about the death penalty, but if prosecutors engage in this practice, it raises constitutional concerns as to only the jury's imposition of the death penalty, not necessarily to the jury's finding of guilt. In *Lockhart v. McCree* (1986), the U.S. Supreme Court clarified that death-qualified juries can decide a defendant's guilt and that there is no cross-section requirement on these grounds. However, in making this decision, the Court majority neglected to understand that death-qualified juries tend to exclude women and people of color at much higher rates, they may be more likely to lead to group think, and they make a jury much more likely to be pro-prosecution. In other words, *Lockhart* makes a jury more partial. Furthermore, then-Justice Rehnquist's mistake was breaking impartiality down to the juror level and not examining the impartiality of the jury as a whole, which would be more in line with the textual command of the Sixth Amendment. A better approach than that adopted by the Court would be to have true jury bifurcation, whereby the jury chosen at the guilt phase cannot be death-qualified. Instead, in these cases we should select one jury to decide a defendant's guilt and then select another jury to determine a convicted defendant's sentence. Potential jurors would not be asked their views on capital punishment when being chosen for the guilt phase of the trial, but potential jurors for the sentencing phase of the trial could be asked such questions to sift out nullifiers. This would protect a defendant's right to a fair trial during the guilt phase, and it would ensure a balanced approach for the prosecution at the penalty phase. Perhaps another way to accomplish this goal would be to have judges do the sentencing in capital cases, like judges typically do in non-capital cases.

That leads us to the requirements for judicial impartiality. *Tumey v. Ohio* (1927) set the early requirement that judges cannot have a direct financial stake in the outcome of the case. *Ward v. City of Monroeville* (1972) further clarified that judges should not have matters at the front of their minds other than the guilt/innocence of the defendant and the relevant case law (i.e.: judges should not be concerned about how the fines from the case will affect the city's finances). Both cases help us understand the need under the Constitution for the separation of powers, whether it is separating the function of prosecution from that of judging, or whether it is the more general separation of executive and judicial functions. Like in *Sheppard*, these cases also demonstrate the potential dangers to impartiality if a judge is overly concerned with reelection.

The trial judge in *Mayberry v. Pennsylvania* (1971) was repeatedly rudely insulted and had his patience tested in ways that were unbelievable. That judge and others in comparable situations need to be able to act immediately to deal with disruptive contemnors, so that the decorum of the courtroom can be properly preserved. However, criminal contempts at the end of a trial raise questions of impartiality and generally require a substitute judge. This is especially the case if the trial judge has been vilified by the contemnor, where the presumption is that a judge cannot help but be biased against that defendant. The statements and actions of the defendants in *Mayberry* were on par with those in the infamous Chicago Seven trial. No judge can be expected to be impartial when sentencing someone who has so rudely demeaned him or her.

Judges should have legal training in order to properly understand the law. This prevents a judge from simply turning to the prosecutor and assuming that person will have the "right" answers. Although the defendant in *North v. Russell* (1976) was denied due process, not all defendants who are tried before non-lawyer judges are denied due process. Non-lawyer judges can be legally trained in ways that do not involve receiving a diploma from a law school. Just like judges with law backgrounds require continuing education, non-lawyer judges can be impartial and protect defendants' due process rights if they receive requisite training. We entrust the decision of guilt versus innocence to jurors who are complete laypersons; we can entrust decisions of guilt/innocence and some questions of law to non-lawyer judges in courts of limited jurisdiction.

Without a doubt, a judge who accepts a bribe is partial in that case. In addition, *Bracy v. Gramley* (1997) taught us that a judge bribed in one case cannot be assumed to be impartial in other cases because the judge may be covering for his or her bribed acquittals by convicting other defendants. This is an important case for judicial impartiality not just because it holds what should be intuitively obvious in that case, but also because it implies that what happens beyond the case in question can affect a judge's impartiality in that case. Although judges can normally be presumed to have properly discharged their judicial duties, that presumption can be rebutted by evidence to the contrary. In *Bracy*, the Court went only so far to say that compensatory bias existed at sentencing, but not at the guilt phase of the trial. Although this was a good start, a completely new trial would have been better, as that would have ensured that the underlying convictions were achieved in a courtroom free from bias. Since there was a financial temptation here, it was similar to the stakes in place in *Tumey*, necessitating a larger remedy than the one provided by the Court. Given the sheer volume of cases that were decided by the trial judge in *Bracy*, not all of them could reasonably be retried, but they should all have been at least revisited with an evidentiary hearing. Since the trial judge was trying to cover up bribes for acquitting defendants accused of homicide, any defendants in those cases surely should have had at least a new trial.

Caperton v. A.T. Massey Coal Co. (2009) provides us with some important lessons on judicial impartiality as well. The case involved more than *Tuney*'s dangers of judicial financial temptations, and it also dealt with more than the *Tumey/Murchison* dangers of judges having prior relationships with parties and engaging in executive functions. The case also introduced the risk of campaign finance affecting the outcome of legal cases. According to the Supreme Court, in these situations one must ask an objective question: will the average person under these circumstances be impartial? This is better than an alternative objective test that would instead ask if a given judge was actually biased, because it is difficult to prove if a private donation was really a payoff. Under the standard articulated by the Court, when a person with a personal stake in a particular case has a significant and disproportionate influence in placing the judge on the case by raising funds or directing the judge's election campaign when the case was pending or imminent, then there is serious risk of actual bias. In these cases, the following criteria are significant: the contribution's relative size in comparison to the total amount of money contributed to the campaign, the total amount spent in the election, and the apparent effect such contribution had on the outcome of the election. While Justice Kennedy emphasized the significant disproportionate influence on the outcome of the election in *Caperton*, what should matter is if the contribution or expenditure is large enough for the judicial candidate to take notice and see it as financial assistance. Kennedy also stressed the timing of the financing, but even prior relationships in years past should be relevant to this inquiry. In the end, the same rule from *Mayberry* should apply to *Caperton* situations: when in doubt, use a substitute judge!

Sheppard, *Caperton*, *Tumey*, and *Ward* collectively raise a problem for judicial impartiality, that of elections. While selecting judges via elections does not inherently lead to judicial bias, absent a strong separation of executive and judicial power there are two situations where a recent or impending election can cause us to doubt a judge's impartiality: high profile cases that occur shortly before an election and contested races that involve large financial contributions. In the former type of case, *Sheppard* provided the remedy of a continuance until after the election. In the latter type of case, however, the election has already ended, so a substitute judge is normally the best remedy. However, in both types of cases another more comprehensive solution has been suggested by Justice Sandra Day O'Connor. In *Republican Party of Minnesota v. White* (2002), O'Connor noted her "concerns about judicial elections generally" because she believed that "the very practice of electing judges undermines" judicial impartiality.[1] According to O'Connor, "if judges are subject to regular elections they are likely to feel that they have at least some personal stake in the outcome of every publicized case. Elected judges cannot help being aware that if the public is not satisfied with the outcome of a particular case, it could hurt their reelection prospects."[2] O'Connor's biggest concern in this regard, in a case decided seven years before *Caperton*, was the amount of funds that judges may have to raise when running for elective office, which "may leave judges feeling indebted to certain parties or interest groups," or at the very least may "undermine the public's confidence in the judiciary."[3] Given these concerns, O'Connor wrote of one alternative, known as merit selection or the Missouri Plan (named after Missouri because it was the first state to adopt this system of judicial selection). According to this selection method,

> Judges are appointed by a high elected official, generally from a list of nominees put together by a nonpartisan nominating commission, and then subsequently stand for unopposed retention elections in which voters are asked whether the judges should be recalled. If a judge is recalled, the vacancy is filled through a new nomination and appointment.[4]

O'Connor concluded that "the Missouri Plan...obviously reduces threats to judicial impartiality, even if it does not eliminate all popular pressure on judges."[5] Although merit selection cannot be constitutionally mandated, it is an additional method that states can individually adopt to help reduce the threat of judges being bought by large campaign donors (especially on appellate courts where the elections are more costly) and to help promote judicial partiality.

Due process also necessitates neutrality in other cases beyond those decided by judges and juries. For these cases, the Court has typically used the framework from *Goldberg v. Kelly* (1970) and the three part test from *Mathews v. Eldridge* (1976). According to *Morrissey v. Brewer* (1972), for a parole revocation process to meet due process requirements there must be (1) a preliminary hearing by an independent officer (i.e.: not the parole officer involved in the case); and (2) a formal hearing by a neutral and detached body, like that of a parole board. Impartiality is further ensured by the requirement that at each stage the decisionmaker issues a written statement listing the reasons for revocation and the evidence relied upon.

Medical licensing boards must also be impartial decisionmakers. Just like *Bracy* taught us that judges are normally presumed to have properly discharged their judicial duties, *Withrow v. Larkin* (1975) taught us that administrative adjudicators are normally presumed to act with honesty and integrity. Still, *Withrow* failed to completely ensure impartiality in medical licensing boards. The Court should have required that the same board cannot serve investigative and adjudicatory functions in the same case. That would have better protected impartiality because not all facts gathered at the investigatory phase will always be relevant at the adjudicatory phase. This would have made *Withrow* consistent with *Morrissey* and *Murchison*. Instead, the Court was too deferential to legislatures, and due process was weakened.

Mental health commitments present special problems, especially when they involve children. The children in *Parham v. J.R.* (1979) were admitted by foster and adoptive parents who were perhaps tired and fatigued. In each case, the children were forced into involuntary confinement without a meaningful hearing before a truly neutral decisionmaker. For most children, their parents will care for them and not want them to be admitted to a mental health facility except as a last resort. Sadly, however, that will not always be the case, as some parents will not have their children's best interests in mind, and some children who are wards of the state may be handled with less than the full attention they deserve. Furthermore, even well-meaning parents will not always know when commitment is helpful or harmful for their troubled children. Coupled with mistakes that could be made by admitting psychologists, there needs to be some oversight by an impartial decisionmaker to ensure that a juvenile being involuntarily committed really needs to be committed. The Supreme Court did not do enough to prevent this scenario from occurring.

Instead, the *Parham* Court resorted to the *Mathews* test to decide what sort of process was due to these children. Although the Court held under this test that a child has a substantial liberty interest in not being confined unnecessarily for medical treatment and that parents cannot always have absolute and unreviewable discretion to decide whether to have a child institutionalized, the Court's decision largely rested on its fear that the state would have to spend additional resources to truly know if a child was admitted erroneously (i.e.: psychologists should not spend more time preparing for hearings instead of helping patients). This is a legitimate concern, but the fact that this outweighed the liberty interest of the children in this case demonstrates the problem of using the *Mathews* test in this context, as it downgrades the importance of the person being confined by the government.

There is a connection between *Parham* and *North v. Russell*, as the Court did not require either judges or medical personnel to need formal and extensive legal training to be eligible to preside over cases that involved people losing their freedom. The difference between these types of cases, however, is that non-lawyer judges can be expected to have some legal training, whereas medical personnel cannot. Given this, Justice Brennan's approach in dissent was better than that of the majority: for a child who is being committed by his or her parents, a physician can determine whether commitment is necessary, but if the child objects to this type of treatment, then a subsequent post-commitment hearing should be held. This would balance the need for immediate care to be given to those needing it, and it would protect the rights of those who are wrongfully committed. For children who are wards of the state, pre-commitment hearings would best ensure that children are treated impartially.

Prison discipline does not give rise to the same level of due process requirements as those necessary for someone accused of crime, but the Court in *Edwards v. Balisok* (1997) stated that a hearing officer who dishonestly suppresses evidence of innocence is unconstitutionally biased. That is not a shocking proposition. The more problematic holding from the Court in that case was that a prisoner may not seek damages under 42 U.S.C. § 1983 for a deprivation of good time credits without due process of law if a judgment in the prisoner's favor would imply the invalidity of the punishment imposed, unless the prisoner can demonstrate that the punishment has already been invalidated. Thus, the Court effectively let the case die on a technicality, and we can never know if Balisok's right to a neutral decisionmaker was, in fact, denied.

Hamdi v. Rumsfeld (2004) rounds out the field of cases where the right to an impartial decisionmaker is at stake. According to the Supreme Court, a citizen held as a suspected enemy combatant must be given a meaningful opportunity to contest the factual basis for that detention before a neutral decisionmaker. The Court again made use of the *Mathews* test, this time to determine that a citizen-detainee challenging his or her designation as an enemy combatant must receive notice of the factual basis for his classification, and a fair opportunity to rebut the government's factual assertions before a neutral decisionmaker. The Court also allowed for military tribunals to hold these hearings. The Court's solution here was better than the Bush Administration's assertion that military interrogators constituted all the process that is due to enemy combatants, but the Court fell short of fully protecting the right to a neutral factfinder. Instead, Justice Scalia's dissent provided the more appropriate answer: in the absence of the suspension of habeas corpus, when indefinite military detention is at stake, a neutral decisionmaker must be an impartial judge and jury in a criminal court; a military declaration is not enough, nor is a military tribunal. This approach is cleaner, simpler, and meets the basic requirements of the Constitution. Although due process is meant to be relatively malleable, the *Mathews* test can be used to justify any detention, and thus should be used only when property interests are at stake, not when liberty interests are in jeopardy.

Yaser Esam Hamdi was able to vindicate his rights because his father filed a writ of habeas corpus on his behalf. This "great writ" has been used by prisoners for centuries to defend their rights in both America and Britain. In this case and in several others described in this book, that writ was filed to help protect the even older rights to due process and a jury trial. Dating back to Magna Carta and passing to the U.S. Constitution, these rights indicate that a person being judged should be entitled to fairness and impartiality. Although these rights have not always been fully honored, they are better protected now than in decades and centuries past. The Court has breathed new life into them in many of these cases that it has decided, and hopefully the justices will continue to ensure that these rights remain in effect and are even stronger in the decades and centuries to come.

Regardless of where it occurs, a lack of impartiality by a legal decisionmaker affects all of us. Martin Luther King, Jr., writing while incarcerated from a jail cell in Birmingham, Alabama in 1963, remarked that "[i]njustice anywhere is a threat to justice everywhere."[6] By rectifying the wrongs in many of these individual cases, the Court has been working to ensure that justice is impartial for all of us, everywhere.

Notes

1. *Republican Party of Minnesota v. White*, 536 U.S. 765, 788 (2002) (O'Connor, J., concurring).
2. *White*, 536 U.S. at 788-89 (O'Connor, J., concurring).
3. *White*, 536 U.S. at 790 (O'Connor, J., concurring).
4. *White*, 536 U.S. at 791 (O'Connor, J., concurring) (internal citations omitted).
5. *White*, 536 U.S. 791 (O'Connor, J., concurring).
6. Martin Luther King, Jr., "Letter from Birmingham Jail," in *A Testament of Hope: The Essential Writings and Speeches of Martin Luther King, Jr.*, James M. Washington, ed., (New York: HarperCollins, 1986), 290.

Catalog of Cases

Addington v. Texas, 441 U.S. 418 (1979)
Apodoca v. Oregon, 406 U.S. 404 (1972)
Argersinger v. Hamlin, 407 U.S. 25 (1972)
Ballew v. Georgia, 435 U.S. 223 (1978)
Barron v. Baltimore, 32 U.S. 243 (1833)
Batson v. Kentucky, 476 U.S. 79 (1986)
Boumediene v. Bush, 553 U.S. 723 (2008)
Bracy v. Gramley, 81 F.3d 684 (7th Cir. 1996)
Bracy v. Gramley, 520 U.S. 899 (1997)
Bracy v. Schomig, 286 F.3d 406 (7th Cir. 2002)
Bracy v. Schomig, 537 U.S. 894 (2002)
Bradwell v. Illinois, 83 U.S. 130 (1873)
Caperton v. A.T. Massey Coal, 2007, W. Va. LEXIS 119
Caperton v. A.T. Massey Coal, 223 W. Va. 624 (2008)
Caperton v. A.T. Massey Coal, 129 S. Ct. 2252 (2009)
Caperton v. A.T. Massey Coal Co., 225 W. Va. 128 (2009)
Citizens United v. FEC, 130 S. Ct. 876 (2010)
Codispoti v. Pennsylvania, 418 U.S. 506 (1974)
Cooke v. United States, 267 U.S. 517 (1925)
Dennis v. United States, 339 U.S. 162 (1950)
Dr. Bonham's Case. 77 Eng. Rep. 638 (C.P. 1610)
Duncan v. Louisiana, 391 U.S. 145 (1968)
Edwards v. Balisok, 520 U.S. 641 (1997)
Federal Election Commission v. Wisconsin Right to Life, Inc., 551 U.S. 449 (2007)
Frank v. Mangum, 237 U.S. 309 (1915)
FTC v. Cement Institute, 333 U.S. 683 (1948)

Gagnon v. Scarpelli, 411 U.S. 778 (1973)
Georgia McCollum, 505 U.S. 42 (1992)
Gideon v. Wainwright, 372 U.S. 335 (1963)
Glasser v. United States, 315 U.S. 60 (1942)
Goldberg v. Kelly, 397 U.S. 254 (1970)
Hamdi v. Rumsfeld, 243 F. Supp. 2d 527 (E.D. Va. 2002)
Hamdi v. Rumsfeld, 542 U.S. 507 (2004)
Hamdan v. Rumsfeld, 548 U.S. 557 (2006)
Hoyt v. Florida, 368 U.S. 57 (1961)
Hoyt v. State, 119 So. 2d 691 (Fla. 1959)
In re Gault, 387 U.S. 1 (1967).
In the Matter of the Application of Mrs. Myra Bradwell, for a License to Practice Law, 55 Ill. 535 (1876)
In the Matter of the Motion to Admit Miss Lavinia Goodell to the Bar of this Court, 39 Wis. 232 (1875)
Irvin v. Dowd, 366 U.S. 717 (1961)
J.E.B. v. Alabama, 511 U.S. 127 (1994)
J.L. v. Parham, 412 F. Supp. 112 (M.D. Ga. 1976)
Johnson v. Louisiana, 406 U.S. 356 (1972)
Larkin v. Withrow, 368 F. Supp. 793 (E.D. Wis. 1973)
Lockhart v. McCree, 476 U.S. 162 (1986)
Mathews v. Eldridge, 424 U.S. 319 (1976)
Mayberry Appeal, 255 A.2d 131 (Pa. 1969)
Mayberry v. Pennsylvania, 400 U.S. 455 (1971)
McCree v. State, 585 S.W.2d 938 (Ark. 1979)
Miller-El v. Cockrell, 537 U.S. 322 (2003)
Miller-El v. Dretke, 545 U.S. 231 (2005)
Moore v. Dempsey, 261 U.S. 86 (1923)
Morrissey v. Brewer, 408 U.S. 471 (1972)
Morrissey v. Brewer, 443 F.2d 942 (8th Cir. 1971)
Murchison, 349 U.S. 133 (1955)
Murray's Lessee v. Hoboken Land & Improvement Co., 59 U.S. 272 (1856)
NLRB v. Donnelly Garment Co., 330 U.S. 219 (1947)
North v. Russell, 427 U.S. 328 (1976)
O'Connor v. Donaldson, 422 U.S. 563 (1975)
Parham v. J.R. 442 U.S. 584 (1979)
People v. Collins, 478 N.E.2d 267 (Ill. 1985)
People v. Collins, 606 N.E.2d 1137 (Ill. 1992)
People v. Witherspoon, 36 Ill. 2d 471 (Ill. 1967)
Pierce v. Society of Sisters, 268 U.S. 510 (1925)
Public Utilities Commission v. Pollak, 343 U.S. 451 (1952)
Republican Party of Minnesota v. White, 536 U.S. 765 (2002)
Richardson v. Perales, 402 U.S. 389 (1971)
Shaughnessy v. Mezei, 345 U.S. 206 (1953)

Sheppard v. Maxwell, 384 U.S. 333 (1966)
State v. Balisok, 843 P.2d 1086 (Wash. Ct. App. 1992)
State v. Balisok, 866 P.2d 631 (Wash. 1994)
Strauder v. West Virginia, 100 U.S. 303 (1880)
Swain v. Alabama, 380 U.S. 20 (1965)
Taylor v. Hayes, 418 U.S. 488 (1974)
Taylor v. Louisiana, 419 U.S. 522 (1975)
Tumey v. Ohio, 273 U.S. 510, 520 (1927)
Ungar v. Sarafite, 189 N.E.2d 629 (N.Y. 1963)
Ungar v. Sarafite, 376 U.S. 575 (1964)
United States v. Maloney, 71 F.3d 645 (7th Cir. 1995)
United States v. Morgan, 313 U.S. 409 (1941)
United States ex rel. Collins v. Welborn, 79 F. Supp. 2d 898 (N.D. Ill. 1999)
United States v. Wood, 299 U.S. 123 (1936)
Village of Monroeville v. Ward, 21 Ohio App. 2d 17 (Ct. App. Ohio 1969)
Ward v. Village of Monroeville, 409 U.S. 57 (1972)
Williams v. Florida, 399 U.S. 78 (1970)
Witherspoon v. Illinois, 391 U.S. 510 (1968)
Withrow v. Larkin, 421 U.S. 35 (1975)
Wolff v. McDonnell, 418 U.S. 539 (1974)

Bibliography

Allison, John R. "Ideology, Prejudgment, and Process Values." *New England Law Review* 28 (1994): 657-743.

American Bar Association. *ABA Model Code of Judicial Conduct* Adopted February 2007 and amended August 2010. http://www.americanbar.org/content/dam/aba/administrative/professional_responsibility/2010_mcjc_final_for_website.authcheckdam.pdf (accessed June 7, 2012).

American Bar Association Commission on Women in the Profession. "A Current Glance at Women in the Law 2011." 2011. http://www.americanbar.org/content/dam/aba/marketing/women/current_glance_statistics_2011.authcheckdam.pdf (accessed May 6, 2012).

And for the Sake of the Kids. "Believe." June 15, 2009. http://www.youtube.com/watch?feature=endscreen&v=qyb8xLTJ6SM&NR=1 (accessed January 29, 2012).

———. "Brothers." June 15, 2009. http://www.youtube.com/watch?v=Xl2wZXJvWk4&feature=related (accessed January 29, 2012).

———. "Tired." June 24, 2009. http://www.youtube.com/watch?v=xL9Lj6WlILg (accessed January 29, 2012).

———. "Wrong Again." June 24, 2009. http://www.youtube.com/watch?v=kzCSMqVMZjI&feature=related (accessed January 29, 2012).

Annals of Congress, Volume 1 (1789).

Authorization for Use of Military Force. S.J. Res. 23 (2001).

Ayres, Ian. "The Twin Faces of Judicial Corruption: Extortion and Bribery." *Denver University Law Review* 74 (1997): 1231-50.

Barratt, Nick. "The Revenues of John and Phillip Augustus Revisited," in S.D. Church, ed., *King John: New Interpretations*. Woodbridge: The Boydell Press, 1999.

Barton, Benjamin H. *The Lawyer-Judge Bias in the American Legal System*. New York: Cambridge University Press, 2011.

"Baseball Bat Slayer of Husband Sentenced to 30 Years in Prison." *Ocala Star-Banner* January 20, 1958, 5.

Bilder, Mary Sarah. "The Corporate Origins of Judicial Review," *Yale Law Journal* 116 (2006): 502-566, 531.

Biskupic, Joan. "Supreme Court Case with the Feel of a Best Seller." *USA Today*, February 16, 2009. http://www.usatoday.com/news/washington/2009-02-16grisham-court_N.htm (accessed January 29, 2012)

Blackstone, William. *Commentaries on the Laws of England, Volume 4*. Chicago: University of Chicago Press, 1769 (1979): 346-47.

Blount, Jim. "U.S. Supreme Court Decision Stopped Crusading Village Mayors." *Journal-News*, February 12, 2003. http://www.lanepl.org/Blount/JBCOLS/documents/5665992053CD8DE5256873837D2697C0BAE3169E.html (accessed August 28, 2011).

Bodenhamer, David J. *Fair Trial: Rights of the Accused in American History*. New York: Oxford, 1992.

Boyer, Allen Dillard. "'Understanding, Authority, and Will': Sir Edward Coke and the Elizabethan Origins of Judicial Review." *Boston College Law Review* 39 (1997): 43-93.

Buckles, Thomas. *Laws of Evidence*. Clifton Park, NY: Thomas Delmar Learning, 2003.

Burg, Michael. "A Message from the President." *The Trial Lawyer: A Magazine for Trial Lawyers & a Voice for Justice*, 2010. http://www.thetriallawyermagazine.com/about (accessed September 18, 2011).

Carnes, Jim. *Us and Them: A History of Intolerance in America*. New York: Oxford University Press, 1999.

Christianson, Stephen G. "Leo Frank Trial." In *Great American Trials: From Salem Witchcraft to Rodney King*, edited by Edward W. Knappman, 267-272. Canton, MI: Visible Ink Press, 2003.

Cichon, Dennis E. "Developing a Mental Health Code for Minors." *Thomas M. Cooley Law Review* 13 (1996): 529-614.

Cogan, Neil H., ed. *The Complete Bill of Rights: The Drafts, Debates, Sources, & Origins*. New York: Oxford University Press, 1997.

Cooper, Cynthia L. and Sam Reese Sheppard. *Mockery of Justice: The True Story of the Sheppard Murder Case*. Boston: Northeastern University Press, 1995.

Cooper, Michael. "Mayor's Courts Lucrative – and Controversial." *Springfield News-Sun*, June 23, 2012, http://www.springfieldnewssun.com/news/crime/mayors-courts-lucrative-and-controversial-1395602.html (accessed July 15, 2012).

Danziger, Danny and John Gillingham. *1215: The Year of Magna Carta*. New York: Simon and Schuster, 2003.

Dash, Samuel. *Intruders: Unreasonable Searches and Seizures from King John to John Ashcroft*. New Brunswick, NJ: Rutgers University Press, 2004.

DeSario, Jack P. and William D. Mason. *Dr. Sam Sheppard on Trial: The Prosecutors and the Marilyn Sheppard Murder*. Kent, OH: Kent State University Press, 2003.

DiBiagio, Thomas M. "Judicial Corruption, The Right to a Fair Trial, and the Application of Plain Error Review: Requiring Clear and Convincing Evidence of Actual Prejudice or Should We Settle For Justice in the Dark?." *American Journal of Criminal Law* 25 (1998): 595-629.

Diller, Paul. "Habeas and (Non-)Delegation." *University of Chicago Law Review* 77 (2010): 585-655.

Dinnerstein, Leonard. *The Leo Frank Case, Revised Edition*. Athens, GA: University of Georgia Press, 2008.

"Distraught Mother Confronts Ciavarella Outside Courthouse." *The Times Leader*. February 18, 2011. http://www.timesleader.com/news/Deliberations-resume-in-CIavarella-trial.html (accessed July 14, 2011).

"Dr. Larkin Gives up State License." *The Milwaukee Sentinel*, January 7, 1976, I18.

Duffy, John. *From Humors to Medical Science: A History of American Medicine*. Urbana: University of Illinois Press, 1993).

Evans, Colin. "Samuel Sheppard Trials: 1954 and 1966." *Great American Trials: From Salem Witchcraft to Rodney King*, Edited by Edward W. Knappman, 471-474. Canton, MI: Visible Ink Press, 2003.

Findley, James "The Debate Over Nonlawyer Probate Judges: A Historical Perspective." *Alabama Law Review* 61 (2.010): 1143-61.

Finn, Scott. "Caperton v. Massey: What a Long, Strange Case It's Been." West Virginia Public Broadcasting, June 9, 2009. http://www.wvpubcast.org/newsarticle.aspx?id=9955 (accessed January 29, 2012).

Flynn, Joseph F. "Prejudicial Publicity in Criminal Trials: Bringing *Sheppard v. Maxwell* into the Nineties." *New England Law Review* 27 (1993): 857-882.

"Former Luzerne Judge Conahan Sentenced to 17.5 years." *The Scranton Times-Tribune*. September 23, 2011. http://thetimes-tribune.com/news/former-luzerne-judge-conahan-sentenced-to-17-5-years-1.1207994 (accessed July 10, 2012).

Frank, Thomas. "Lock 'Em Up: Jailing Kids Is a Proud American Tradition." *The Wall Street Journal*. April 1, 2009. http://online.wsj.com/article/SB123854010220075533.html (accessed July 14, 2011).

Freedman, Eric M. "Leo Frank Lives: Untangling the Historical Roots of Meaningful Federal Habeas Corpus Review of State Convictions." *Alabama Law Review* 51 (2000): 1467-1540.

Friedman, Lawrence M. *A History of American Law*. New York: Touchstone, 1973.

Fukurai, Hiroshi, Edgar W. Butler, and Richard Krooth. "Where Did Black Jurors Go? A Theoretical Synthesis of Racial Disenfranchisement in the Jury System and Jury Selection." *Journal of Black Studies* 22 (1991): 196-215.

Garner, Bryan A., ed. *Black's Law Dictionary*. St. Paul, MN: West, 2009.

Gibeaut, John. "Issues that Don't Go Away: High Court's Agenda Features Batson Challenge and Alleged Prosecutor Misconduct." *ABA Journal* 88 (Nov. 2002): 40-41.

Gillespie, Richard. "Buying a Judicial Seat for Appeal: *Caperton v. A.T. Massey Coal Company, Inc.*, is Right out of a John Grisham Novel." *Journal of the National Association of Administrative Law Judiciary* 30 (2010): 309-352.

Ginsberg, Benjamin, Theodore J. Lowi, and Margaret Weir. *We the People: An Introduction to American Politics*. New York: Norton, 2011.

Goldstein, Leslie Friedman. "Hoyt v. Florida." In *The Oxford Companion to the Supreme Court of the United* States, edited by Kermit L. Hall. New York: Oxford University Press, 2005.

Grob, Gerald N. *The Mad Among Us: A History of the Care of America's Mentally Ill*. New York: The Free Press, 1994.

Grossman, Joanna L. "Women's Jury Service: Right of Citizenship or Privilege of Difference?." *Standford Law Review* 46 (1994): 1115-1160.

Hardaway, Robert and Douglas B. Tumminello. "Pretrial Publicity in Criminal Cases of National Notoriety: Constructing a Remedy for the Remediless Wrong." *American University Law Review* 46 (1996): 39-90.

Heise, Kenan. "William Witherspoon: Beat the Chair 15 Times." *Chicago Tribune*, March 6, 1990. http://articles.chicagotribune.com/1990-03-06/news/9001190215_1_electric-chair-william-witherspoon-killing (accessed May 26, 2012).

Hodes, W. William. "What Ought to be Done—What Can Be Done—When the Wrong Person is in Jail or about to Be Executed: An Invitation to a Multi-Disciplined Inquiry, and a Detour about Law School Pedagogy." *Loyola of Los Angeles Law Review* 29 (1996): 1547-83.

Howard, A.E. Dick. *The Road from Runnymede: Magna Carta and Constitutionalism in America*. Charlottesville: University Press of Virginia, 1968.

———. *Magna Carta: Text and Commentary*. Charlottesville: University of Virginia Press, 1998.

Hudson, Jr., David L. *The Rehnquist Court: Understanding Its Impact and Legacy*. Westport, CT: Praeger, 2007.

Hurter, Jerry. "Don Quixote Judge and Case Celebre: Kangaroo Court Tyranny K.O.'d Sixty-One Years Ago." *Cincinnati Magazine*, March 1988: 43-44.

Jackson, Robert H. "Why Learned and Augustus Hand Became Great." Annual Bar Dinner, American Bar Association. Waldorf-Astoria Hotel, New York, New York, December 13, 1951.

Janoski, Dave. "Ciavarella, Conahan Withdraw Guilty Pleas." *The Citizens' Voice*. August 24, 2009. http://citizensvoice.com/news/ciavarella-conahan-withdraw-guilty-pleas-1.208291#axzz1S6aJWL7n (accessed July 14, 2011).

Jensen, Trevor. "Thomas J. Maloney, 1925-2008: Judge Was Convicted of Rigging Cases." *Chicago Tribune*, October 22, 2008. http://truthinjustice.org/judgemaloney.htm (accessed June 10, 2012).

"Justice Warren McGraw." McGraw 4 Justice, 2004. http://www.nurelm.com/examples/warren_mcgraw/ (accessed January 29, 2012).

Juvenile Law Center. "Luzerne County 'Kids-For-Cash' Juvenile Court Scandal." http://www.jlc.org/luzerne/ (accessed July 14, 2011).

Kasper, Eric T. "The Influence of Magna Carta in Limiting Executive Power in the War on Terror." *Political Science Quarterly* 126 (2011-12): 547-78.

Katcher, Susan. "Legal Training in the United States: A Brief History," *Wisconsin International Law Journal* 24 (2006): 335-75.

Kemp, Donna R. *Mental Health in America: A Reference Handbook*. Santa Barbara, CA: ABC-CLIO, 2007.

Kerber, Linda K. *No Constitutional Right to Be Ladies: Women and the Obligations of Citizenship*. New York: Hill and Wang, 1998.

King, Martin Luther, Jr. "Letter from Birmingham Jail," in *A Testament of Hope: The Essential Writings and Speeches of Martin Luther King, Jr.* James M. Washington, ed. New York: HarperCollins, 1986.

Kishlansky, Mark. "Tyranny Denied: Charles I, Attorney General Heath, and the Five Knights' Case." *The Historical Journal* 42 (March 1999): 59-60.

Klarman, Michael J. "The Racial Origins of Modern Criminal Procedure." *Michigan Law Review* 99 (2000): 48-97.

Koehn, Melissa L. "The New American Caste System: The Supreme Court and Discrimination among Civil Rights Plaintiffs." *University of Michigan Journal of Law Reform* 32 (1998): 49-104.

Lahav, Pnina. "The Scholarship of Lawrence M. Friedman: The Republic of Choice, the Pledge of Allegiance, the American Taliban." *Tulsa Law Review* 40 (Summer 2005): 599-626.

Lanzarone, Michael R. "Professional Discipline: Unfairness and Inefficiency in the Administrative Process." *Fordham Law Review* 51 (1983): 818-37.

Latourette, Audrey Wolfson. "Sex Discrimination in the Legal Profession: Historical and Contemporary Perspectives." *Valparaiso University Law Review* 39 (2005): 859-909.

Lazarus, Edward. "A Death Penalty Case the Supreme Court May Review Shows the Dysfunction of the Federal Judiciary When It Comes to Capital Punishment." *FindLaw*, June 24, 2004. http://writ.news.findlaw.com/lazarus/20040624.html (accessed April 29, 2012).

Leaf, Samuel M. "How Voluntary is the Voluntary Commitment of Minors? Disparities in the Treatment of Children and Adults under New York's Civil Commitment Law." *Brooklyn Law Review* 62 (1996): 1687-1730.

Le Clercq, Frederic S. "The Constitutional Policy That Judges Be Learned in the Law." *Tennessee Law Review* 47 (1980): 689-741.

Lee, Randy. "Twenty-Five Years after *Goldberg v. Kelly*: Traveling from the Right Spot on the Wrong Road to the Wrong Place." *Capital University Law Review* 23 (1994): 863-1002.

Levy, Leonard W. *Origins of the Bill of Rights*. New Haven: Yale University Press, 1999.

Liptak, Adam. "Judicial Races in Several States Become Partisan Battlegrounds." *The New York Times*, October 24, 2004. http://www.nytimes.com/2004/10/24/politics/campaign/24judicial.html (accessed January 29, 2012).

———. "Motion Ties W. Virginia Justice to Coal Executive." *The New York Times*, January 15, 2008. http://www.nytimes.com/2008/01/15/us/15court.html (accessed January 29, 2012).

———. "U.S. Supreme Court Is Asked to Fix Troubled West Virginia Justice System." *The New York Times*, October 11, 2008. http://www.nytimes.com/2008/10/12/washington/12scotus.html (accessed January 29, 2012).

Logan, F. Donald. *A History of the Church in the Middle Ages*. New York: Routledge, 2002.

MacLean, Nancy. "The Leo Frank Case Reconsidered: Gender and Sexual Politics in the Making of Reactionary Populism." *The Journal of American History* 78 (1991): 917-948.

Madison, James. *The Federalist No. 10*. Edited by Jack N. Rakoye. Chicago: University of Chicago Press, 1956.

"Man Pleads Guilty after Verdict Tossed." *USA Today*, March 20, 2008. http://www.usatoday.com/news/nation/2008-03-20-3755575938_x.htm (accessed May 3, 2012).

Mansfield, Cathy Lesser. "Disorder in the People's Court: Rethinking the Role of Non-Lawyer Judges in Limited Jurisdiction Court Civil Cases." *New Mexico Law Review* 29 (1999): 119-200.

Markon, Jerry. "Hamdi Returned to Saudi Arabia; U.S. Citizen's Detention as Enemy Combatant Sparked Fierce Debate." *Washington Post*, 12 October 2004, A2.

Martin, David L. *Running City Hall: Municipal Administration in America*. Tuscaloosa, AL: University of Alabama Press, 1990.

McGirk, Jan. "Fighting Terror." *Boston Globe*, Nov. 17, 2002, A30.

Metzger, Gillian E. "Abortion, Equality, and Administrative Regulation." *Emory Law Journal* 56 (2007): 865-906.

Meyer, Robert G. and Christopher M. Veaver. *Law and Mental Health: A Case-Based Approach*. New York: The Guilford Press, 2006.

Mish, Frederick C., ed. *Merriam-Webster's Collegiate Dictionary*. Springfield, MA: Merriam-Webster, 2009.

Moeckli, Daniel. "The Selective 'War on Terror': Executive Detention of Foreign Nationals and the Principle of Non-Discrimination." *Brooklyn Journal of International Law* 31 (2006): 495-534.

Morihara, Kimberly. "An Evaluation of the Summary Contempt Power of the Court: Balancing the Attorney's Role as an Advocate and the Court's Need for Order." *Hawaii Law Review* 19 (1997): 145-75.

Nahari, Mihal. "Due Process and Probation Revocation: The Written Statement Requirement." *Fordham Law Review* 56 (1988): 759-82.

Neubauer David W. and Henry F. Fradella. *America's Courts and the Criminal Justice System*. Belmont, CA: Wadsworth, 2011.

Ohio Historical Society. "*Tumey v. Ohio*." *Ohio History Central: An Online Encyclopedia of Ohio History*, 1999-2011. http://www.ohiohistorycentral.org/entry.php?rec=563 (accessed August 28, 2011).

Olshansky, Barbara J. *Democracy Detained: Secret Unconstitutional Practices in the U.S. War on Terror*. New York: Seven Stories Press, 2007.

Oney, Steve. *And the Dead Shall Rise: The Murder of Mary Phagan and the Lynching of Leo Frank*. New York: Pantheon Books, 2003.

Orth, John V. *Due Process of Law: A Brief History*. Lawrence, KS: University Press of Kansas, 2003.

"Pennsylvania: Mixed Verdict for Disgraced Judge." *The New York Times*. February 18, 2011. http://www.nytimes.com/2011/02/19/us/19brfs-Judge.html?_r=1&ref=markaciavarella (accessed July 14, 2011).

Pitts, Jr., Leonard. "Kids Denied Due Process." *The Miami Herald*. February 27, 2011. http://www.miamiherald.com/2011/02/27/2086108/kids-denied-due-process.html#storylink=misearch (accessed July 14, 2011).

Pollock, Adam L. "Using Parole to Constitutionally Reconcile the Criminal Punishment Goals of Desert and Incapacitation." *University of Pennsylvania Journal of Constitutional Law* 8 (2006): 115-141.

Pozen, David E. "The Irony of Judicial Elections." *Columbia Law Review*, 108 (2008): 265-330.

Provine, Doris Marie. *Judging Credentials: Nonlawyer Judges and the Politics of Professionalism*. Chicago: University of Chicago Press, 1986.

Purdum, Todd S. "After the Attacks: The White House; Bush Warns of a Wrathful, Shadowy and Inventive War." *New York Times*, September 17, 2001. http://www.nytimes.com/2001/09/17/us/after-attacks-white-house-bush-warns-wrathful-shadowy-inventive-war.html (accessed September 18, 2011).

Rakove, Jack N., ed. *James Madison: Writings*. New York: Library of America, 1999.

Raveson, Louis S. "Advocacy and Contempt: Constitutional Limitations on the Judicial Contempt Power; Part One: The Conflict between Advocacy and Contempt." *Washington Law Review* 65 (1990): 477-593.

Revelson, Paul. "Nothing But Trouble: The Ohio Legislature's Failed Attempts to Abolish Mayor's Courts." *University of Dayton Law Review* 35 (2010): 223.

Robertson, David Brian. "Madison's Opponents and Constitutional Design. *The American Political Science Review* 99 (2005): 225-243.

Rozelle, Susan D. "The Principled Executioner: Capital Juries' Bias and the Benefits of True Bifurcation." *Arizona State Law Journal* 38 (2006): 769-807.

Rubinkan, Michael. "Pa. Judge Gets 28 Years in 'Kids for Cash' Case." *Forbes*. August 11, 2011. http://www.forbes.com/feeds/ap/2011/08/11/general-us-courthouse-kick backs_8618656.html (accessed August 11, 2011).

Ryan, Jr., Bernard. "*Moore et al. v. Dempsey* Appeal." *Great American Trials: From Salem Witchcraft to Rodney King*, edited by Edward W. Knappman, 300-303. Canton, MI: Visible Ink Press, 2003.

Sanders-Rivera, Melissa. "Must Read/This is what PRISON is...." Illinois Inmates Support, April 28, 2005. http://dir.groups.yahoo.com/group/illinoisinmatesupport/ message/1818 (accessed June 10, 2012).

Schwartz, Bernard. *The Great Rights of Mankind: A History of the American Bill of Rights*. Madison: Madison House, 1992.

Segal, Elizabeth A. *Social Welfare Policy and Social Programs: A Values Perspective*. Belmont, CA: Cengage Learning, 2010.

Sigerist, Henry E. "The History of Medical Licensure." *Journal of the American Medical Association* 104 (1935), 1057-60.

Snyder, Franklyn Bliss. "Leo Frank and Mary Phagan." *The Journal of American Folklore* 31 (April 1918): 264-266.

Sonsteng, John O. with Donna Ward, Colleen Bruce and Michael Petersen. "A Legal Education Renaissance: A Practical Approach for the Twenty-First Century." *William Mitchell Law Reivew* 34 (2007): 303-472.

Spurr, Stephen J. "Sex Discrimination in the Legal Profession: A Study of Promotion." *Industrial and Labor Relations Review* 43 (1990): 406-17.

Stephen, Robert S. "Prejudicial Publicity Surrounding a Criminal Trial: What a Trial Court Can Do to Ensure a Fair Trial in the Face of a 'Media Circus.'" *Suffolk University Law Review* 26 (1992):1063-1106.

Stewart, Kay. "'Good' reversal followed 'unfair' trial." *Louisville Courier-Journal*, November 6, 2005. http://www.courier-journal.com/article/20051106/NEWS01/511 060406/-Good-reversal-followed-unfair-trial (accessed May 3, 2012).

Stockley, Grif. *Blood in Their Eyes: The Elaine Race Massacres Of 1919*. Fayetteville, AR: University of Arkansas Press, 2001.

The 9/11 Commission Report: Final Report of the National Commission on Terrorist Attacks upon the United States. New York: Norton, 2004.

The Supreme Court of Ohio. "Judicial System Structure." http://supremecourt.ohio.gov/ JudSystem/ (accessed August 27, 2011).

Terry, Timothy R. "Lawyers, Guns, and Money: What Price Justice?." *Journal of Law and Criminology* 88 (1998): 1087.

Thorne, Samuel Edmund. *Essays in English Legal History*. London: Hambledon Press, 1985.

Underwood, Richard H. "Perjury: An Anthology," *Arizona Journal of International and Comparative Law* 13 (1996): 307-79.

United States Courts. "Juror Qualifications, Exemptions and Exclusions." *Federal Courts*. http://www.uscourts.gov/FederalCourts/JuryService/JurorQualificaitons.as px (accessed April 22, 2012).

Urbina, Ian. "Despite Red Flags About Judges, a Kickback Scheme Flourished." *The New York Times*, March 27, 2009. http://www.nytimes.com/2009/03/28/us/28judges.html?_r=1 (accessed July 14, 2011).

U.S. Bureau of Labor Statistics. "CPI Inflation Calculator." 2011. http://www.bls.gov/data/inflation_calculator.htm (accessed April 16, 2012).

"U.S. Nationals Detained as Unlawful Combatants." *American Journal of International Law* 96 (2002): 981-83.

Wasserman, Rhonda. *Procedural Due Process: A Reference Guide to the United States Constitution*. Westport, CT: Praeger, 2004.

Watts, Mikal C. and Emily C. Jeffcott. "A Primer on *Batson*, Including Discussion of *Johnson v. California*, *Miller-El v. Dretke*, *Rice v. Collins*, & *Snyder v. Louisiana*." *St. Mary's Law Journal* 42 (2011): 337-410.

Welsh, Nancy A. "What Is '(Im)Partial Enough' in a World of Embedded Neutrals?." *Arizona Law Review* 52 (2010): 395-471.

Werner, Tiffany A. "*Edwards v. Balisok* — Is the Court Washing Its Hands of Prisoners' Due Process Rights?." *Seton Hall Law Review* 28 (1997): 650-81.

West Virginia Humanities Council. "Brent Benjamin." *The West Virginia Encyclopedia*, November 22, 2010. http://www.wvencyclopedia.org/articles/2319 (accessed January 29, 2012).

Wisconsin Court System. "For Attorneys: Admission to Practice Law in Wisconsin, Diploma Privilege 2012." March 7, 2012. http://www.wicourts.gov/services/attorney/bardiploma.htm (accessed June 4, 2012).

Wisconsin SCR 60

Wisconsin Statute § 19

Wisconsin Statute § 757

Wisconsin Statute § 990

Young, Rowland L. "Supreme Court Report." *American Bar Association Journal* 57 (April 1971): 367-72.

———. "Supreme Court Report." *American Bar Association Journal* 59 (January 1973): 72.

Index

Addington v. Texas, 160, 163
Afghanistan, 183-84, 190
Albright, Justice Joseph, 124
Alito, Justice Samuel, 127
Al Qaeda, 182-83, 184, 191
American Bar Association (ABA), xiv-xv, 1, 11, 13, 38, 57, 103
American Psychiatric Association, 170
anti-Semitism, 29, 31-34
Argersinger v. Hamlin, 105
A.T. Massey Coal Co., 121-24, 131
Authorization for the Use of Military Force (AUMF), 183

Bailey, F. Lee, 25, 27
Balisok, Jerry Bibb, 175-79, 199
Barron v. Baltimore, 5
Batson, James, 43, 52-53
Batson v. Kentucky, 41, 43-46, 48-53, 65, 75, 194
Benjamin, Justice Brent, 122-24, 125-27, 130, 131
Bill of Rights, xvi, 5, 10, 182. *See also individual constitutional amendments*
Black, Justice Hugo, 70-71
Black's Law Dictionary, 12
Blackstone, William, 3
Blankenship, Don, 122-24, 126-27, 130-31
Blythin, Judge Edward, 24-27
B'nai B'rith, 29
Booher, G. Donald, 139-40, 141, 143, 144-45
Boumediene v. Bush, 190
Bradley, Justice Joseph, 56
Bradwell, Myra, 55-57
Bradwell v. Illinois, 55-57, 60
Brandeis, Justice Louis, 38
Brennan, Justice William, 15, 75, 86, 143, 159, 167-70, 199
Bracy, William, 111-19
Bracy v. Gramley, 111-19, 196, 198
Breyer, Justice Stephen, 50-51, 185
bribed judges, xiii-viv, 108, 111, 114-19, 196
Brough, Gov. Charles Hillman, 36, 37
Burger, Chief Justice, 45-46, 95, 97, 105-7, 140-44, 163-67, 169-70
Bush, Pres. George W., 182-83
Bush Administration, 184-85, 188-90, 199

campaign finance, 123, 126-27, 129-30, 196-97
Camp X-Ray, 183
Caperton, Hugh M., 121-22, 123-27
Caperton v. A.T. Massey Coal Co., 121-32, 196-97
challenge for cause, 3, 42
change of venue, 26, 33, 193
Charles I (king), 7
Ciavarella, Mark A., xiii-xvi
Citizens United v. FEC, 129
Clark, Justice Tom C., 25-26
Codispoti, Dominic, 91-92, 94, 96, 97, 99
Coke, Sir Edward, 7, 10, 13, 148
Collins, Roger, 111-15, 117-19
Combatant Status Review Tribunals (CSRTs), 189-91

Commentaries on the Laws of England, 3
compensatory bias, 117-19, 196
Conahan, Michael T., xiii, xv-xvi
conflict of interest, xiv-xv, 2, 123-24, 127-30
Conley, Jim, 30-31, 36
Connecticut Declaration of Rights, 8
Constitution of the United States. *See individual constitutional amendments*; Bill of Rights
contempt of court, 89-99, 128, 152, 195
continuance, 24, 26, 115, 193, 197
Cooke v. United States, 90
coroner's inquest, 24
Curtis, Justice Benjamin, 10

death-qualified juries, 47, 67-77, 194-95
Delaware Declaration of Rights, 4
Detainee Treatment Act (DTA), 190
Diagnostic and Statistical Manual of Mental Disorders, Fourth Edition (DSM-IV), 170
Dix, Dorothea, 160
Dorsey, Hugh Mason, 31-32
Douglas, Justice William, 70-71, 96-97, 143-44
Doumar, Judge Robert G., 184-85
Dr. Bonham's Case, 6-7, 147-48
due process, xv-xvi, 2, 5-11, 13, 15-16, 21-22, 26-27, 29, 32-34, 37-38, 42, 64, 69, 81-86, 89, 96-98, 101, 104-8, 111, 116-17, 119, 123-31, 137, 139-40, 142-45, 147-48, 150-52, 154-55, 160-63, 166-69, 171, 175-79, 181-82, 184-89, 191, 193-95, 197-200; Fifth Amendment and, xv, 6, 9-11, 163; Fourteenth Amendment and, xv, 5-6, 10-11, 22, 32, 34, 36, 38, 42-44, 61-65, 67, 73, 75-76, 81, 83, 89, 97, 104, 116-17, 123, 125-26, 128-31, 140-41, 143-44, 148, 152, 163, 194; procedural, xv-xvi, 11, 144, 150, 163, 185
Dugan v. Ohio, 86
Duncan v Louisiana, 5, 42, 60, 61, 62, 64, 194

Edward I (king), 3
Edwards, Gary, 176
Edwards v. Balisok, 175-79, 199
Eighteenth Amendment, 82
Eldridge, George, 163
enemy combatants, 11, 181, 183-91, 199
equal protection, 42-44, 64, 113, 194. *See also* Fourteenth Amendment
ethics. *See* judicial ethics

federalism, 33, 38
Federalist No. 10, 1, 10
Field, Justice Stephen, 56
Fiok, Judge Albert A., 91-98
Fifth Amendment, xv, 6, 9-11, 163. *See also* due process
First Amendment, 14-15, 27, 129, 131, 193
Fourteenth Amendment, xv, 5-6, 10-11, 22, 32, 34, 36, 38, 42-44, 61-65, 67, 73, 75-76, 81, 83, 89, 97, 104, 116-17, 123, 125-26, 128-31, 140-41, 143-44, 148, 152, 163, 194. *See also* due process; equal protection
Frank, Leo, 29-39
Frankfurter, Justice Felix, 98
Frank v. Mangum, 29-39, 42, 51, 193
The Fugitive, 21

gag order, 26, 193
Gault, 160-61, 163
Geneva Conventions, 190
Georgia v. McCollum, 46
Gideon v. Wainwright, 105
Ginsburg, Justice Ruth Bader, 189
Glasser v. United States, 42
Goldberg v. Kelly, 15-16, 142-43, 197
Goodell, Lavinia, 56-57

Hamdan v. Rumsfeld, 190
Hamdi, Esam Fouad, 183-84
Hamdi, Yaser Esam, 183-91, 200
Hamdi v. Rumsfeld, 181, 183-91, 199

Harlan, Justice John Marshall, 60-61, 70, 97-98
Hart, Judge William T., 118
Heck v. Humphrey, 177
Henry III (king), 2
Holmes, Justice Oliver Wendell, Jr., 29, 34-35, 38
Hoyt, Gwendolyn, 58-61, 65
Hoyt v. Florida, 55, 58-65, 194
Hughes, Justice Charles Evans, 34, 38

Illinois Supreme Court, 55-56, 114
impartiality, xv-xvi, 1-6, 8-16, 21-22, 24-27, 29, 32-35, 38-39, 42-46, 48-49, 51-53, 55, 60-65, 67-77, 82-83, 85-87, 89-91, 96-99, 104, 106-8, 111, 116, 119, 123-31, 137, 142-45, 148, 151-52, 155, 162, 169-71, 177-78, 184, 189, 193-200; of decisionmakers, 10-11, 13, 142-45, 148, 151-52, 155, 162, 169-71, 178, 184, 193, 198-200; defined, 12-16;of judges, 11, 13-15, 82-83, 85-87, 89-91, 96-98, 104, 106-8, 111, 116, 119, 123-31, 137, 170, 177, 189, 193, 195-97, 199; of juries, 2-6, 8-11, 12-14, 16, 21-22, 24-27, 29, 32-35, 38-39, 42-46, 48-49, 51-53, 55, 60-65, 67-77, 99, 137, 189, 193-95, 199; Sixth Amendment Jury Clause and, xv, 5-6, 12, 22, 42-44, 55, 60-64, 68-69, 75, 193-95. *See also* neutrality; unbiased
Innocent III (pope), 1-2,
Irvin v. Dowd, 12-13, 193

Jackson, Justice Robert H., 1, 11
J.E.B. v. Alabama, 65
Jefferson, Thomas, 21
John (king), 1-2, 7, 107
judges. *See* impartiality, neutrality
judicial elections, 15, 24, 26, 122-23, 126-27, 129, 131, 193, 195, 196-97
judicial ethics, xiv-xv, 14, 108, 124, 129, 131
judicial independence, 1, 11, 101, 106, 127
Judiciary Act of 1789, 63
juries. *See* impartiality, neutrality
juror qualifications, 63, 67
jury selection, 24, 41-53, 59-65, 68-77, 194
jury shuffle, 48, 50, 51, 52, 194
juvenile courts, xiii-xiv, 159-71, 186, 198

Kennedy, Justice Anthony, 122, 124-27, 185, 196
King, Martin Luther, Jr., 200
Ku Klux Klan, 29, 35

Lamar, Justice Joseph, 38
Langdell, Christopher Columbus, 102
Langnes, Herbert, 91, 96, 97, 99
Larkin, Duane, 149-56
law school. *See* legal education
legal education, 57, 58, 82, 102-4, 108, 170, 195
Lockhart v. McCree, 67, 72-77, 194

Madison, James, 1, 5, 10
Magna Carta, xvi, 1-3, 5-10, 107-8, 200
Mahon, John, 22, 24
Maloney, Judge Thomas J., 112, 114-19
Marshall, Justice Thurgood, 45-46, 48, 50, 67, 75-76, 106, 143, 172
Maryland Act for the Liberties of the People, 8
Maryland Declaration of Rights, 4, 8
Mathews v. Eldridge, 163-65, 171, 185-86, 189, 197-98, 199
Mayberry, Richard, 91-99
Mayberry v. Pennsylvania, 89, 91-99, 195, 197
Maynard, Justice Elliot, 123-24
mayor-judges, 81-87, 106, 128, 155
Massachusetts Body of Liberties, 8
Massachusetts Constitution, 9
McCree, Ardia, 72-73, 75-77
McDonnell, Robert, 115, 117-18
McGraw, Justice Warren, 122-23, 126-27
medical licensure, 6-7, 147-50, 153-54, 156, 169-70

mental health commitments, 11, 159-71, 198, 199
Military Commissions Act (MCA), 190
Miller, Justice Samuel, 56
Miller-El, Thomas, 46, 48-53
Miller-El v. Dretke, 41, 46, 48-53, 194
Minnesota Supreme Court, 14
mistrial, 25-26, 193
Mobbs, Michael, 183-84, 188
Mobbs Declaration, 183-84, 187, 190
Moore v. Dempsey, 29, 36-39, 41-42, 193
Morrissey, John J., 138-39, 141, 143, 144-45
Morrissey v. Brewer, 137-45, 151-52, 155, 197-98
municipal court, xiv, 81-82, 89, 103, 108
Murchison, 125-28, 151-53, 196, 198
Murray's Lessee v. Hoboken Land & Improvement Co., 10

National Association for the Advancement of Colored People (NAACP), 37
neutrality, xv-xvi, 2, 6-7, 11, 12-13, 15-16, 34, 41, 44-46, 50-51, 56, 69, 81, 85-86, 98-99, 101, 106-8, 116-17, 119, 125, 137, 141-45, 150, 159, 161, 165-71, 178-79, 181, 184-91, 193-94, 197-99; of decisionmakers, xv-xvi, 6-7, 11, 15-16, 137, 141-45, 150, 159, 161, 165-69, 171, 178-79, 181, 184-91, 193, 197-99; defined, 12-13, 15-16; of judges, xvi, 6, 11, 15, 34, 81, 85-86, 98-99, 101, 106-8, 116-17, 119, 125, 170, 190; of juries, 41, 45, 50, 69, 194. *See also* impartiality; unbiased
New Hampshire Constitution, 9
New Jersey Constitution, 103
New York Constitution, 9
non-lawyer judges, 101, 102-8, 154, 170, 195-96, 199
North, Lonnie, 104-8
North Carolina Declaration of Rights, 4, 8
Northern Alliance, 183-85, 187
North v. Russell, 101, 104-8, 166, 170, 195, 199

Oakes, 160
O'Connor, Justice Sandra Day, 15, 185-88, 193, 197
O'Connor v. Donaldson, 160
Ohio Supreme Court, 25, 81-82, 86
Operation Greylord, 114-15
Owens, Judge Wilbur D., Jr., 162-63, 164

Parham v. J.R., 159, 161-71, 186, 198-99
parole, 48, 137-45, 151, 170, 197-98; and revocation, 138-45, 151, 197-98
Pennsylvania Constitution, 4, 8-10
peremptory challenge, 3, 14, 43, 45-48, 50-52, 65, 70, 73, 194
Petition of Right, 7
Phagan, Mary, 30-32, 35-36
Pitney, Justice Mahlon, 32-33
Powell, Justice Lewis, 43-45, 49
prejudicial pretrial publicity, 13, 21-27
prison disciplinary procedures, 11, 145, 175-79, 199
Prohibition, 82
Public Utilities Commission v. Pollak, 98
Pugh, A.R., 82-85

racial discrimination, 6, 31, 36-37, 41-53, 55, 67, 74, 194
Rehnquist, Justice/Chief Justice William, 45, 64-65, 73-76, 86, 115-17, 185, 194-95
Republican Party of Minnesota v. White, 13-15, 129, 193, 197
res judicata, 123
Roan, Judge Leonard, 31-33, 35
Roberts, Chief Justice John, 127-31
Russell, Judge C.B., 104-7

Scalia, Justice Antonin, 14-15, 127, 177-79, 188-89, 191, 199
September 11, 2001, 181-83, 186

sequestration, 25-26, 193
sex discrimination, 6, 55-65, 67, 74, 194
Shays's Rebellion, 5
Sheppard, Marilyn, 22-23
Sheppard, Sam, 21-27, 33
Sheppard v. Maxwell, 21-27, 42, 193, 195, 197
Sixth Amendment, xv, 5-6, 12, 22, 42-44, 55, 60-64, 68-69, 75, 193-95. *See also* impartiality
Slaughterhouse Cases, 56
Slaton, Gov. John, 35
Souter, Justice David, 49-50, 51, 189
South Carolina Constitution, 9-10
Starcher, Justice Larry, 123-24
Stevens, Justice John Paul, 15, 75, 167, 188
Stewart, Justice Potter, 69-72, 101, 106-7
Strauder v. West Virginia, 41, 44, 45, 58
Struble, Judge Stanley, 83
Supreme Court of the United States. *See names of individual cases and justices*
Swain v. Alabama, 42-43
Swano, William, 114-16, 118
Swayne, Justice Noah, 56

Taliban, 183-84, 191
Taft, Chief Justice William Howard, 38, 83-86, 90, 128
Taylor, Billy J., 61-65
Taylor v. Louisiana, 55, 61-65, 194
Thomas, Justice Clarence, 51, 127, 185
trial by jury. *See* Sixth Amendment
trial *de novo*, 104, 105, 107
Tumey, Ed, 82-85
Tumey v. Ohio, 81-87, 106, 119, 124-28, 131, 155, 171, 195, 196, 197

unbiased, xv-xvi, 12-14, 33. *See also* impartiality; neutrality
Ungar v. Sarafite, 90-91
Uniform Code of Military Justice, 190
United States v. Wood, 12

Vermont Constitution, 4
Vermont Declaration of Rights, 9
Virginia Declaration of Rights, 4, 8-9
voir dire. *See* jury selection

Ward, Clarence, 85-86
Ward v. City of Monroeville, 81, 85-87, 106, 107, 155, 171, 195, 197
War on Terrorism, 181, 183, 185
Wersal, Gregory, 14
West Virginia Supreme Court of Appeals, 122-24, 125, 127, 130-31
White, Chief Justice Edward, 38
White, Justice Byron, 62-64, 70, 86, 151-55
Wisconsin courts, xiv-xv, 56-57, 87, 108
Wisconsin Supreme Court, 56-57
Witherspoon, William, C., 68-71
Witherspoon v. Illinois, 67-72, 74-75, 77, 194
Withrow v. Larkin, 147, 148-56, 169-70, 198
Wolff v. McDonnell, 145
Wood, Tana, 176

www.ingramcontent.com/pod-product-compliance
Ingram Content Group UK Ltd.
Pitfield, Milton Keynes, MK11 3LW, UK
UKHW041124071026
15587UKWH00009B/191

9 780739 177211